A Life
on the
Road

OTHER BOOKS BY CHARLES KURALT

On the Road with Charles Kuralt
North Carolina Is My Home
Dateline: America
To the Top of the World

CHARLES KURALT

A Life on the Road

G. P. PUTNAM'S SONS • NEW YORK

G. P. Putnam's Sons
Publishers Since 1838
200 Madison Avenue
New York, NY 10016

Library of Congress Cataloging-in-Publication Data

Kuralt, Charles, date.
    A life on the road / Charles Kuralt.
        p.   cm.
        1. United States—Description and travel—1960–1980.   2. United
    States—Description and travel—1981–   3. United States—Social life
    and customs—1945–1970.   4. United States—Social life and
    customs—1971–   5. Kuralt, Charles, 1934–   —Journeys—United
    States.   6. Television journalists—United States—Biography.
    I. Title.
    E169.02.K8685   1990   90-39461 CIP
    917.304′92—dc20
        ISBN 0-399-13488-3

Printed in the United States of America

1   2   3   4   5   6   7   8   9   10

This book is printed on acid-free paper.

For
Ina Bishop Kuralt
and
Wallace Hamilton Kuralt,
my mother and father

Acknowledgments

I am grateful to Karen Beckers for helping me open up old cornerstones and dig up time capsules from my CBS News past; to Isadore Bleckman for reading the manuscript and correcting some of my recollections, and for poring through shoe boxes of memory to find photographic souvenirs of our travels together; to Bernard Birnbaum for discovering other evidence of my life on the road and spending much of his own time in the sorting and printing of pictures; to the CBS Photographic Department for generously opening its files; to Joseph Bellon for his dependable representation of me as literary agent; and to Neil Nyren, publisher of G. P. Putnam's Sons, editor and friend, who did not *really* begin to lose patience with me until the manuscript of this book was three years overdue.

Contents

Foreword

ROAD, *n*. A strip of land along which one may pass from where it is too tiresome to be to where it is futile to go.

—Ambrose Bierce

There is no contentment on the road, and little enough fulfillment. I know that now. I am acquainted with people who live settled lives and find deep gratification in family and home. I know what I have missed, the birthdays and anniversaries, the generations together at the table, the pleasures of kinship, the rituals of the hearth.

And still I wander, seeking compensation in unforeseen encounters and unexpected sights, in sunsets, storms and passing fancies. I long ago exasperated those closest to me. I beg their forgiveness for all the experiences we didn't have at home together. It's too late for me to put down roots and join the Rotary.

I come from wandering tribes, Norse and Celtic on my mother's side it seems, nomad Bavarians on my father's, ancestors become Scots–Irish and Slovenian by the time of their immigration to America. As far as I can tell, none of them stayed anywhere for long. My brother, Wallace, overcame these vagabond genes to settle happily for life in Chapel Hill, North Carolina, and raise a large and loving family. My sister, Catherine, a beautiful woman, wife and mother of two, is an ornament of domesticity on Bainbridge Island, Washington. All the itinerant impulses of our lineage seem to have concentrated in me. They still goad me. No train leaves the station that I do not want to catch.

I have not set out to write an autobiography. That book would have to refer in detail to many mentors—Ransom Gurganus, who interested me

11

in journalism when I was seven or eight years old; Anne Batten of Alexander Graham Junior High School in Charlotte, North Carolina, who gave me encouragement; Professor William Geer of the University of North Carolina, who opened my eyes and heart; Rolfe Neill, who taught me to make up a page—and to many friends and colleagues of CBS News, Tom Spain, Irv Drasnin, Shad Northshield, Hughes Rudd, Russ Bensley, Burton Benjamin, Bill Leonard, Bill Small and Gordon Manning among them, who are mentioned here in passing or not at all. An autobiography would be about those who have touched and changed me and about those I love. This book isn't that one.

This one is simply an incomplete remembrance of roads taken, breakdowns, misdirections, potholes and detours. If the traveler expects the highway to be safe and well graded, he might as well stay home. The little roads without numbers are the ones I have liked the best, the bumpy ones that lead over the hills toward vicinities unknown.

I started traveling as the youngest CBS News Correspondent, only twenty-three. Thirty-three years later, I look around the newsroom and find no other reporter in the place who was there then except Harry Reasoner—and since he went away to ABC for a few years, I find to my surprise that in terms of consecutive years of employment, I am the old geezer of the on-the-air staff. I knew I was growing older out in the byways, and shorter of breath. I have noticed my thoughts turning to former companions and foregone pleasures. But I am not tempted to give up my seat in the "On The Road" bus for a rocking chair, not yet. Bierce was right about the futility of the destination, but he did not take into account the joy of the trip. I keep thinking I will find something wonderful just around the next bend.

The bookshelf of my grandmother's house contained a set of books, *The Complete Works of Robert Louis Stevenson*. I took down one of the books, *Songs of Travel*, when I was a little boy, and learned a poem in it:

> *Wealth I ask not, hope nor love,*
> *Nor a friend to know me;*
> *All I ask, the heaven above*
> *And the road below me.*

A Life on the Road

1

WANDERLUST

Before I was born, I went on the road. The road was U.S. 17, south from Jacksonville, North Carolina, through the Holly Shelter Swamp to Wilmington, where the hospital was. My father backed the Chevrolet out of its place in the hay barn next to the farm cart and helped my mother into the front seat on the afternoon of September 9, 1934. He made the trip in little more than an hour, barely slowing down for the stop signs in Dixon, Folkstone and Holly Ridge. I was born the next morning with rambling in my blood and fifty miles already under my belt.

We lived on my grandparents' farm off and on for a while there during the Depression. A sandy road passed in front of the house and a logging path through the pine woods behind it. I always wondered where the roads went, and after I learned that the one in front went to another farm a mile away, I wondered where it went from there. Once, playing in the woods, I surprised a flock of wild turkeys, which went flying down the logging road and out of sight. I remember wanting to go with them. Whenever I hear the Judy Garland lyric "Birds fly over the rainbow— Why then, oh why can't I?" it's those turkeys I see flying.

My mother was a schoolteacher and my father was getting started in what seemed to him the right job for the times, helping out poor people. There was no shortage of poor people to help out in the thirties, of course. My father, who had earned a Phi Beta Kappa key at the University of

15

North Carolina and had planned to become a big businessman, became a social worker instead. He found employment in several of President Roosevelt's alphabet agencies, the CCC, the ERA, the WPA, then went back to the university at Chapel Hill, took some graduate courses in social work, and accepted a job with the state Department of Public Welfare. We moved from one town to another in eastern North Carolina, and I loved every move. I began to find out where the roads went.

My father's job as field supervisor for the state required him to travel to the small-town county seats to visit the local welfare offices. Since my mother was busy teaching school, somebody had to take care of me. The solution—a little troublesome for my father, I imagine, but perfect for me—was for him to take me with him on his trips.

We rolled along the country roads to the old tidewater towns, Edenton and Plymouth and New Bern and Swanquarter, my father smoking Tampa Nuggets and spinning yarns for my amusement. He tried a little history on me, thinking to improve my mind: "The people here didn't like the British governor, and had a fight with the British at this bridge." He filled me with local lore: "At Harkers Island over there, they make wonderful strong boats and go to sea in them." He taught me to read the Burma-Shave signs: " 'Twould Be More Fun . . . to Go by Air . . . but We Couldn't Put . . . These Signs Up There. Burma-Shave." We stopped in the afternoons to fish for a few minutes in roadside creeks turned black by the tannin of cypress trees, my father casting a red-and-white plug expertly with the old bait-casting rod he carried in the trunk, and patiently picking out the backlashes that snarled the reel when I tried it. We stopped for suppers of pork chops, sweet potatoes and collard greens at roadside cafes, and rolled on into the night, bound for some tourist home down the road, my father telling tales and I listening in rapture, just the two of us, rolling on, wrapped in a cloud of companionship and smoke from his five-cent cigar.

I wanted never to go home from these trips, and when we did go home, I contrived longer trips to farther-away places, trips of the mind. In a field within walking distance of our farm, a small detachment of U.S. Marines was setting up a tent camp, forerunner of what was to become Camp LeJeune, the sprawling Marine base that eventually changed Jacksonville forever. On hot summer mornings, I used to walk barefoot down the sandy road to the tent camp towing a red wagon filled with quart jars of milk from our cows and sugar cookies my grandmother had baked and wrapped in wax paper. It never took more than a few minutes to sell out my stock of milk and cookies to the Marines. If they didn't have money, I accepted souvenirs. Somewhere in my folks' attic, there must still be a cigar box containing sharpshooter medals, uniform buttons and globe-and-anchor emblems from the pith helmets of those Marines. Most of them were young enlistees, I suppose, who had never traveled farther than a few miles from home, but the cadre was composed of old sergeants who told me casual tales of service in places I had trouble imagining, places where the people spoke other languages entirely, they told me, places with names like the Philippines and Nicaragua and the Canal Zone. I learned to seek out the three-stripers when I wanted to hear good traveling stories. I learned the words of their song, "From the halls of Montezuma to the shores of Tripoli . . ." More than anything else, I wanted to wear a Marine pith helmet and go to the halls of Montezuma. I asked a jolly fat sergeant named Carpenter if he had ever been there. He always called me "Charlie, my boy." "Charlie, my boy," he said, "I'll tell you the truth. I've never even figured out where Montezuma might be. But if the United States Marines decide to send me there, I'll send you a penny postcard." I asked Sergeant Carpenter how old he was when he joined the Marines. "Charlie, my boy," he said, "I was a grand old man of sixteen." You had to be sixteen, he said. I was only six.

In school, I proved to be a below-average student in all forms of mathematics, and later in such subjects as chemistry and biology, but I was good at reading—I had started early on the Burma-Shave signs—and I was fascinated by history and geography, subjects that were still taught in public school in those days. Indiscriminately, I read the works of writers who had traveled, including everything I could find of Richard Halliburton's. I knew the capitals of all the states. The ones I most wanted to go to were Montpelier, Vermont, and Olympia, Washington, for they were the ones that sounded most distant and wondrous.

I entered contests that promised travel as a prize. In 1947, when I was twelve, to my surprise, I won one of these competitions—or rather, finished second for the second straight year, which proved to be just as good as winning. We lived in Charlotte, North Carolina, then, where my father had become the county welfare superintendent. *The Charlotte News* sponsored an annual baseball writing contest for students on the subject "My Favorite Hornet." The prize was a road trip with the Charlotte Hornets, our Washington Senators' farm team. Baseball was my passion and regularly I spent my Saturdays in the old green grandstand watching the Hornets play, but it was the trip I was after. My essay on "bouncing" Bobby Beal, the third baseman, was judged good enough that I was invited to accompany the winner, an older boy named Buddy Carrier. We were to ride in the bus with the team and take turns covering six games in Asheville, North Carolina, and Knoxville, Tennessee. I loved it. I loved the easy chaperoneship of manager Cal Ermer, who assigned Buddy and me the same curfew that applied to the team—one A.M.! I loved listening to the banter of the players on the bus, sitting in the dugout during the games and hanging around the hotel lobbies with my heroes. I loved being away from home, in places I had only heard about. Asheville! Knoxville! A good-natured country pitcher named Sonny Dixon played catch with me on the field before each game began and took to introducing me to players on the other teams as "Flash Kuralt, our traveling big-time sports writer." I loved that, too. But best of all was climbing up to the press box as the game was about to end and pecking out my story on the battered portable typewriter I had borrowed for the trip from a caseworker in my father's office, then, downtown after the game, swaggering into the Western Union office, tossing the copy across the counter and saying to the clerk the words I had been instructed to say by Ray Howe, the *Charlotte News* sports editor. They are words that still give me a little thrill of importance all these years later. I did my twelve-year-old best to growl them like a veteran.

The words were:

"*The Charlotte News*. Press rate collect."

After that summer, in my imagination, I was an experienced traveling reporter. I covered junior high school basketball and football for the newspaper, frustrated by the state law and the parental discretion that agreed I wasn't yet old enough to drive a car to the games. Not that I had a car to drive, of course. My parents wouldn't even give me permission to own a motorbike. I rode the crosstown bus with my notebook showing out of my pocket and my typewriter prominent by my side, or yielded with embarrassment to a ride to the gyms or football fields in the back seat of my parents' car, where the *children* always sat. I made this humiliation tolerable by imagining, there in the back seat, that I was flying across an ocean in a DC-3, checking over my notes for a big story while on the way to Constantinople or Khartoum.

At fourteen, I won another contest and got another trip. It was a speaking contest this time, called the "Voice of Democracy." Not very many kids entered; not very many had a wanderlust like mine. As one of four national winners, I got to give my speech in the House of Burgesses in colonial Williamsburg, Virginia, at the spot where Patrick Henry said, "If this be treason, make the most of it!" My speech, as I remember, was along the same oratorical lines. From Williamsburg, I went to Washington with the other winners to meet President Truman in the Oval Office of the White House. I was gratified to notice that the double-breasted blue suit the President was wearing was just like the one I had bought for the occasion back home at Belk's Department Store. As we took notes, the President gave us his broad Missouri smile, and treated us like grownups, which I appreciated. But I knew I really wasn't a White House correspondent yet, because the woman holding my arm and smiling nervously back at Mr. Truman was my mother. I couldn't wait to be sixteen and off on my own, without any parent tagging along, to the halls of Montezuma. Or at least, on my sports assignments, to the Piedmont Junior High School gym.

On the dirt roads out in the country near our house, I learned to drive—with my father sitting beside me again, in the passenger's seat this time—and I started nagging my parents to lie about my age so that I could get a driver's license early.

"We could go to jail for that," my father said.

"Nobody would ever find out," I said.

Eventually, to end these daily arguments, and with what must have been a sigh of defeat, my father gave me a notarized statement in which he swore that my birthday was June 1. It was really September 10.

With that precious, fraudulent document in my hands, the only palpable lie my father ever told, I hastened to the courthouse to apply for a driving test. For years afterward, because of the spurious date of birth on my driver's license, I was listed in employment, military draft and bank records as three months older than I actually was.

At the time, all that mattered was that I was sixteen in the eyes of the Department of Motor Vehicles of the State of North Carolina and fit to drive a car alone. Naturally, the first thing I did was plan a trip.

My friend Landon Smith and I acquired a twelve-year-old motorcar, originally a 1938 Chevy, I think, but patched up during World War II by somebody who had access to parts from various other makes, a kind of Pontiacrolet or Chevifordmobile. We salvaged a working radio from a wrecked Olds in a junkyard, and when we found it wouldn't fit in the dashboard of our car, hung it *under* the dash where it swung from coat-hanger wire, banging the shins of the front-seat passenger. That summer, with gears clashing, chassis squeaking and radio swinging, and with my lying license in my pocket, we headed for California.

Our vague idea was to explore the Rockies and the Golden West, make a great loop north, perhaps to Canada, and end up at midsummer in Evanston, Illinois, where I had a scholarship to attend a writing program for high school students at Northwestern University. We nursed the car along slowly to save fuel and because we had promised our worried parents not to drive fast. We breakfasted on nickel Cokes and peanut butter crackers and supped on cold cans of pork and beans. We slept in the car, beside the road or in truck stops or abandoned drive-in movie lots after the last movie had ended.

We had badly overestimated nearly everything: the soundness of our vehicle, the distance we could travel in a day on country roads, the adequacy of the supply of dollars we kept hidden under the floor mat in case of holdup, and our own immunity to homesickness. We saw we'd never make it to California. We crossed the Mississippi with the car coughing noticeably on the upgrades and our money and our spirits running low. We were having arguments about trivial things, like whether it was legal to turn right on red lights. Landon said yes. I said no. Neither of us had the slightest idea. Was it harmful to the transmission to keep the car from rolling backward when stopped on a hill by manipulating the clutch and accelerator instead of using the brakes? I said no. Landon said he was going to get out of the car if I kept doing it. We were having crises of inexperience. At Jefferson City, Missouri, we turned sharp right onto U.S. 54 and steered for Chicago. There, my pal Landon found a room on the North Side and a job selling hot dogs on the street to make enough money for his trip home alone. I checked into the YMCA Hotel on Wabash Avenue to await the start of my summer classes in Evanston.

I was given a room that would have had a beautiful view of Lake Michigan but for the intervening mass of the Stevens Hotel. The joy of the tourist returned to me. I happily wandered the streets of my first big city, peeking through the open doors of the strip joints at night, reading the *Tribune* with my fifty-five-cent breakfasts in the morning. (This was the *Tribune* of Colonel Robert McCormick, and I had read and laughed at the *New Yorker* magazine "brightener" quoting a *Trib* news story on a giant excavation: "The hole will be so great that the Tribune Tower would fit into it," to which *The New Yorker* replied, "How about Thursday?") I discovered that jazz musicians, returning to their rooms at the Y after their gigs, often gathered in the basement recreation room of the hotel for jam sessions in the predawn hours. If the musicians noticed the fifteen-year-old white kid sitting on a folding chair off to one side, soaking up their sounds at three o'clock in the morning, they never said anything.

At last came the day when I took the el to Evanston, "Home," announced a big sign on the station platform, "of the Women's Christian Temperance Union." I remember not one thing I might have learned in the next six weeks at the Northwestern High School Institute. I remember walking on the manicured campus and watching sailboats in the distance on the blue lake. I remember The Huddle, an upscale coffee shop where college students laughed and chatted. I remember girls, the most desirable and unapproachable creatures imaginable, many driving convertibles. Northwestern's streets and walks and lawns and dormitories seemed to me a Hollywood version of a college campus, and I seemed to myself a big-boned country boy from the South, a hick kid after all. I wanted to acquire at least a thin veneer of the sophistication I saw all around me, but I didn't know where to begin. And then the summer ran out and it was too late. I caught the train to Gary, Indiana, lugged my big Samsonite suitcase to the side of a highway and started hitchhiking home, relieved to have cultivation and refinement behind me and the romance of the road ahead.

A friendly elderly couple took me as far as Fort Wayne, driving at a stately pace in their big De Soto, questioning me about my family and background. A truck driver drove me through the night so as to have somebody to talk to, dropping me off south of Louisville as the sun came up.

Of the rides I got after that, the one I remember was a long one through the Kentucky hill country with a kindly and demented evangelist in a pickup truck with a loudspeaker mounted atop the cab. He slowed down as we passed through each hamlet so that he could exhort the citizens to come to God lest sulfur and flame overtake them right there on the main street of Roxanna or Redbush or Rockhouse, Kentucky. There was no room in the passenger seat for me, for that was where he kept his microphone and amplifier between villages, so I rode contentedly in the back of the pickup with my feet propped up on my suitcase, watching the mountain curves recede behind the truck, feeling free.

All these years later, I wonder if I haven't patterned my life after that of the daft old man in the pickup truck, who wandered where the back roads took him, the means of amplification close at hand. My job at CBS has turned out just the same, though the preacher had a more confident message.

Riding along that day in the back of his truck, near the end of my first trip away from home alone, I returned the wave of a man who stood up from his work in his vegetable patch to watch us pass. I saw a barefoot young woman in a calico dress pinning sheets to a clothesline. I saw a cluster of old men studying the moves in a game of checkers on the front porch of a one-pump gas station. The road retreated, mile after mile. I was perfectly happy.

When we paused for a few minutes at a sleepy county seat for the old preacher to pass out religious leaflets, I went into the courthouse to find a bathroom. Walking down the halls, I looked into offices and saw people at work at typewriters and adding machines. I felt terribly sorry for them. They were going to work there at their desks all that day, and the next, and the next, and half a day on Saturday, and return to those same desks and office machines on Monday morning.

I walked out and found the preacher at the wheel waiting for me. I climbed into the back of the truck and we pulled away and picked up speed and left that town behind us. The sun was shining, and I could feel the wind in my hair.

2

RADIO DAYS

"I'm going down to the Texan on Lex. Anybody want anything?"

It was my first night on the job for CBS News. I was a writer on the radio overnight shift, midnight 'til eight A.M. A desk assistant—copyboy in newspaper language—made his inquiry to the newsroom at large.

"Sure," said the writer at the next desk, digging into his pocket for money. "Bring me a prune danish and a large light."

"What about you?" the kid asked. The kid was older than I was. He was looking impatiently straight at me. I did not understand anything that had been said. "Texan," "Lex," "danish" and "light" were all New York words I had never heard before.

"Sure. Same thing," I said.

What came back, from an all-night diner called The Texan on Lexington Avenue, was a sweet roll and a big cardboard cup of coffee with cream. After a few nights of listening to the three A.M. food orders given by the other writers, I learned that what I really wanted was a twisted chunk of sweet fried dough and coffee with sugar and cream (more cream than in a "dark" coffee, but not as much as in a "light").

In other words, "a cruller and a regular."

I had a lot of catching on to do.

This was May 1957. I was twenty-two years old and not exactly a man of the world. I had spent four years at the University of North Carolina, my father's old school at Chapel Hill, studying history and working at *The Daily Tar Heel*, the student-owned newspaper. In the spring of my junior year, I printed up some posters and ran for editor on a pro-integration (the state's schools were still segregated then, including the university), anti–Joe McCarthy, anti–big-time sports platform. On election day, I beat the sports editor for the job by a handful of votes. The first thing I did was call my old high school girlfriend, Sory Guthery, on the telephone. She was in school at Greensboro down the road.

"I won!" I said.

"Great!" she said.

"The job pays thirty dollars a week," I said.

"So?"

"So that's enough to live on. Let's get married!"

We were married in Charlotte in August, in a big church wedding. She was twenty, and I was almost twenty myself.

We moved into a cabin, a former tenant house, beside a cornfield a few miles out of Chapel Hill on the road to Raleigh. Our senior year I remember as pure joy. We studied history and read poetry together in the mornings; in the afternoons, I wrote my editorials, often trying them out on Sory by telephone before sending them to the printer.

I flailed about at tradition, in the best tradition of student editors. Racial integration was the theme I adopted as a crusade. The Supreme Court's "Brown vs. Board of Education" decision had come out mandating an end to school segregation and I kept urging the North Carolina legislature to get on with it, starting with the university. "We see no reason in human history or in the human heart why this state school should not belong to all the state's citizens," that kind of thing. The all-white legislature, of course, was trying to figure out ways around the court decision at the time. I was afraid nobody was paying any attention to *The Daily Tar Heel*, so I had copies shipped over to the capital every day. Finally, I had the satisfaction of being called a "pawn of the Communists" on the legislature floor.

At night, Sory sometimes stood over the composing stone with me to watch the editorial page take shape. Always, with two or three other sleepy members of the newspaper staff, I waited until the old flatbed printing machinery cranked up at one A.M. or so and the first copies of that morning's *Tar Heel* came off the press. Then we usually went out to the cabin to admire the paper and drink coffee and talk about the next day's issue until late into the night, Sory sometimes excusing herself to get some studying done. As for me, the newspaper used up so much of my time that I started dropping courses. By the time the spring quarter arrived, I had dropped them all; I was editor of the student newspaper, but—nobody in the administration building seemed to notice—no longer a student. Graduation proceeded without me. I didn't care. I had found my career.

We moved back to Charlotte and I took a job on the afternoon newspaper, *The Charlotte News*, the paper whose sportswriting contest I had entered years before. The *News* was a wonderful place to work, with a heritage of reporters that included such famous ones as Harry Ashmore, Burke Davis, Marion Hargrove and W. J. Cash, who had gone on to write the greatest of books about the region, *The Mind of the South*. I became a general assignment reporter and after a few months, Tom Fesperman, the managing editor, gave me a daily column to write, "People," about the ordinary folk of the city, cops or kids or cabdrivers. I worked hard on all my assignments, but especially hard to make the "People" column interesting and readable. I thought *The Charlotte News* was the best paper in the state, and I assumed I'd work my way up there, perhaps becoming the star reporter or an editorial writer someday.

One Sunday afternoon in March 1957, however, the phone rang at the house. It called me in from the backyard, where I was walking around looking for signs of early blooming daffodils. The man on the line said he was John Day, calling from New York. He said he was director of news at CBS. He said he had read about my winning a prize for newspaper reporting, the Ernie Pyle award, and wondered whether I had any interest in writing for radio.

"Well, sir," I said, "I've always admired you people at CBS, but I don't think there's enough going on down here in Charlotte to write about for radio."

"I don't mean there," the man said. "I mean here. Would you like to come to New York to talk about a job?"

I couldn't believe what I was hearing. "Well," I said, "I suppose I would, yes."

"Can you come tomorrow?" he asked.

"No," I said, "I have to go to work tomorrow. I have to work on the state edition tomorrow, see, which means they'll be expecting me at six-thirty. You understand *The Charlotte News* isn't a real big paper and they'll be shorthanded if I don't show up."

The man on the other end of the line chuckled and said, "Sure, I understand. How about later in the week?"

"Well, I'll ask for a day off," I said. "Could I call you tomorrow or Tuesday?"

"Sure," he said. "The number is PLaza 1-2345. Ask for me."

I was very much impressed by the phone number. I thought CBS must be the big time, all right, to have a telephone number like that.

My wife came in from outside to see who had called. I told her it was CBS News in New York, maybe offering a job. She said, "I bet it was Emery Wister kidding you about having the big head over that Ernie Pyle award."

Emery Wister sat at the desk next to mine in the newspaper office down on Fourth Street. He was a good reporter, but fun-loving. He was capable of a trick like this. I could just hear him the next morning telling everybody how I'd said I couldn't come to New York right away because I had to work on the state edition. I picked up the phone and asked for New York information. When the operator came on the line, I said, "What's the number for the Columbia Broadcasting System, please?"

After a pause, she said, "PLaza 1-2345."

At least that much checked out, and the next morning Emery Wister didn't say a thing. I asked Tom Fesperman if I could have Friday off.

Sory and I had a one-year-old daughter by this time. Sory asked, "Do we want Lisa to grow up in New York City?" It was a pretty good question. But I thought of Irving Berlin escaping the squalor of the Lower East Side to become the toast of Broadway. I thought of Fred Astaire dancing on a penthouse terrace. I said, "Kids do grow up there, I guess." My wife said, "Well, you decide."

That Thursday afternoon, I flew to New York on an Eastern Airlines Constellation and took a taxi to the Blackstone Hotel. "That's where we put up our people who come in from abroad," John Day had said. I was to see him at nine o'clock Friday morning.

The Blackstone was a shabby-genteel old institution somewhere in midtown. My room for the night was on a high floor, the fifteenth or so, a higher floor than I had ever been on in my life. When I stepped over to the window and looked down at the street below, full of tiny pedestrians and toy cars, it made me dizzy. I knew New Yorkers lived at such altitudes, but I couldn't even get to sleep up there. I lay awake listening to the sirens that seemed never to stop, police cars, fire trucks and ambulances, sirens close by and far away. It seemed to me that some terrible calamity must have struck Manhattan for there to be so much loud urgency down in the streets. I wondered if it could be a Russian air raid. I lay there worrying about the sirens until the sun came up. When I got dressed and left the hotel, none of the fast-walking people on the sidewalk seemed to be aware of all the trouble their city had been in during the night. I walked down the street, talked with John Day for a few minutes, and accepted a job as a writer at CBS News in New York for $135 a week.

Then I bought a copy of *The New York Times* and turned to the real-estate ads to see if there was any such thing in the city of New York as a ground-floor apartment.

I found the next best thing eventually, a second-story walk-up in an old wooden house on Middagh Street in Brooklyn. The paint was peeling off the walls a little bit, but the kitchen window afforded a partial view of the Brooklyn Bridge and the Manhattan towers. Downstairs lived a dour modern artist named Charles Duback. Upstairs lived a jovial folk singer, Lee Hays of The Weavers quartet, blacklisted and unable to find employment at the time because of alleged left-wing associations in his peripatetic past. Duback worked below, creating vast geometric canvases nobody wanted to buy. Lee Hays worked above, composing songs on his guitar that nobody wanted to listen to. I was the only person in the house who ever put on a necktie and went to work, which sort of ruined the Bohemian style of the place.

Often, I left for the office a few hours early and walked all the way, across the great bridge ("How could mere toil align thy choiring strings!" asked Hart Crane) and through the crowded streets of Chinatown or Little

Italy ("I hear America singing, the varied carols I hear," sang Whitman) and up one of the great avenues. Everywhere, I heard poetry. New York, which was, I suppose, nearly as squalid and rude then as it is now, seemed saucy and inviting to me. On those long walks, I consumed the city hungrily, inhaling the foreign smells and listening to the music of the streets until I arrived at work almost delirious from what I had smelled and heard and seen.

The newsroom where I labored was on the seventeenth floor of the CBS Building, 485 Madison Avenue, at the corner of 52nd Street. On higher floors were the offices of Dr. Frank Stanton, the longtime President of CBS, and of William S. Paley himself, the founder of the company and Chairman of the Board. The only floor I ever saw was 17, which was exciting enough, even in the stillness of the late hour when I arrived for work. On the way from the elevator to the newsroom was a closed blue door on which was lettered in gold: "MR. MURROW."

Of course, all these notables were out on the town or at home in bed during my working hours. I rarely even laid eyes on any of the important people at CBS, and the first time I did, I was sorry. I came to the building during daylight hours to attend some sort of staff meeting and followed a distinguished white-haired gentleman into an open elevator. A uniformed doorman came rushing over, pressed the button for the twentieth floor and stepped respectfully out of the car. I pressed 17. The doorman looked at me aghast. He leapt back into the elevator, turned a key that cancelled the floor selections, pressed 20 again and hustled me out by the arm. The door closed. I could hear the elevator starting up.

"What's wrong?" I asked.

"That was Dr. Stanton, buddy," the doorman said. "He goes up alone, and he don't stop on the way."

I felt bad that I didn't know Dr. Stanton. On the other hand, I felt good that he didn't know me.

My job, a task for the good of the company which no doubt escaped Dr. Stanton's attention, was to roll through reams of wire copy from the AP, UP and Reuters machines, read the night's cables from CBS News's foreign bureaus, rewrite all this into a five-minute newscast for an announcer, Bob Hall, to read on the air at two A.M.—and then do it all over again for the newscasts of three, four, five and six A.M. This did not require much thinking, but it required very fast typing. As soon as I ripped a script out of my typewriter, I tossed it onto the desk of a fierce, eagle-eyed editor named Maggie who sat like a schoolmarm at the head of the class, dying to find the slightest factual or grammatical error in the copy so she could sing out a correction as she blue-penciled the page. Maggie's corrections were so loud they made everybody jump. I dreaded them, partly because I didn't have time to anticipate them. While she was reading over my two o'clock copy, I was already rattling away at the typewriter again, desperately getting a head start on the three o'clock show.

"Clarke!" Maggie roared one night. *"Clarke!* With an *e!"*

A truck driver named Clarke had been killed by a freight train at a railroad crossing in Indiana. This sort of local misfortune would be ignored by CBS News during the daytime when things were happening, but on the overnight we might make it a lead. I had rendered the name of the victim "Clark."

I said, "What the . . ." and stopped. What I was going to say was, "What the hell difference does it make on the radio?" but thought better of getting into an argument with the infallible Maggie.

A couple of hours later, three bells rang on one of the wire machines. You learned to listen for the bells—one bell for a routine story; three for a bulletin or correction; five for a flash, an event of earthshaking significance. We never heard five bells on the overnight. This time it was a correction. The correct spelling of Clarke's name, it said, was "Clark."

Maggie was looking at the machine over my shoulder. I turned around and smiled at her. She said, "Don't smile at me, you smart-ass kid!" and walked back to her desk. The importance of the story really didn't justify it, but I put Clark into all the rest of my newscasts that night just for the pleasure of typing his name.

I really didn't feel like a smart-ass kid. I felt like a North Carolina boy a long way from home. The other writers on the overnight were all older and experienced, most of them jaded newspaper rewrite men between jobs. They came and went. I was just starting out, eager to make a good impression on my bosses and learn how to be a sophisticated New

Yorker all at once. One of my co-workers, a man with tired eyes who studied the *Racing Form* at night and spent his afternoons at Belmont Park, persuaded me that inasmuch as we finished work at eight A.M., that was our cocktail hour. For a few mornings there, I went with Eddie to a dark Irish bar on West 52nd Street that opened its doors at eight in the morning. Since he ordered martinis, very cold, straight up with a twist of lemon, that's what I ordered, too. I loved the feeling of amity and urbanity these morning martinis induced, but I hated what followed, the tipsy walk in the bright sun to the IND station at Madison and 53rd, the scruffy, unwashed and unshaven descent into the underground against a tide of freshly dressed and beautiful young women hurrying up the escalator on their way to work, and the struggle to stay awake on the rattan subway seat on the bumpy trip home to Brooklyn.

"Tough night?" Sory would inquire sympathetically. She was usually still in her bathrobe, feeding the baby at the kitchen table.

"Yep," I'd reply, "tough night," and head for the front bedroom of the old house, already taking off my coat and tie. We had no air-conditioning and the room was always hot that summer. I slept a few sweaty hours and woke up with a hangover in midafternoon. It wasn't long before I realized I was going to have to find some other way to become a cosmopolitan New Yorker. The nights at work were not so tough as I pretended to my wife, but the mornings were murder. I wasn't man enough to drink breakfast with Eddie.

Instead, I started hanging around the office after my work was done to watch them put together the "World News Roundup." This was real journalism. In those days in this country, anybody who wanted to hear a serious news report in the morning had to tune in to that one fifteen-minute radio program. On television, the news was quick and skimpy, sandwiched in among puppets and pet monkeys and cute weather reports. The other radio networks did their best to compete, but none of them could call on the roster of great reporters who worked for CBS News. Eric Sevareid, Charles Collingwood or Alexander Kendrick reported to the "Roundup" from London each morning, David Schoenbrun from Paris, Richard C. Hottelet from Bonn, Winston Burdett from Rome, Daniel Schorr from Moscow. There might be contributions from Robert Trout,

Ned Calmer or Larry LeSueur. Never before or since has any broadcast news organization assembled a staff approaching the style and expertise of that one. In the decades that followed, network news staffs doubled and redoubled, the glitter of television put radio in the shade, new technologies revolutionized broadcasting—but after the "World News Roundup" of the fifties, news on the air only went downhill.

The program was moderated by calm Dallas Townsend, seated at a heavy table of polished wood in a small square room known as Studio 9, with one window looking into the newsroom and another into the control room. Townsend wore a cumbersome headset and spoke into a large black microphone, the same mike Edward R. Murrow used in the evenings. Tape recording had been invented, but nobody at CBS News trusted it yet, so all the reports on the "World News Roundup" came in live, the ones from abroad via shortwave radio. The correspondents checked in minutes before the program started—"Schoenbrun, you'll be first up this morning, are you there?" "Schoenbrun here"—and their reports were juggled into the broadcast by an engineer with patch cords hung around his neck and his hands on the dials and switches of a giant control board known as the "piano."

There was an old Western Union clock on the wall of the control room, the kind that automatically reset itself to a time signal that came in on the hour. At eight A.M. straight up, a red light came on, the director threw a cue and an announcer said:

"This is the CBS 'World News Roundup,' with reports from our correspondents at home and overseas. From our newsroom in New York, here is CBS News Correspondent Dallas Townsend."

I wasn't experienced enough to be invited to work on the "World News Roundup," of course, but nobody minded if I sat in a corner of the control room and watched the engineer play his flawless concert on the piano, and listened to the director calling in these heroes of mine from the ends of the earth. I was dazzled by them. They seemed to me giants among men. I ached to become one of them someday, but I knew that even if I lived to be—well, fifty!—I could never attain their worldly experience or finesse. It was enough just to think that now I worked at the same place Sevareid and Collingwood and Burdett worked, the same place

Murrow worked! I didn't have a single thing to do with the "World News Roundup," but I never left the control room after the program ended without a glow of secret pride. It was better than martinis in the morning.

The other thing I was proud of—I didn't see any contradiction in this—was my union card. On the newspaper back home, I had become the twenty-year-old President of the Charlotte local of the Newspaper Guild. Nobody else much wanted the job. The union was weak (it has entirely disappeared from newspapers in North Carolina now) and the local president had the onerous duty of sassing the publisher from time to time, which was considered hazardous to career advancement. But I was steeped in labor union lore, knew a few old union songs and had read the column Heywood Broun wrote in the *New York World-Telegram* before founding the Newspaper Guild in 1933:

"There should be a newspaper writers' union. Beginning at nine o'clock on the morning of October 1, I am going to do the best I can to help in getting one up. I think I could die happy on the opening day of the general strike if I had the privilege of watching Walter Lippmann heave half a brick through a *Tribune* window."

I even went to night school to take a course in collective bargaining, only to discover that collective bargaining at the *News* went this way:

I: "We think starting pay for reporters ought to be raised from fifty-five dollars a week to sixty."

Brodie Griffith, executive editor: "Starting pay is going to remain fifty-five dollars a week. Is that clear?"

I: "Yes, sir. But it is not enough."

Mr. Griffith: "Probably not. What else would you like to discuss?"

Not having much luck at my own paper, I went down the street to the other one, *The Charlotte Observer*, which suffered no unions at all outside the pressroom. I secretly organized a disgruntled group of circulation employees, signed them right up in the Newspaper Guild and then wrote a letter to the *Observer*'s management to break the news and ask for a union representation election at the paper. The *Observer* called the circulation employees in and told them they were fired. I figured I needed some help. I called the Newspaper Guild's national office in New York and told them what I had done. "You have done *what?*" exclaimed the man on the other end of the line. The national office flew a professional organizer down the next day to apologize to the *Observer* bosses and get all those circulation guys their jobs back. I was relieved, of course, but also disillusioned. I didn't think that was the way unions were supposed to work.

In New York, I assumed, unions would be different, full of camaraderie and resolution. I looked forward to attending the monthly meetings of my new union, the Writers Guild of America. I knew it had been founded not long before, a spin-off from the national Screen Writers Guild, with whose left-wing leadership many New York writers had quarreled. I was going to become an active union member, I was sure of that. We paid one percent of our take-home pay in union dues. At my first meeting, there was only one topic of discussion: After a member's dues assessment reached $1,000 in a single year, shouldn't there be a cutoff? Some said yes, some said no. I did the arithmetic and realized that this union was wrangling over the union dues of members who made more than *one hundred thousand dollars a year!* What kind of union was that? It was, of course, a union which represented famous writers like Paddy Chayefsky, J. P. Miller and Reginald Rose. I left there thinking of my fights with Brodie Griffith over five dollars a week. I never went to another meeting of the Writers Guild. I figured all those rich guys didn't need any help from me.

I worked the radio overnight through the summer, except for a wonderful week in August. Edward R. Murrow ordinarily composed his own nightly radio commentary, but Ed Bliss, a gentle and scholarly man, wrote the summary of the day's news that Murrow read to open the broadcast. When Ed Bliss took a short vacation, I was drafted to replace him for a week as Murrow's writer.

I worried about it all weekend, arrived early on Monday morning and spent the day writing and rewriting the news as it clattered in on the press service machines, hearing Murrow's voice in my head as I worked. The great man wandered into the newsroom from his office in late afternoon with his commentary in hand and looked about inquisitively. I was ready. I jumped up, my heart pounding a little, and introduced myself.

"Good," he said in that famous deep voice. We entered the studio and swapped scripts. Murrow started timing and editing my copy. I was supposed to copyread what *he* had written, but I knew I wasn't going to suggest any changes, not in the copy of Edward R. Murrow, not to his face! I kept sneaking peeks to see how much of my work he was changing. Not very much, a word here and there. I turned my attention back to his commentary. It was about the French war in Algeria, well reasoned as always, tightly written. I read with interest—and then, in the middle of the second page, I found a grammatical error. It was a small error of the sort people make in conversation, a subject that didn't strictly agree with its predicate or some such thing. I can't remember, but I *can* remember thinking, all right, what the hell do I do now?

What I did was circle the offending word lightly in pencil and wait for Murrow to finish timing what I had written for him. When he looked up, I handed him his commentary. Trying to keep my voice from breaking, I pointed to the mistake.

"It's wonderful, Mr. Murrow," I said. Then, casually, "I just wondered about this one word."

He glanced down. He fixed it with a few strokes of his pen. He looked up at me and nodded.

He said, "Good catch."

I exhaled. No veteran ever said two kinder words to a beginner.

After the same copyreading ritual the next evening, in the few minutes before Murrow went on the air, he questioned me about my background. I told him I was from North Carolina, knowing it was the state where he was also born. He brightened and spoke a bit about his memories of Polecat Creek in Guilford County and about his Quaker forebears. He asked me about my experience in journalism. Of course, that led only to a very short conversation, but it was the beginning of an amiable interest in my career that was typical of Murrow's generosity toward all the younger staffers. Frequently at the end of the day, he'd say, "Well, we've done as much damage as we can do for one day. Shall we have a drink?" It was a general invitation to all within the sound of his voice, and we all accepted when we could, because we knew we were going to have more than a drink. We were going to have a seminar on broadcast journalism, how things were done and how they ought to be done, with the greatest broadcast journalist of all as moderator.

I couldn't resist telling Murrow that he had appraised my writing once before, when he was a judge of the "Voice of Democracy" contest and I was a schoolboy winner. He seemed delighted by this news and repeated it around the office. For the rest of his years at CBS and even afterward, Murrow made a habit of sending me, as he sent others, notes of encouragement and brief praise.

After his death, Janet Murrow told me she thought her husband had been interested in me because I was from North Carolina, from a place not unlike Polecat Creek. Whatever the reason, and in spite of all his preoccupations, I felt that he never lost his benevolent concern for me. One night that first week, a wartime friend from Europe met him at his office as I was passing on the way to the elevator. Murrow introduced me.

"This," he said, "is my colleague Charles Kuralt."

After that, going back to the radio overnight wasn't so bad.

At the end of my shift one Friday morning in early September, I waved good-bye to one of the good writers and part-time editors on the staff, John Merriman. "See you Sunday night, John," I said. "No, you won't," he said. "You'd better check the assignment schedule." They posted writers' days and hours on a bulletin board in the corner. I never looked at it because, except for the five days with Murrow, my days and hours had remained the same—twelve midnight 'til eight A.M. Monday through Friday. I walked over there and looked, thinking it was John who had been reassigned. It said "Kuralt: Monday–Friday, 11 A.M.–7 P.M., 70 E. 45."

"What's this?" I asked John.

"It's television," he said.

Television. I didn't know anything about television. Television was in another building, and another world. It occurred to me that I had irritated Maggie once too often and was being sent down to the minor leagues. But John Merriman said I should think of this as a promotion. He said they were going to try me out on the television network's big news program, the *CBS Evening News* with Douglas Edwards. One of Doug Edwards's writers, Bill Crawford, was taking a one-year sabbatical to accept a fellowship to Columbia University. I was to be his replacement.

I stood there wondering how any of the daytime bosses knew about me. Later I learned that the management had canvassed all the editors for suggestions, and that John Merriman, after checking with Murrow, had told them a young prospect was buried on the radio overnight. That morning, all he said was, "Look at it this way. Now you get to sleep at night."

3

THE GREENHORN KID

*I*f commuters hurrying through Grand Central Station to catch the six-thirty to Scarsdale on weekday evenings in the late 1950s had ever looked up at the great arched windows of the terminal, they would have seen an odd sight—a line of people running along a catwalk high up in the arches. It might have been a chase scene in an Alfred Hitchcock thriller. What it was was merely the *CBS Evening News* staff trying to get the show on the air on time.

The program was prepared on the 45th Street side of Grand Central in an office building of heroic proportions with high ceilings and echoing marble halls, a structure meant by Commodore Vanderbilt, who put it there, to last for the ages. (Lesser mortals tore it down later and built a mediocre skyscraper on the spot.) The broadcast went on the air from the 42nd Street side of the terminal nearly three blocks away, in a cavernous space the Commodore must have intended to be a ballroom. CBS turned it into a television studio. (I believe it's a tennis court today.) The fast route from the office to the studio was along the catwalk several stories above Grand Central. We hardly ever finished preparing the show on time, so we had to run.

Don Hewitt, the director, who later became famous as the impresario of *60 Minutes*, led the race, shouting instructions to his assistants, Fred Stollmack and Dave Dewey, as he ran. Next came Doug Edwards, the star, with Kleenex tissues flapping from his collar to keep his makeup off his shirt. Doug's secretary, Petie Baird, sprinted behind him, putting his script in order on the run. Bill Porter, the editor, huffed and puffed along in front of Alice Weel, one of the writers, and I gamely brought up the rear with the film editors, Tom Micklas and Len Raff, who were carrying reels of film to the projectionist. This was the entire staff of the biggest news program in television, all in a footrace against the clock. Douglas Edwards frequently delivered the evening's lead story in an urgent pant. People thought he was trying to make the news sound important. Really, he was just trying to catch his breath.

I loved working on the show. The hours were good—nobody showed up until ten or eleven in the morning—and there was so little writing to be done for a fifteen-minute broadcast that Alice and I could discuss our approach to the news and then rewrite and polish our few paragraphs right down to the immutable deadline of six twenty-five P.M. Alice Weel chewed pencils while she was thinking. If she was thinking hard, she could go through a dozen pencils a day. She was a good, methodical writer and her desk was always littered with the remains of Eberhard Faber #2s. She taught me how to write to film. Where *she* learned, I don't know, but, "Don't write captions," she'd say, "don't point out what people are seeing. They can see what they're seeing. Just write the story to flow along with the film. And don't ever let your words fight the pictures. Pictures are so strong that in a fight, they always win."

Don Hewitt was restless, excitable, impatient. He kept urging the motorcycle couriers who brought film in from the airport to figure out ways of making the trip faster. One day, in reaction, one of the messengers brought his Harley-Davidson up in the elevator and roared down the hall right into Don's office to dump a film shipment on his desk. Live coverage of events was rare in those pre-satellite days, but Hewitt bought land-lines to bring the news in live whenever possible. In the studio, he was forever tinkering with camera angles, trying to work out the perfect size ratio of Doug's on-screen face to the pictures that appeared behind him. He invented the "super," the little sign on the screen that identifies people and places without breaking the flow of the news. He invented the "double-projector" story, a technique of on-the-air editing; it permitted the director to choose picture from one film projector and synchronized sound from the other and to create dissolves and other effects that would have taken a week to achieve in a film lab. Hewitt was not a writer, but he knew what he liked, and what he liked were snappy beginnings and amusing endings. Hewitt's innovations became conventions of television news programs everywhere. The evening news was being invented, and Don Hewitt was its Edison.

From my working place on the Edwards show, I could look across the wide hall into the television newsroom where the assignment desk was located. On quiet days, I wandered over there to see how this desk worked. It was staffed by "reporter-contacts," a title that went back to the movie newsreel days when the lordly cameramen were accompanied by underlings who went about collecting facts and getting names spelled right. A reporter-contact at CBS was not a correspondent by a long shot. His main duty was to assign free-lance cameramen to cover fires, train wrecks and beauty contests. Occasionally, if no correspondent was available, a desk reporter might be lucky enough to go out on a story himself. On the assignment desk, people were always quitting or being fired, rarely promoted. But I made friends over there, Phil Scheffler and Harry Reasoner and Bob Schakne. They were the new generation. They did not owe their jobs to Murrow or any of the other titans of CBS News. Their interest was the new medium, television, which the great correspondents disdained. Most of the desk men had lately come from newspaper jobs as I had, and from my safe haven across the hall, I began to envy them the uncertainty and commotion of their lives.

Reporting was what I really wanted to do, and they, at least, had a chance once in a while to cover the news. Reasoner was even sent on a big story, President Eisenhower's dispatch of federal troops to Little Rock to enforce school integration there. Day after day, he sent back magnificently reported stories. Sitting in the peaceful office writing the lead-ins to his reports, I realized I'd rather be in turbulent Little Rock with Reasoner.

"You're crazy," Hewitt said when I told him I was thinking of applying for a job on the assignment desk. "That's a dead-end job." Ralph Paskman, the crusty taskmaster of the desk who always said everything at the top of his voice, said, at the top of his voice, "You're a greenhorn kid, you're lucky to have a job, and you should stay where you are!" He warned that if I moved to the desk, I'd have to take a cut in pay.

But I think Paskman was touched that I wanted to work for him. He was so tough and unforgiving that nobody else wanted to. When the next vacancy came along, he called me aside. "The job's yours if you still want it," he growled. "Come to work at midnight Sunday." I was back on the overnight, and starting all over again.

Paskman didn't want to be awakened at home unless the world was coming to an end, so for a while there, between midnight and eight A.M., all the decisions about national news coverage for the CBS Television Network were in the hands of a twenty-three-year-old ex-cub reporter from *The Charlotte News.* "God help you if you screw this up," Paskman had said, so I kept a scrupulous typewritten log: "2:36 A.M. Woman calls to say drunks making a racket outside saloon on W. 43rd St. Passed. Suggested she call NYPD." CBS had no bureaus outside New York and Washington in those days, so if a dam broke somewhere or a grain silo exploded, we had to hope it happened within range of a stringer camera-man whose name could be found in a thumb-worn Rolodex file along with comments on his past performance: "Caution against panning" and "Give us close-ups for a change" and even "Do not hire if *anybody* else available." I kept an eagle eye on the wire machines for postmidnight calamities that justified leaping to the Rolodex and assigning a camera-man before NBC could get to him. To Paskman, wasting money on cameramen was a sin—after all, CBS paid these guys $25 per assignment and replaced their film free—but getting shut out on a story was a *cardinal* sin.

After a few weeks, Paskman called me at home one afternoon to give me my own first assignment, that night's Chinese New Year celebration. "You can do it on your way in to work," he said. Somehow, I had thought I'd have more time to prepare for my big moment. I hurried to the Brooklyn library, read everything I could about the Chinese way of counting time, and scribbled notes to myself on the subway. I met a staff cameraman named Al Gretz on Mott Street. Gretz set up his heavy, 1,200-foot Auricon sound camera in the middle of all the horns and firecrackers, and with a knot in my stomach and a battery-powered light in my eyes, in my best imitation of the way I thought Murrow would have done it, I delivered into the microphone a sober lecture on the traditions of the Chinese New Year.

I finished and Al turned off the light. I asked him, "What do you think?" He said, "I couldn't hear what you were saying in all this racket, but you sure looked grim. I think this is supposed to be fun."

I said, "Maybe I'd better think of something else to say." We stood there in the middle of the street while I thought.

After a while, Gretz said, "If you will watch the camera and keep anybody from knocking it over, I think I will just have a quick drink in that bar over there."

Paper lions went dancing by, blaring bands passed, confetti fell from the rooftops, strings of firecrackers exploded. The minutes ticked away. I stood in the street alone, trying, and failing, to write a script in my head. I was blowing my first assignment. I might never have another one. I needed a typewriter and a little peace and quiet.

Gretz came back from the bar. "Ready?" he said. "Sure," I said. The light came back on. As I looked toward the camera and opened my mouth to say something, anything, a cherry bomb exploded at my feet with a deafening bang. I jumped and exclaimed, "Wow, that one nearly got me, Al!"

They used thirty seconds of film of the Chinese New Year celebration on the late local news that night, including this much from the reporter on the scene:

"Wow, that one nearly got me, Al!"

They were my first words on the air for CBS News.

My next appearance was even shorter and even sillier. Marilyn Monroe came to town with her husband, Arthur Miller, to promote a new movie. A camera crew and I elbowed our way through a mob of other reporters in a hotel ballroom until I made it to her side. She was wearing a low-cut gown with sequins all over it. She was gorgeous and perspiring. The camera rolled. A surge of the crowd pushed us tightly together.

I said, "Good afternoon, Miss Monroe."

She smiled and said huskily, "Oh, isn't it *hot* in here?"

Grinning foolishly, I wiped my forehead and said, "It sure is!"

She turned away, looking for a way out of the crush, and I couldn't reach her again. That was my interview with Marilyn Monroe. It went on the air in its entirety.

I covered a "cleanup" of Times Square, with Radio City Music Hall Rockettes wielding brooms, a press agent's idea of a compelling story. Even in those innocent days, the film was judged too hokey to inflict on CBS's audience. It was discarded. Nobody but me even remembers that the event took place.

The Brooklyn Dodgers announced plans to move to Los Angeles. In retaliation, a longtime Brooklyn congressman named Emanuel Celler started promoting a third major league for baseball, the Continental League, with a team that would play in Ebbets Field. I went to his office, drew him out on this subject at great length, and watched back in the editing room as they cut my precious interview down to a sentence or two.

I covered the opening of the Ringling Brothers Circus and made a lyrical, carefully memorized speech to the camera with acrobats performing over my shoulder; but then a lion escaped from his cage and sauntered briefly through the lobby of Madison Square Garden before being recaptured. They put the lion on the air, naturally, instead of me. I was beginning to get discouraged.

One night, just at the change of shifts on the assignment desk, Bob Schakne and I were shooting the breeze beside the teletype machines when the bells rang and a short notice moved on the city wire. It said: "Editors: An aircraft is reported down in the East River. Staffing. Will advise." We both reached for phones and called Idlewild and LaGuardia airports. Nobody claimed to know anything, but I could hear a commotion in the background at the LaGuardia tower. Schakne said, "Might be a Piper Cub. Might be nothing. But maybe one of us better get out there just in case." He called a cameraman named Pat Kinghan who lived near LaGuardia and sent him on his way. Then he turned to me.

"You want to go?" he asked.

I said, "Sure, I guess so."

Schakne said, "Well, I do, too, but one of us has to stay here on the desk." He pondered this problem for a couple of seconds and said, "I'll flip you for it."

He took a quarter out of his pocket. "Call it," he said.

"Heads," I said.

He slapped the coin on the back of his hand. It came up heads. Schakne turned back to the phones. I grabbed my coat and hat and a windup Kudelski tape recorder and ran out the door.

About five minutes past the Midtown Tunnel, the taxi I was riding in bogged down in traffic. Radio stations had broadcast the news of a plane crash and half the population of Queens was trying to get to the airport to see it. The cabdriver said, "Nothing I can do for you, pal. We're in it, that's all." I paid him off, jumped out of the cab and started waving my press pass, hitching rides with cars in whichever lane of traffic seemed to be moving.

After a couple of minutes of this, getting nowhere, I saw a motorcycle coming up from behind, working its way between the lanes. I stepped in front of its headlight. The rider was a tough-looking guy in a studded leather jacket. I said, "Look, I'm a reporter. I have to get to LaGuardia in a hurry, and it looks like you're my only hope." He jerked his thumb toward the saddle behind him. "Hold on," he said. I climbed aboard, clutching my tape recorder and holding my knees in tight to keep from banging them into the cars on either side. He gunned the bike forward. He drove that thing like a stunt rider, squeezing through impossibly narrow spaces at full speed, and in no time, he banked hard right onto the LaGuardia Airport grounds.

"Where do you want to go?" he hollered back at me. Off in the distance, I could see a cluster of lights at the end of a runway, the revolving red lights of police cars and a searchlight aimed into the darkness of the river.

"I want to go there," I said, "but . . ."

Behind us, a fire truck gave us a blast of its horn and headed for an open gate onto the field. The motorcycle driver slowed to let the fire truck pass, then fell in behind the truck and roared right through the gate and across the taxiways and runways to the cluster of emergency vehicles at the water's edge.

"Jesus," I said, "that was a hell of a ride."

I reached into my pocket. All I had left was a five-dollar bill and some loose change. I handed him the five. "It's all I have," I said. He handed it back.

"Forget it," he said.

"By the way," he said, "what's going on?"

I said, "A plane crash, I think."

A New York cop came over to us from the crowd around the trucks and police cars. "What do you think you're doing here?" he snarled. I showed him my press card. He turned to the motorcycle rider. "And what about you?" he asked. The bike rider nodded to me and said, "I'm with him." The cop said, "Don't get in the way," and walked off.

I didn't see the motorcycle rider again. I never even got to thank him. A big portable generator was roaring to power the searchlight. People were hollering to one another in confusion. More emergency trucks kept arriving. I looked around and realized I was the only person on the scene who wasn't wearing a uniform. I turned on the tape recorder, walked up to a police sergeant, waited until he finished shouting into a radio and then asked him what he could tell me.

"American Airlines," he said. "One of their new planes, four-engine turboprop coming in from Chicago. Hit the water. There are survivors. That's all I know."

"How do you know there are survivors?" I asked him.

He stared at me.

He said, "Just walk over there and listen."

I walked away from the sound of the generator into the darkness along the shore. When I was far enough away, I could hear occasional faint shouts coming from out in the river and see the searchlight lingering on floating bits of debris. Some of the passengers were alive in the water and calling for help, but the searchlight couldn't seem to find them. A couple of police launches inched through the darkness in the middle of the river, fanning the water with their own tiny spotlights, and I could see what looked like a small fishing trawler tacking back and forth. Everything seemed to be happening in slow motion. The muffled cries from the river became less frequent.

I stood there alone in the dark. I didn't know what to do. I felt like crying.

Finally, I remembered the tape recorder. I turned it on and aimed the microphone at the river, wondering if it would pick up the distant calls for help. Then I spoke into it, trying to describe the sound of the voices in the darkness, the deliberate movement of the boats, the frustration of the would-be rescuers on shore. I remembered to mention that there was a tugboat strike in New York at the time, otherwise many more harbor craft would be out there on a night like this looking for survivors.

After I had said everything I could think of into the machine, I realized I had failed to get the name of the police sergeant I'd talked to a few minutes before. I walked back toward the crowd of emergency vehicles to try to find him and ran into Pat Kinghan, our cameraman, just arriving. He was out of breath from carrying his heavy equipment across the field.

"They're not letting anybody out here," he said. "I had to climb a fence. How the hell did you get here so fast?"

"I got a ride," I said.

Kinghan shot a fast hundred feet of film of the lights and the fire trucks and said, "We'd better get out of here before they throw us out." I shouldered his tripod and one of his batteries and we headed back across the maze of runways for the terminal. It took a long time to get there. On the way, Kinghan said, "We better go in and talk to people who were waiting for the plane." I hadn't thought of that. I didn't want to do it. What could I say to people who knew their relatives might be dead out there in the river? But when we reached the terminal building, Kinghan ran right up the stairs into the American Airlines waiting room and I followed.

It was worse than I imagined it would be. Twenty or thirty people stood in shock or sat on benches with their heads in their hands. Some of them were sobbing uncontrollably. When they saw Kinghan setting up the camera, several turned away. I whispered, "I'm not going to try to talk to them, Pat. I just can't."

But two or three, then half a dozen of the people crowded around us. They *wanted* to talk, to ask what we knew, to tell me how long they'd been waiting and how they heard the news of the crash. An airline official came over to try gently to intervene but they ignored him. They wanted to share their fears with somebody.

"I am Mr. Warren from Flatbush," one man said with dignity. "It's my wife. She only went to Chicago for two days to visit her mother. You haven't heard, have you, anything about a Mrs. Warren?"

I felt awkward. I wanted to leave and give these people back their privacy.

"I'm sorry," I said. "I do think there are going to be some survivors."

"Let us pray you are right," Mr. Warren said.

Other reporters and camera crews were showing up. A CBS motorcycle messenger came running through the door. He came up to me and said quietly, so nobody else could hear, "Don Hewitt has lined up a big tugboat and a tape crew, and they're on the way to the scene. We're way ahead of everybody else. Paskman says for you to break off right now and get into the office with whatever you've got."

Pat Kinghan ripped the film magazine from his camera and handed it to me. He said, "Take good care of that, kid." I grabbed the magazine of unprocessed film and followed the courier out to his motorcycle for my second wild ride of the night. We reached the office in fifteen minutes, and half an hour later, I went on the air with the first pictures and description of the crash scene, an incomplete story of the accident, but— I was only beginning to understand how important this was in television news—the *first*.

After that, working with a film editor who matched my tape recording to Pat Kinghan's pictures, I put together a more coherent version of the story for the morning news program. There were the lights on the river and the indistinct cries for help. There was Mr. Warren asking about his wife. I was relieved that the pictures and sound were all there, but when we projected the finished story, I felt like crying again. I had to look away from the screen.

"Go home," Ralph Paskman said gruffly. "You did okay."

It was the middle of the morning. I walked down into the Grand Central subway station to wait for the shuttle to Times Square and the Seventh Avenue Express to Brooklyn. I bought an early edition of an afternoon newspaper with the plane crash splashed all over the front page. Inside, the paper listed the names of a few survivors the police boats had picked up. Mrs. Warren's name wasn't in there.

My head ached and my chest felt full. I wondered if I might be having a heart attack. I knew that real reporters were aggressive while covering a big story, and exhilarated afterward. I had been reluctant and meek, only going on the story because I won a coin toss, only getting to the scene because a nameless motorcycle rider took me onto the airfield without asking, only doing the interviews at the terminal because Pat Kinghan told me I had to. And now that it was over, I didn't feel exhilarated. I felt sad.

Well, it was all my secret. I went home and went to bed.

A few days later, the President of CBS News, Sig Mickelson, called me into his office.

"We'd like to offer you a job as a correspondent," he said.

CBS News Correspondent was the title held by Murrow, Sevareid and Collingwood. Only one correspondent had ever been promoted from the assignment desk, and that was Harry Reasoner just a few weeks before. But Reasoner was a seasoned reporter in his thirties. I was not yet twenty-four years old. I had just proved to myself that I didn't have what it took to cover a big story. As I opened my mouth to speak, Sig Mickelson held up his hand.

"Think about it," he said. "Talk it over with your wife. You'd be based in New York, but the job would involve an awful lot of traveling."

I don't know how I'd have answered him if he hadn't said that last word.

"Traveling."

I took the job on the spot.

4

GLOBE-TROTTING

I already had a New York City press shield. It said "Bearer is entitled to pass police and fire lines wherever formed." Now, CBS News issued me a green air travel card, good for ticket purchases to any destination on earth. I regarded these credentials as icons, the confirmation of worldly attainment. I didn't have much time to indulge my newfound self-importance, however. The Eisenhower era was ending, the world was changing out there, and CBS News was woefully short of legmen. I was sent running.

My first assignment was to cover the beginning of something—the opening of the new St. Lawrence Seaway, which permitted seagoing vessels twice the length of a football field to sail right into the middle of the continent. I was the first person to enter the seaway, standing in the bow of the first ship. At Chicago, that ship unloaded steel bars from Japan almost in the shadow of the Gary, Indiana, steel mills. In my story, I said something about coals to Newcastle, making much of a ship bringing Japanese steel up the seaway for sale in Gary. I did not imagine that other ships would someday bring Japanese automobiles for sale in Detroit.

Then I was sent off to cover the end of something—one of the last lynchings in the deep South. A twenty-three-year-old black man, Mack Charles Parker, accused of raping a white woman, was taken from his jail cell in Poplarville, Mississippi, on the eve of his trial. A mob of masked white men dragged him by his feet down the steps of the county jail, leaving a trail of blood from his head on the stairs.

Ten days later, Mack Charles Parker's body was found floating in the Pearl River. By that time, I knew the names of every man in the lynch mob and had even been to see a couple of them, my first experience at looking murderers in the face. It had taken the FBI about a day to solve the crime and provide a complete report to the county prosecutor. Working together, a UPI reporter and I managed to "borrow" the FBI report for a few hours one night and copy it in longhand. The killers named were ignorant backwoods tung tree growers, a former lawman, a fundamentalist preacher. The whole county knew them. The all-white county grand jury refused to indict any of them. Those still living are probably walking around free to this day in Pearl River County, Mississippi.

I left Poplarville feeling sick. I haven't been back there. When crossing southern Mississippi, you can avoid that one county seat by swinging up through Hattiesburg or going south along the coast by way of Biloxi, and all these years later, one way or the other around Poplarville is the way I always feel like going.

Most of the rest of that summer I spent among empty farmhouses, screen doors banging in the wind, weeds growing in the corn stubble. I was in the Great Plains for the first time, wandering through Nebraska, Kansas and Oklahoma to chronicle the death of family farms.

My cameraman and guide was Wendell Hoffman, a rangy, grown-up farm boy who had taught himself how to use a Bell & Howell Filmo and the big, awkward Auricon sound camera. Wendell had rambled all over the world for CBS News as a free-lance cameraman, but he insisted on making his home in Manhattan, Kansas, where he lived with his wife, Doretta, dean of the Department of Home Economics at Kansas State, and a houseful of growing sons. When he wasn't shooting film for CBS, Wendell was out on the land, trying to make a farm of his own pay off, changing his crop from corn to hogs to Christmas trees depending on his mood and his calculations of national demand. He was a wonderful cameraman, but I don't think he ever made it as a farmer. It was Wendell who had suggested a series on the spreading failures among small farmers, and it was from Wendell that I learned much in my first summer as a CBS News Correspondent about hard work, pain and disappointment in rural America. I also discovered the satisfying camaraderie that can develop between a cameraman and a correspondent working together toward a common goal. In Wendell's battered station wagon, we drove thousands of miles together in the summer of 1959, stopping at small-town grocery stores for supplies of baloney, mayonnaise and white bread from which to make our lunches, sending stories back to New York every few days, driving on, soaking up the feelings of the vast, rolling land under the big sky.

Next thing I knew, I was chatting with Nikita Khrushchev in a silage pit on a farm outside Coon Rapids, Iowa.

"You look a little tired," I said to Nikita Khrushchev.

"No, no," he said. He put a beefy hand on my shoulder. "I do not sleep eight hours a night," he said. "If you sleep eight hours and live for sixty years, that's twenty years of sleep!" He waited for this remark to be translated. He shook a finger at me and repeated reprovingly, "Yes, twenty years of sleep!"

Khrushchev was on the final leg of a grumpy tour of America. In New York, he was needled by the crowds. In California, he complained that they showed him the backsides of dancers doing the can-can on a movie lot when what he really wanted to do was go to Disneyland. In Des Moines when they gave him his first hot dog he said it would have gone down a lot better with a cold beer.

But now on Roswell Garst's hog farm, wearing a fedora with the brim turned up and a suit with sleeves that were too long for him, the Premier of the Union of Soviet Socialist Republics was having a roaring good time at last, traipsing in the silage pit, reaching down for handfuls of corn shucks to throw at the news photographers when they crowded too close, bawling insults at the big mob of reporters. My job was to stay at Khrushchev's elbow come what may, holding a radio transmitter with a great long whip antenna, so that no remark could go unrecorded.

Farmer Garst said, "Well now, Mr. Premier, you should know that Iowa produced something above 700 million bushels of corn this year. . . ."

Khrushchev said, "The Ukraine, you know, is the most fertile land on the earth."

Garst said, "Well, we could produce even more corn in Iowa if the government didn't pay us to produce less."

Khrushchev said, "The big American corporations don't want to see farmers get too rich, isn't that it?"

"Well, not exactly," Garst said. "You see . . ."

Nikita Khrushchev wasn't listening. He was waving his arms, shouting at the reporters again and cutting up for the cameras. In the maelstrom, I lost my place at his side, slipped in the wet silage and fell down. When I looked up, all I could see was the rump of the Soviet Premier as he climbed out of the pit and headed toward the Garst farmhouse for lunch. I thought, this is the man the whole free world is afraid of? He's a clown, that's what he is. And we, I reflected, brushing corn silks off my pants as the horde of my fellow reporters and photographers thundered away after Khrushchev and Garst, we're clowns, too.

The only trouble was, I was beginning to enjoy life in the center ring. The political primaries of 1960 were coming on and I was enlisted in the ragtag band of reporters who crisscrossed the country as political camp followers. I didn't let my prejudices show through in my reports, but I found myself pulling hard for the joyful liberal, Hubert Humphrey, against the rich young interloper, John F. Kennedy. I felt personally forsaken when Kennedy, pouring his father's money into the race, ended Humphrey's presidential hopes for that year with a victory in the grimy cities and lonely hollows of West Virginia. Harry Reasoner got to cover that one. After the voting, Robert Kennedy came over to Humphrey headquarters in Charleston to escort the loser to Kennedy headquarters a few blocks away where Humphrey was to publicly congratulate the winner. Up on the stage, a country singer, refusing to give up, whanged away at his guitar and loudly sang a Humphrey anthem we had all heard a hundred times: "I'm for Hubert Humphrey, he's for you and me . . ." Bob Kennedy put his arm around Humphrey's shoulder. They walked out into the night, Humphrey still smiling bravely. I always thought he would have been a great President.

CBS News did not yet have bureaus all over the country, not even in Los Angeles or Chicago. The correspondents whose names everybody knew covered London or Paris or stuck to their radio essays from Washington. That left the whole United States of America to Harry Reasoner and me. We were pals, Harry and Charlie, CBS's good soldiers, willing to go anywhere and cover anything. It didn't matter if one of us outworked the other on a story so long as between us we made NBC and ABC look bad. Reasoner and I listened to John F. Kennedy's ringing acceptance speech at the end of the Democratic convention in Los Angeles that July and then drove straight through to Chicago without stopping to sleep, in order to be ready for the Republican convention which was about to begin. Afterward, I trailed Richard Nixon through Texas, Wyoming, Washington and California, then went off to cover Kennedy in Ohio, Illinois and Michigan.

We watched the campaign transform the campaigners. Richard Nixon, Eisenhower's vice president, started out projecting an image of calm and maturity, trying to play both experienced statesman and regular fellow, telling homey stories about his boyhood employment in a general store, about a toy train his family couldn't afford to buy him for Christmas; by the end of the campaign, rattled by Kennedy's attacks on the Republican Party, he seemed grim and angry. His speeches became defensive and indignant and sometimes a little out of control.

Kennedy, on the other hand, was stiff and businesslike at the outset of the campaign, hacking the air awkwardly with his right arm as he punched his points across in speeches; but as the summer ended and fall came on, the impatient, over-serious candidate gave way to a relaxed and smiling one who could joke with his staff and then go out and respond to the cheers of the crowds. Moreover, he became easily accessible to reporters. If we needed a moment alone with Kennedy to fill out a story we were working on, all it took was a word to Pierre Salinger, his press aide. Kennedy gave dozens of these private interviews; Nixon avoided them. Kennedy seemed to enjoy the give-and-take with the reporters; Nixon suspected us and kept us at arm's length. After Richard Nixon's narrow defeat in November, he accused the press of being secretly on Kennedy's side. By that time, I am sure, he was right. I always have believed that the outcome of that election might have been different had Nixon been able to put his feet up at the end of the day and relax with the reporters, explaining his positions over a glass of scotch and a cigar. But he was not the drinking, smoking, explaining sort, or the relaxing sort either. I think it cost him the Presidency in 1960.

In the middle of the Presidential campaign, CBS News started a new Friday night program, *Eyewitness to History*, with the avowed intention of covering the big news story of the week wherever in the world it occurred. I was pulled off the campaign and installed as the youthful anchorman. I bought a trench coat and waited for the phone to ring.

"The Congo," Les Midgley, the *Eyewitness* producer, said on the phone, and I was off to the Congo. A more experienced globe-trotter, Ernest Leiser, and I played gin rummy for seventeen hours as we throbbed across the Atlantic toward west Africa in a DC-7, then flew eight more hours down the coast into the Heart of Darkness. But even Joseph Conrad's story, even the dying Kurtz crying out "The horror! The horror!" had not prepared me for the chaos and danger of the place. The Belgians, under world pressure, had suddenly given up their dominion over a land of 14 million, leaving behind not one doctor, not one judge, not one engineer or economist. In a sovereign nation newly "free," there were no courts, no lawyers and no law. Terror ruled the streets of the old Belgian capital and tribal rivalries erupted into warfare in the bush. Soldiers of the former Force Publique raced about in jeeps, frenzied, armed and belligerent. There was no safety anywhere. The Congo was a bad dream.

The first night I spent in Léopoldville, now Kinshasa, all the reporters in the hotel were rounded up by soldiers banging on doors with rifle butts. We were forced into the lobby and required at gunpoint to prove we were not Belgians by presenting our documents to noncommissioned officers who could not read. One reporter showed the only identification he had—his Italian driver's license, which had also served to get him into the country after a trip across the Congo River from Brazzaville in a dugout canoe. The next day, as a group of reporters gathered in the street outside the house of Premier Patrice Lumumba to wait for a promised interview, guards pointed excitedly to one of those waiting, grabbed him, took him aside and began clubbing him. There was nothing the other reporters could do to help. The victim was an Algerian journalist friendly to Lumumba who had made the mistake that morning of putting on a web belt and brass buckle to hold up his pants. Spotting the belt, which was similar to those worn by Belgian officers, the guards had taken the poor man for a spy. Without asking any questions, they beat him to death with their rifle butts and left him lying there in the street. When this was reported to Lumumba an hour later, he shook his head and laughed.

Capricious death overtook others, too. One morning, I watched a young American reporter, Henry J. Taylor, Jr., leave the hotel in a jeep to join a column of troops out in the countryside who were said to be loyal to Joseph Kasavubu, the President of the country. That night, we heard that the column had been ambushed and that Taylor had been killed—victim of a poisoned arrow in the chest. I was deeply shaken. I wanted to go home.

Instead, I let myself be talked into going to Matadi, the port city on the Congo River a day's drive away. It was John Tiffin, a dashing English cameraman for CBS, who talked me into it.

"Nobody's been there, you know," he said. "Rumors of a massacre. Abandoned streets and all that. Hell of a story." He produced a taxi driver willing to make the trip and a big American flag to stretch across the hood of the car. "Who'd do harm," he asked with a smile, "to two nice fellows under the protection of the Stars and Stripes?"

He got his answer in the first village we came to. A barefoot man with a rifle stepped in front of the car and signaled us to pull over.

"We better stop!" I shouted to the driver.

"Step on it!" Tiffin shouted louder. *"Allez-y! En avant!"*

The driver accelerated straight toward the man with the gun, who leapt aside as we ducked to the floor of the car. We looked back to see him squeezing off wild shots in our direction. The bullets all missed and the car careened around a corner and back to the open road.

I sat up slowly. I said, "What if he radios ahead?"

Tiffin said, "The bloke doesn't even have shoes. It's a safe bet he doesn't have a radio."

In Matadi, we didn't find any evidence of a massacre. What we found instead were Congolese randomly strolling about in their neighborhoods as if on holiday, and in the former white district, sepulchral silence. I still see Matadi sometimes at night in my dreams of the world after Armageddon. The business section held only broken, looted stores. In the residential districts where 1,800 Europeans had lived, the houses were empty. It took the Belgians eighty years to construct Matadi—and a few panic-stricken hours to clear out and leave the city to the river and to the Congolese. We walked about among artifacts of the white man's civilization, curious relics now—a swing for the children, an outdoor theater for amusement, a tennis court for exercise, all empty and irrelevant. The Congo, about to become Zaire, had no use for swings, theaters and tennis courts at the moment. A mailbox sign said "Dr. von Dreesche." The doctor, whoever he may have been, had abandoned his car on the dock with those of his neighbors and sailed for Antwerp.

I didn't feel sorry for the Belgians. I knew their record of cruel colonialism; the penalty for petty thievery once had been loss of the thieving hand, and hundreds of Congolese now walked around handless. But I felt terribly sorry for the country the Belgians had left behind. In Matadi, I had a vision of the future of black Africa, and it was a gloomy vision, silent and despairing.

Tiffin and I found lodging for ourselves and the cabdriver at the Metropole Hotel above the river, an old building with rooms arranged around an open courtyard. The French owner of the hotel had sent his family to safety and stayed on to try to protect his property. He helped carry our bags up to the rooms in the otherwise nearly empty building, wryly apologizing for the absence of the hotel staff, and let us borrow his shortwave radio receiver.

"Now," Tiffin said, fiddling with the tuner, "the ace trick is to dial the Beeb."

It took him only a few minutes to find a BBC newsreader dryly reciting the day's developments in the Congo. Lumumba and Kasavubu were still feuding. There was a report of fighting in Katanga Province. "And in the vacated port city of Matadi, officials of the Force Publique have threatened to direct their artillery against a hotel, the Metropole, which they describe as a hiding place for Belgian saboteurs."

We looked at each other in shock. "Time for a word with the management," Tiffin said. We ran down the stairs to the Frenchman's office to tell him what we had heard.

"Oh, yes," he said wearily. "They have been saying this for several days now. What can one do?"

What Tiffin and I did was stay awake the rest of the night. Sometime after midnight, a truculent squad of obviously drunken soldiers stormed into the hotel courtyard shouting for the Frenchman to come out. When he did, the soldiers surrounded him menacingly, poking him with the barrels of their rifles. Tiffin and I looked down at this frightening scene from a dark balcony above. My impulse was to get out of there somehow and hide. Tiffin's was to grab his camera and a portable light.

"What the hell are you doing?" I whispered.

" 'The heart of danger,' " he said, " 'is where we shall find safety.' It's a Chinese proverb." He handed me the light. "Turn it on when I say. Let's go."

He led the way calmly down the stairs and addressed the sergeant who seemed to be in charge. *"Bon soir, Monsieur le Commandant. Je suis journaliste américain.* Light, please!" I pressed a button and flooded the courtyard with light. The soldiers looked about uncertainly as Tiffin proceeded to film them as if they were a winning Liverpool soccer team—wide shot, close-up, with special attention to the sergeant, captain of the team. The soldiers assumed something like military bearing. One or two of them grinned self-consciously. After a couple minutes of this, the sergeant said a word to the French hotel owner and led his squad smartly out of the hotel and down the street. "Kill the light, please," Tiffin said to me.

Often afterward, I have heard the argument that television news can never quite be true to life because the camera's presence alters events. Well, it did that time, thank God.

We headed back to the capital with our film of Matadi, the deserted port and the midnight callers. On the way, we stopped at roadside grocery stores looking for Players cigarettes, Tiffin's brand, which were unavailable in the ransacked stores of Léopoldville. We finally were able to find two precious tins of Players in the rural grocery of a woman who kept a shiny long-barreled six-shooter on the counter to guard her stock from looters. She agreed to part with the cigarettes if we would also buy a chicken. We struck the deal. She went out back and caught the chicken, which the taxi driver placed, untrussed and cackling, in the trunk. Tiffin tossed the Players in his shoulder bag. Cash, smiles and handshakes were exchanged, and we departed in an air of satisfaction all around. The driver, for all his bravado on the trip down, took a long detour on dirt roads on the way back to avoid the village of the barefoot rifleman. We arrived in Léopoldville feeling smug and successful with a chicken in the trunk.

The next morning, I hired an illegal launch to take me across the river and out of the country. Weeks later, when I saw John Tiffin again, he told me that a few nights after we left Matadi, the Metropole Hotel had been shelled to the ground.

He also told me he had rationed the priceless Players so that only one cigarette was left on the morning of his own departure. He took it out as he was being ferried across the river, lighted it, and tossed the empty tin into the Congo. A crocodile rose from the depths, crushed the tin in its jaws and disappeared into the brown water.

I knew I would need a stopover on the way back to New York. I flew from Brazzaville to Paris, arriving in the midst of the morning rush hour with the dust of the Congo still on my clothes. I had never been to Paris before. I took a taxi to the Hotel Raphael, where David Schoenbrun, the Paris bureau chief, had reserved a room for me. The hotel proved to be small and extremely elegant. I was shown to a room with a crystal chandelier hanging from the ceiling and a rich Bokhara rug on the floor. The white sheets of a canopied feather bed were turned down and waiting for me.

I drew back the heavy draperies, opened the French doors and stepped out onto a balcony that overlooked the Avenue Kleber. I was dirty, unshaven and exhausted. I looked to my right and saw a beautiful woman dressed in a terry-cloth robe standing on the balcony of the room next door. It was Leslie Caron.

"Good morning, Miss Caron," I said. Without a word she turned, swept back into her room and closed the doors.

I laughed to myself. I had been to Africa and been shot at. I was alive. I was in Paris. There was a movie star in the room next door. It was a beautiful, clear, cool morning. It was my twenty-sixth birthday.

I left the balcony, took a long, hot shower and slept the day away.

"Cuba," Les Midgley said on the phone, and I went off to Havana with Wendell Hoffman. In the days when Fidel Castro was still a guerrilla in the Sierra Maestra, Wendell had undertaken a long, dangerous journey into the mountains on foot to secure the first film interview with him. Now that Castro was in command of the country, Wendell thought CBS might have a certain *entrée* to the centers of power. We wasted a lot of time hanging out in designated bars in the small hours of the morning waiting for a promised rendezvous with Fidel. To Wendell's disgust, this meeting never materialized. As booby prize, I was awarded an interview with Che Guevara. He was going to become a martyr and a legend, but in the second year of the Cuban Revolution, Che struck me as a pompous braggart.

"New Orleans," Midgley said, and a few hours later I was in the midst of a screaming mob of white parents trying to prevent a six-year-old black girl named Ruth Nell Bridges from entering a public school. The little girl wore a pretty yellow dress and held the hands of two strapping U.S. marshals as she walked up the steps of the William Frantz School with the cruel, loud insults of all those white people in her ears. When she came out after school, the crowd was even larger and louder. Wendell Hoffman and I walked down the steps with her, with the camera aimed, not at the little girl, but at the howling throng on the sidewalk. "This," I said, as the camera moved through the crowd, "is what the only Negro student in the only truly integrated school in the deep South sees and hears every afternoon." It was a forceful and appalling bit of film. Shooting it cost Wendell a rotten egg on his jacket.

The Frantz school was "truly integrated" only because a handful of white parents refused to join the boycott that kept all the other white youngsters at home. One of these was a man named James Gabrielle who accompanied his six-year-old daughter Yolanda to her first-grade class every day through the jeering, threatening gauntlet. "Hold your head up," he told his daughter. "They can't keep you from going to school." After school one day, Wendell Hoffman and I followed James Gabrielle and Yolanda back to the public housing project where they lived. The little girl was crying.

"Don't cry," her father said. "You have to do this again tomorrow."

"I know, Daddy," she said.

James Gabrielle's shirt was torn and he was steaming. I told him what he was doing seemed courageous. He said, "Well, I wouldn't say courageous. I am just not going to have a goddamn mob tell me what to do with my child."

I wonder whether Ruth Nell Bridges and Yolanda Gabrielle, first-grade classmates, became friends. I wonder whether they remember each other. They should, because they did something important together. Deep South school integration had to start somewhere. It started with two brave little girls in New Orleans.

A few days later, Midgley said, "Laos." I left on a Friday night, flew twenty-seven hours on Pan Am and Royal Air Lao, and stepped out into a country just emerging into the thirteenth century—except for all the guns and airplanes. King Savang Vatthana's troops were fighting Communist rebels in the Plain of Jars, gingerly, at a distance, with artillery. Unmarked transport planes flew all over the country, Russian planes bringing guns and rice to the rebels and American planes bringing guns and rice to the Royal Lao Army, a few thousand loyal Meo and Hmong tribesmen. Neither army seemed to want to hurt anybody, and neither needed more guns, but the United States had solemnly committed $50 million a year to guns for our Laotians and the Russians probably that much or more for theirs, so the guns kept coming in.

On the outskirts of Vientiane, I saw a neat little cinderblock building with a sign that said "Indiana Telephone Company." I knocked on the door. The man who answered said, "Yep, we're under contract to improve the phone service in the country. If you'll excuse me, we're awfully busy right now." But there wasn't any phone service in the country. I figured I had just met the CIA station chief.

At night, the Indiana Telephone Company employees congregated in a bar downtown to drink beer and dance with the local girls. In the distance, the sound of the artillery went on all night. I thought it would make a great sequence on film if I stood outside in the street and listened to the guns and then walked into the Lido Nightclub where the music was playing and everybody was dancing, ignoring the war. But when I tried it, it didn't work. The minute I walked into the place with the camera rolling, all those "telephone workers" covered their faces, dived under the tables or ran out the back door, and the band stopped playing. Even the musicians worked for the CIA.

I visited a couple of *boun*s at rural temples, Buddhist church socials with dancing on the grounds. I drove to the royal capital, Luang Prabang, on a highway being built with millions of American dollars, passing at the place where the paving ran out a sign warning travelers to turn around, Communists ahead. I made this trip in a Mercedes-Benz. I don't know what they were doing there, but there were hundreds of Mercedes-Benzes in Vientiane, some of them for hire, so I hired one.

A few other Western reporters trickled into the country while I was there. We met nightly on the veranda of the Continental Hotel and talked about our illnesses. We all had taken care to drink only the bottled water provided in the rooms, but still we all felt sick. A *Time* magazine reporter had to be evacuated to Bangkok with a severe case of dysentery. Finally one morning, Keyes Beech of the *Chicago Daily News*, an old Asia hand, solved the mystery. He caught the room boy from the hotel filling the bottles at the filthy town well. When Beech remonstrated with him, the young man shrugged and smiled an innocent Laotian smile. "The Europeans like their water in bottles," he said.

"If Laos fell to the Communist Pathet Lao," I said on the air, "pro-Western Thailand and South Vietnam could no longer be considered safe, so the stakes in this secret war are high: the future of Southeast Asia." In truth, I thought the "secret war" had all the elements of a comic opera. But I wasn't sure enough of my judgment to report it that way. It was the first war I had ever attended. For all I knew, all of them were like this.

When I reached Hong Kong on the way home, I reported to Les Midgley by telephone.

"Well, chum," he said, "I'm sorry to tell you, but you've been bumped out of the sled."

"What does that mean?" I asked.

"You're not the anchorman of *Eyewitness* anymore," he said.

"What have I done wrong?" I asked.

"Not a thing as far as I'm concerned," he said. "It seems to be Aubrey's decision." Jim Aubrey was the head of CBS Television "across town," a man known to underlings as the Smiling Cobra. I had never even met him.

"Aubrey thinks our ratings might go up if somebody more mature anchors the show," Midgley said. "Mickelson argued for you, I think, but he lost. We're going to have a new anchorman."

"Who's it going to be?" I asked.

"Fellow named Cronkite," Midgley said.

So that is how Walter Cronkite got his first big break in television.

Cronkite was a solid, experienced wire service reporter who had distinguished himself as a combat correspondent in World War II and decided during the Korean War to try his hand at broadcasting. I liked and admired him, and figured he was a lot more logical choice than I had been to anchor *Eyewitness* in the first place.

I said this to Midgley and then asked, "What's going to happen to me?"

"You'll still be in the field," Midgley said. "We want you on every story. Nothing's going to happen to you, except that you won't ever have to come home anymore."

"Okay," I said. "Now let me tell you what we got in Luang Prabang."

I found that I didn't mind being kicked out of the studio—which was just as well, because it was good practice for all the studios I was going to be kicked out of in the future. I knew I could get along fine without makeup, lights and camera, even without fame and fortune, as long as they didn't take away my air travel card, the green one, the one that lets you go everywhere in the world.

5

THE RUNAWAY CRUISE SHIP

*T*he new President, John F. Kennedy, sent his Secretary of State, Dean Rusk, to a SEATO meeting in Thailand; I went along. There was a steel strike in Pennsylvania; I covered it. Ambassador Adlai Stevenson made a tour of South America; I traveled with him, discovering a new country every day. I woke up those mornings staring at hotel room ceilings and trying to remember whether I was in Bangkok, Bethlehem or Bogotá. Wherever I was, it wasn't Brooklyn, where I was supposed to live.

My wife had another baby. We talked by phone and agreed to name her Susan. I stopped by the hospital to admire Susan and then caught another flight to somewhere else. I was drunk with travel, dizzy with the import of it all, and indifferent to thoughts of home and family. Pretty soon, I no longer had a home or family. Sory and I agreed to separate. We did that by phone, too. She moved back to North Carolina with Lisa and Susan. I gave up the apartment, put my few possessions into storage, and flew off to the Dominican Republic with a camera crew to cover the final fall of the Trujillo dynasty. This was callous and unfeeling behavior, of course. The thought of missing a breaking story had become more intolerable to me than the thought of letting our lives fly apart. It was much later that the burden of guilt settled upon me, and much too late.

My passport, fattening with fanfold inserts, grew to the thickness of a paperback novel. I still listed my residence as "New York, N.Y." on the visa applications and airline landing cards, but for a long time, I had no residence at all except for whatever room I happened to be staying in for the night. I didn't want a place to live; I had nothing to do there. I didn't want days off; I had no way to fill empty days. All I wanted was stories, the wilder the better.

A wild one came along. A luxurious Portuguese cruise ship, the *Santa Maria*, with 600 souls aboard, including about forty American vacationers, was hijacked in the Caribbean by a band of Portuguese rebels. Their leader, a stouthearted old crackpot named Henrique Galvao, put a boat ashore in Venezuela with members of the ship's crew who were wounded when the pirates stormed the bridge, then steered the *Santa Maria* for the open sea.

My assignment—and that of dozens of other reporters from all over the world—was to get to that ship somehow. But first we had to find it. The *Santa Maria* just vanished into the South Atlantic. For several days, U.S. Navy reconnaissance planes crisscrossing the ocean and U.S. Navy destroyers steaming in search patterns turned up nothing. It began to be a little embarrassing. I interviewed an admiral. "It's a big ocean out there," he said.

I flew to Caracas, found the ship's purser who had just been put ashore, and persuaded him to give me his first interview:

"Did you talk to Galvao yourself?"

"Yes, before I leave the ship, I talk to him."

"What did he tell you?"

"He told me you go ashore but during four or five days, you don't speak about this."

"He told you not to talk to anybody?"

"No, not talk about this. He said if you talk and come ships or planes to catch me, I sink the ship together with passengers."

"Do you think he meant it?"

"Yes, he's serious. It's not a joke."

The U.S. State Department protested to CBS News that this interview should not have been broadcast because it might have "upset" the

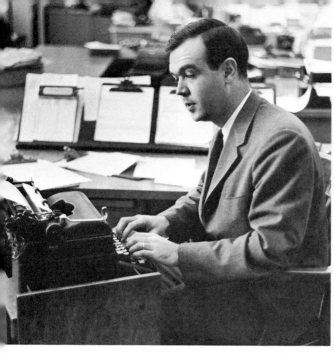

On the Desk at CBS News, 1958. (*CBS News.*)

With Mike Wallace at the Democratic National Convention, 1960. (*CBS News.*)

On the Léopoldville–Matadi road, 1960.

John Tiffin filming in Matadi, Congo, 1960. (*Charles Kuralt.*)

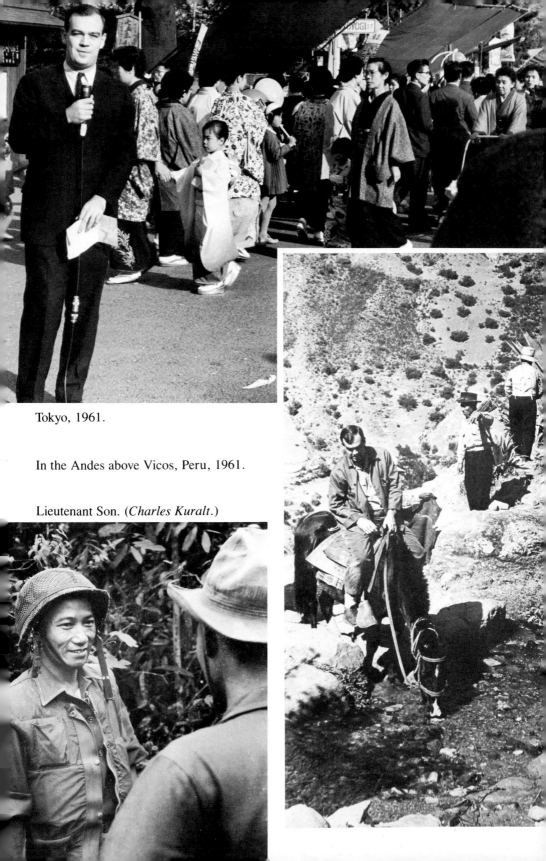

Tokyo, 1961.

In the Andes above Vicos, Peru, 1961.

Lieutenant Son. (*Charles Kuralt*.)

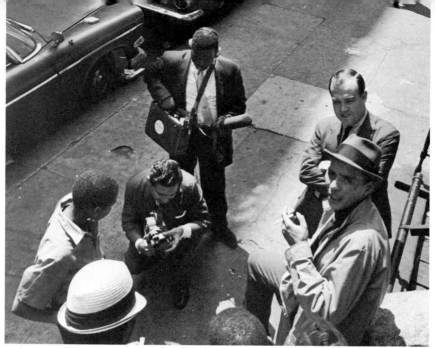

117th Street, New York, with cameraman Herb Schwartz. (*CBS News.*)

Campaign '64. (*CBS News.*)

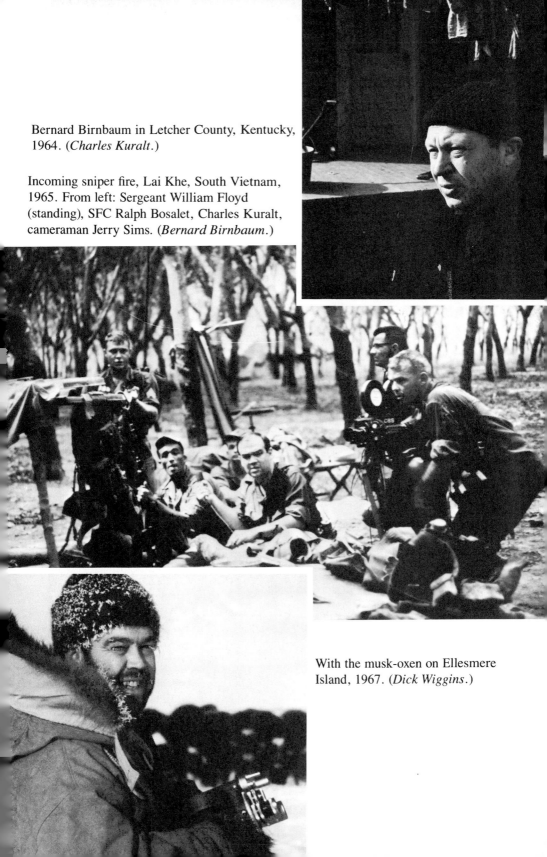

Bernard Birnbaum in Letcher County, Kentucky, 1964. (*Charles Kuralt.*)

Incoming sniper fire, Lai Khe, South Vietnam, 1965. From left: Sergeant William Floyd (standing), SFC Ralph Bosalet, Charles Kuralt, cameraman Jerry Sims. (*Bernard Birnbaum.*)

With the musk-oxen on Ellesmere Island, 1967. (*Dick Wiggins.*)

The Travco at Grizzle's Grocery, 1968.

Dinner at home, 1968. From left, Larry Gianneschi, Jim Wilson, Bill Lewis. (*Charles Kuralt*.)

Mr. Norris feeds the deer,
Colorado, 1969.

Larry and Izzy.

Breakdown: Changing tires on the Cortez. From left, Charles Kuralt, Larry Gianneschi, Izzy Bleckman, Charlie Quinlan.

Breakdown: Izzy unclogging the fuel line. (*Charles Kuralt*.)

rebel captain Galvao. I wondered how the old pirate could be upset by something he couldn't see aboard a ship the U.S. Navy couldn't find.

Frustrated reporters gathered in cities all over the rim of the South Atlantic. Some went to Africa on the theory that the *Santa Maria* was headed for one of the Portuguese colonies. Others collected in Caracas and Trinidad.

When a search plane finally spotted the *Santa Maria* one morning, she was discovered to be about 400 miles north of the big bulge in the South American continent. By fabulous good luck, a CBS News cameraman, Herb Schwartz, happened to be aboard the Navy Constellation that made the sighting. He persuaded the crew to remove the door and hang on to his belt to keep him from falling out as he made the first pictures of the runaway cruise ship, footage every news organization in the world was dying for.

Back on the ground, as the plane refueled and Herb reloaded his camera for the next flight over the ship, an envious cameraman from UPI Movietone, an old friend of Herb's, admitted defeat on the story and offered to ship Herb's film to CBS for him. Herb gave him the film cannister with many thanks and took off on another run with the Navy. The film was purloined by UPI Movietone, which offered it to its worldwide clients the next day. CBS News had to buy a copy like everybody else.

"THROW YOUR FILM IN THE WATER BEFORE GIVING IT TO UPI FOR SHIPPING," Ralph Paskman cabled.

Herb's feelings were hurt. He cabled back, "EYE FLY 48 HOURS WITHOUT SLEEP, RISK LIFE HANGING OUT PLANE DOOR, OBTAIN EXCLUSIVE FIRST FOOTAGE OF SANTA MARIA, SHIP FILM BEST WAY EYE KNOW HOW, AND THIS IS ALL THANKS EYE GET."

Paskman cabled, "NEXT TIME DON'T RISK YOUR LIFE FOR UPI."

I took a look at a map of the *Santa Maria*'s position and headed for Recife, Brazil, on the chance that when the ship finally stopped running, it might be in that Portuguese-speaking port. When I got there, I found the waterfront hotel filling up with reporters from many countries who had made the same guess. Ernest Leiser, my old traveling companion to the Congo, came down from New York to join me, but we still felt shorthanded.

"SCHEFFLER ON WAY FROM GUATEMALA," Paskman cabled.

Phil Scheffler had switched over from the assignment desk where I first met him to join our little band on *Eyewitness* as reporter-producer-bon vivant. He had been in Guatemala City doing spadework for a future story, but he was a whiz with the airline schedules and I knew he and his camera crew would make it to Brazil in no time.

A day passed. News reports speculated the *Santa Maria* was Recife-bound, all right.

"WHERE SCHEFFLER?" I asked Paskman.

"ON WAY FROM MIAMI," he replied.

Phil had calculated that the fastest way south to Recife was north to Miami, the hub of South American airlines. This was the long way around, but it made sense.

Leiser boarded an American warship, USS *Gearing*, which called in Recife for provisioning before heading out to sea, to try to intercept the *Santa Maria* and escort the cruise ship into port. I felt awfully alone on shore.

"WHERE SCHEFFLER?" I cabled.

"BUENOS AIRES," Paskman replied.

Buenos Aires was 2,500 miles *south* of Recife! But Scheffler was good. He had those airline schedules down cold, I knew that. It had to be that the fastest connections to Recife that day were through Buenos Aires, that's all.

Another day passed. By now, the *Santa Maria* was dead in the water a few miles offshore while the renegade captain, Galvao, negotiated with the U.S. Navy and the Brazilian government. Up on the hotel roof with a pair of strong binoculars, I thought I could actually *see* the ship on the distant horizon. Any hour now, the impasse might be resolved, the passengers might be freed, and I'd have to cover the whole complicated event by myself.

"WHERE SCHEFFLER?" This time I was agitated.

"MADRID," Paskman replied.

Madrid?

What had happened was that Phil and his camera crew had made a tight connection in Buenos Aires to an international flight of Aerolíneas

Argentinas. In the rush to get them aboard, the airline had neglected to check their documents. When the plane landed in Rio de Janeiro, they had stayed aboard. When the plane landed in Recife and they headed impatiently through Brazilian Immigration, an official asked them politely for their disembarkation cards.

"What disembarkation cards?" Scheffler asked.

"Carteira verde," the man said. "Green card. The airline gave it to you in Buenos Aires."

"Oh, well," Phil said, "they must have forgotten. Here, we'll fill out the cards now."

"No," the man said. "You must have green cards upon arriving in Brazil."

"Or what?" Phil asked.

"Or you may not enter this country," the man said firmly.

Phil had been traveling two days from Guatemala. He was tired. He hit the ceiling. He screamed at the immigration officers, he screamed at the airline clerks. He threatened to call the U.S. Consulate, and would have done so except that the telephones were all just on the other side of the immigration barrier, inside the country, and he wasn't allowed inside the country. Phil shouted, cajoled, harangued, spoke of the urgency of his mission, pointed out the absurdity of the situation. He banged on the table, he showed his passport, he showed his press credentials. The immigration officer was interested only in seeing a little green card.

The Aerolíneas plane was about to leave. Brazilian law stated that anyone lacking proper documents for entering the country must depart on the same aircraft that brought him. Phil refused to board. Soldiers were summoned. They pointed their rifles. Phil boarded.

The plane's next stop was Dakar, West Africa. Phil and the crew didn't have documents to get off there, either. They flew on thousands of miles to the next stop—Madrid.

Phil called Midgley by telephone to explain the situation and ask for instructions.

"Come home," Midgley said.

But the plane to New York encountered a blizzard and was diverted to Montreal. Having traveled from Miami to Buenos Aires to Rio to

Recife to Dakar to Madrid to Montreal, Phil took the train home to New York in a February snowstorm, still wearing the Palm Beach suit he had put on four days before in Guatemala City. In the annals of fruitless journalistic travel, Phil's 17,000-mile expedition to three continents is writ large, but to this day, he changes the subject when anybody brings up the *Santa Maria*.

The reporters on land began a hectic scramble to reach the ship, but Galvao's armed pirates repelled all boarders from the sea. Two plucky French photographers, demented by competitiveness, decided to board from the sky. They hired light planes to fly them over the ship and bailed out by parachute, aiming for the *Santa Maria*'s deck. Both missed and landed in the sea. Some humanitarian instinct stirred in Captain Galvao's breast; he ordered them fished out and taken aboard.

I went down to the Recife waterfront and chartered a forty-foot sailboat owned by an elderly Argentine couple who were on the last leg of a circumnavigation of the world. At a stately five knots, Herb Schwartz and I were conducted to sea under sail aboard the yawl *Gaucho*. It took forever to reach the *Santa Maria*. When we did, I used a megaphone to shout questions to the passengers as our sailboat tacked back and forth under the ship's stern. They yelled back that the ship was running low on food and water and that they had been told they would be freed the next day at Recife. I had a big international scoop—and no way to send it from the sailboat.

One of the French parachutists aboard the *Santa Maria* had the same problem. He decided to use me to get his story out. We played a seagoing game of pitch and catch out there. He threw me a knotted handkerchief with a weight and a note inside. It asked in several languages, "Who are you?" I held up a big yellow CBS News film bag for identification. On our next pass under the stern, he dropped a bag of his own. I leaned overboard and caught the bag one-handed just before it dropped into the sea. It contained several cassettes of 35mm color film, the exclusive pictures aboard the *Santa Maria* he had leapt from the sky to get, and two rolls of unprocessed motion picture footage. There was another note, this one written in red ink, in capital letters.

It said: "GOD WILL PUNISH YOU IF YOU DO NOT DELIVER THIS FILM IMMEDIATELY TO *AGENCE DALMAS*, PARIS."

When the good ship *Gaucho* finally returned to the dock in Recife, I sped to the airport and faithfully shipped the man's film to his French picture agency. By way of CBS News, New York. The pictures were sold by Dalmas to magazines and television networks all over the world. But first, they showed up on CBS.

The old UPI trick.

6

LIEUTENANT SON

*T*hat spring, Les Midgley said something that came within an inch or two of costing me my life. He said, "Vietnam."

It was April 1961. My notes on the trip say "Approx. 500 U.S. military advisers here." No U.S. news organization yet considered the Vietnam War important enough to open a permanent bureau in the country. A visit by an American television crew was so unusual that when Los Angeles cameraman Fred Dieterich and I arrived at the Saigon airport, the South Vietnamese government sent a chauffeured Citroën to pick us up and take us comfortably into the city. The government arranged a palace interview with President Ngo Dinh Diem for the next morning.

Diem was an elected President who had turned into an autocrat, ordering mass arrests of his opponents and censoring the press in the name of victory over the Communists. His army was fighting a brutal war in the jungles and rice fields, and was slowly being worn down. In the interview, Diem discussed the plight of his country in plain language, without any of the diplomatic obfuscation I had expected. He made a frank pitch for U.S. military aid.

When Vietnam was partitioned in 1954, he said, 900,000 people fled to the South. Most of these were anti-Communist refugees, he said, but among them were about 10,000 *Việt Nam cong-san*, trained Communist troops under orders to hide out among the people and terrorize them.

"Kill the village chief," he said, "kill his deputy, frighten the people, control the village. That is their tactic. And now the Vietcong are being reinforced directly by uniformed cadres from Hanoi. This is a stealthy invasion, supported by China and the Soviet Union. To combat it, our government needs much military aid from the United States."

I suggested that as a former French colony, South Vietnam might expect help from France.

"France has no will," Diem said bluntly. "Only your country has the will to defend freedom in the world. If the United States also loses its will, there will be no freedom in Vietnam."

Ngo Dinh Diem gave me pretty good history that day. Pretty good prophecy, too.

I found Saigon the most seductive of cities. The war in the country-side had not yet had any effect on the capital. All the people I met, teachers, newspapermen, waiters and cabdrivers, were friendly and considerate. The women were beautiful, I thought, gliding along in their diaphanous costumes, and the spring weather was lovely, and the sidewalk cafes delightful. I walked along the tree-shaded avenues during the day and, lying in bed under the lazy ceiling fan in my room in the old Majestic Hotel, listened to the sounds of the river traffic at night. As hordes of Western reporters were to do in years to come, I fell in love with Saigon. This is worth defending, I thought. If this sunny, beguiling city ever falls to the Communists and becomes gray and regimented, there just isn't any hope for civilization.

Every day, I dropped by the government press office to badger an official there for permission to go out into the country on a military operation. "Too dangerous," he said at first; then, "Maybe"; then when he saw I wasn't going away, finally one day, "Tomorrow. Lieutenant Son will pick you up at your hotel at noon. Be prepared to be gone for several days."

Fred Dieterich placed his gear in the back of a Vietnamese Army jeep the next day and climbed into the back seat. I sat up front with the driver, Lieutenant Son, a neatly turned out young Ranger officer who had spent a few months in training in the United States. My poor French and his poor English were enough to permit us to talk to each other as we drove north out of town. Young as he was, Lieutenant Son turned out to be a veteran of warfare. He came from a nationalist family, he said. He and two brothers had been members of the Viet Minh army that expelled the French, and Son himself had taken part as a teenaged foot soldier in the final siege of Dien Bien Phu in 1954. "But we want a free country," he said. "My family did not fight the French in order to be ruled by Ho Chi Minh." He shrugged and smiled. "So now, we fight on. You will find many like me in the Rangers."

We spent the night in an abandoned warehouse in the provincial town of Bencat with Lieutenant Son and his outfit, the 150th Ranger Company. Son introduced us to the men in his platoon. We shook hands formally with each of them and then he made a speech to them. "I tell them to take care of you tomorrow," he said with a grin.

As night came on, Son brought us food, rice and meat in a pungent sauce. "What is it?" I asked. "I don't know how to say it," he said, and laughed. "Anyway, don't ask." He gave Fred and me cots to sleep on while he and his men rolled out bedding on the floor. "I don't like this," I said. "We are prepared to live exactly as you do." He held up his hand. "You are our guests," he said.

The officers met in a corner of the building to study a map under the glare of a bare light bulb hanging from the ceiling. The next morning, three platoons of Rangers were to move south into a pocket of land between the Saigon River and a canal, hoping to trap what they thought was a small group of Vietcong at a place called An Dien. Lieutenant Son's platoon was to be the center column. "We don't go on trail," Son said to me apologetically. "I am sorry, but you will get muddy feet."

We set out in trucks before dawn. After a short trip, the trucks stopped beside a patch of thick woods. The men quietly put on their helmets and hoisted rifles and cartridge belts in the dark. Artillery opened up somewhere behind us, firing 155-millimeter shells over our heads as we walked into the woods toward—what? I had no idea. Toward whatever was in there.

When the sun came up, I could see that we were passing occasional clusters of empty houses in the forest. "Nobody home," Son said. "Afraid of us, afraid of enemy. Always run away."

The artillery fire stopped. The morning became silent, except for the sound of about thirty pairs of boots moving over the ground. We emerged from the woods, climbed a barbed-wire fence and slogged through a mile of rice fields. Freddy Dieterich and I walked a few steps ahead of the point man, turning to film the platoon advancing toward us. The day was beginning to get hot. I thought, well, nothing's going to happen. At least, we're getting some good film of troops in the field.

Just as we reached the high ground of an earthen dike, a sudden rattle of automatic weapons burst from a tree line on the other side of a small stream, about half a mile away. The firing grew and grew in volume and intensity until it sounded like one long sustained explosion. We could see men running at the edge of the trees and hear their shouts.

Lieutenant Son shouted orders to his troops. "Ambush!" he said to me. "Other platoon fall into a trap. They need us now." He drew his .45 pistol and, waving it overhead, led his men toward the battle. The soldiers followed him at a run, waded the stream and rushed to the edge of the trees. Fred Dieterich and I had everything we could do to film the running soldiers and record the sound of the fighting without being left behind.

By the time we reached the tree line, the shooting had stopped, except for isolated bursts of fire from deep inside the forest. I saw bodies of dead men sprawled everywhere at the edge of the woods, most of them Rangers but two wearing the loose black pajamas of the Vietcong. One of the dead VC had a heavy Browning automatic rifle lying beside him. The other was armed only with a sword.

Lieutenant Son stopped his platoon at the tree line. On his orders, each of the men took out a pocket handkerchief and tied it around his left arm. Son produced handkerchiefs for Fred and me. "So we don't shoot at each other in there," he explained. "We go in slow now. You stay with me."

The soldiers fanned out along the tree line and on Son's signal, we entered the forest. We crept fifty yards in, a hundred yards, each soldier alert for the slightest movement ahead. We came upon more bodies. We passed a wounded Ranger trying to stop the bleeding in his more seriously wounded buddy's chest; Son stopped for an instant to speak to him and then led us on, slowly, wordlessly. Fred Dieterich whispered to me, "This is scary as hell."

We came at last to a dirt road leading to a large clearing in the forest. In the clearing were a small, run-down temple and a roofless house. Son motioned to four of his soldiers to search the buildings. They banged open the door of the temple with their rifle butts and barged in. Empty. They cautiously surrounded the house and then entered it. Empty. The searchers rejoined the rest of us in the center of the clearing. We formed a rough circle, each man peering into the silent woods.

And then all hell broke loose. The forest around us just detonated. We were surrounded by a clatter of gunfire, deafeningly loud. It took me a second or two to realize that all the shooting was taking place only a few yards away, and was aimed at us. I looked around for cover, but there wasn't any except for a shallow depression in the center of the clearing. Fred Dieterich and I fell into this slight hollow together. We could see figures in the trees taking aim and firing at us. Incredibly, Fred flipped his camera turret to the long lens, raised himself to his elbows, aimed and fired back at them.

"Stop that!" I hollered. "Get your head down!"

Fred Dieterich said calmly, "Charlie, I figure this is it. We might as well take pictures to show what happened to us."

"The hell with that!" I shouted. "This is *not* it! Keep your head down!"

Seeking to rescue the first platoon from an ambush, we had walked into an ambush ourselves. Even with my own head down, I could look around and see that we were in terrible trouble. Several of the Rangers had been shot down in the initial volley and lay surrounding us in the clearing, dead or wounded. Those still on their feet were fighting back bravely, however. One rushed straight into the woods with his weapon firing until he was dropped by enemy fire. He fell with his finger still tight on the trigger, his gun pumping bullets into the sky. Others formed a perimeter and poured a steady volley of return fire into the woods. Lieutenant Son had taken a bullet in the arm, but he was still in action, kneeling on the ground beside his radio operator, cranking the handle of the magneto-operated radio, trying to call battalion headquarters for reinforcements.

Fred Dieterich and I crawled the few yards over to him to film the attempt. Bullets spattered the ground around us. Son ignored them and kept cranking. But it was useless. No answer came. We were out of radio range.

Then the radio operator, a kid no more than seventeen or eighteen years old, performed the most astounding act of courage I have ever seen. Without a word, he reached into his pack, found a coil of wire and attached one end of it to the radio antenna. He ran to a tree, uncoiling the wire as he ran. Holding the other end of the wire in his mouth, he climbed the tree with bullets whizzing around him, tied the wire to a high branch, shinnied back down the tree and made it back to his radio unscratched. He cranked the handle furiously. Lieutenant Son, lying beside the radio, spoke into the microphone, reached battalion headquarters and started reading coordinates from a map. He handed the mike back to the radio operator. "Stay down," he said to Fred and me. "It's okay. They send the paratroopers."

The firing eased off. I could no longer see any VC in the woods, although occasional shots still crisscrossed the clearing from somewhere. Two of Son's men bandaged his arm and then the three of them crawled about with a medical pack to see whether they could do anything to help the other wounded. They dragged several wounded men to the cover of the temple wall, where most of them went into shock and died while we waited for the promised paratroopers.

Son was up and walking around the clearing now, encouraging his surviving soldiers. He came over and knelt beside Freddy and me. "We are nearly out of ammunition," he said. "You should know this. I don't think we will be attacked again, but if we are . . ."

A single shot was fired from the woods. It hit Son's helmet in the back center and exited the front. He pitched forward into me and fell to the ground.

The wound looked so small at first. I cradled his head on my chest. I picked up a handful of leaves from the ground and tried to stuff them into the wound to stop the bleeding.

The shot that killed Son was the last one I remember being fired that day. The paratroopers arrived, riding in trucks. The VC disappeared into the woods, carrying their dead and wounded with them. We went a few miles down the road to a rural schoolhouse to regroup. There was a poster on the floor, which I picked up and later had translated. It said: "Do not give Communists rice. Do not give Communists information. Do not let Communists into your house." The poster was on the floor because the Communists had wrecked the schoolhouse the night before.

A Colonel, the commander of the Rangers, arrived at the school-house in a jeep. He lined up the 150th and told them, "You are a courageous company. You held off an enemy force five times greater than you. Don't think about the dead. You fight for a great cause and you will prevail."

But nineteen members of the company were not there to hear him. They were killed that day. Among them were two officers, Lieutenant Son and his company commander. I saw at least eleven wounded; there may have been others.

The Colonel assigned an armored car to drive Fred Dieterich and me back to Saigon. We reached the safety of the graceful city in little more than an hour. We clattered down the broad avenues. Bicyclists pedaled here and there. The sidewalk cafes were crowded. We arrived at the front door of the Majestic Hotel before dark and walked through the lobby toward the elevators, carrying our gear. People turned to look at us because we were so dirty and out of place. I had Lieutenant Son's blood all over my shirt.

I never was able to get Son out of my mind. Through all the years of the Vietnam War, I thought of him. I returned to Vietnam several times, went out into the countryside with troops again—they were American troops by then—and was present when other good men were killed in jungle clearings. As the war dragged on inconclusively and American casualties mounted, it became the fashion in the United States to say that those American boys were dying for nothing. All my friends agreed it was an immoral war, imperialist America against "the Vietnamese people."

I never thought so. The Vietnamese people I met wanted nothing to do with warfare. They wanted to be left alone to live peacefully. But they weren't being left alone. They were being invaded by an army from the North, sent by a government they hated. I thought of Son, who wanted so much for Vietnam to be free that he was willing to go on fighting for the idea long after his fighting days should have been over. I thought of the men of the 150th, the one who charged into the woods firing his rifle, the one who climbed the tree with the radio antenna in his teeth. I thought, I still think, that justice and virtue resided with those brave men. I hated going back there later and hearing them called "gooks" by my own countrymen.

The ones who lived through it—not many of the Rangers did—have presumably been "re-educated" now. Lovely, languid Saigon has become Ho Chi Minh City. The wound of the Vietnam War is healing in America. In America, most people don't remember the war very well or take into account any longer the wishes of "the Vietnamese people."

I go to the Vietnam War Memorial sometimes when I am in Washington. There are names of some men I knew carved on the black marble. I think of them. Son isn't up there, of course, but I think of him, too.

I only knew him for a day.

I never even learned the rest of his name.

7

RIO

I came back to New York for a few days when the *Eyewitness* season ended in the spring of 1961, and one of my bosses, Blair Clark, took me to lunch. He asked, "What do you think is going to be the big story of the next few years?"

"Latin America," I said.

It was the wrong answer, as things turned out, but Blair Clark said, "Right! Fidel Castro is going to try to communize the hemisphere, with plenty of help from the Russians and Chinese. I know that Jack Kennedy is determined to stop them by pouring billions into the Alliance for Progress."

"How do you know?"

"Jack told me."

Blair Clark moved in impressive circles.

He sketched a scenario of coming Cold War confrontations in the Central American jungles and the valleys of the Andes. It sounded like a CIA briefing, which may have been where Blair got it.

"You know who's covering Latin America for us?" he asked.

"Nobody," I said.

"Wrong," he said. "You are."

"I've forgotten my high school Spanish," I said.

"It'll come back to you," he said. "I want to start a Latin American bureau right away and get on this story fast. You can open the office anywhere you want to, as long as you do it within thirty days. What do you say?"

What could I say? I was CBS's good soldier, willing to go anywhere and do anything. I was getting divorced, I had no ties to New York anymore, I liked the idea of taking on twenty countries in one gulp, and I was sure my boss was right when he said the U.S.–Cuban face-off was going to spread all over the hemisphere. I chose Brazil, the "sleeping giant" of South America, as the logical base for reporting this coming struggle, and it didn't take me thirty days to get there. I filled one suitcase with my clothes, another one with volumes of Latin American history and diplomacy, and went off to Rio studying Spanish and Portuguese phrase books on the plane. I found a hotel room on Copacabana Beach, rented an office downtown on Rua Mexico across the street from the U.S. Embassy, had business cards and stationery printed up identifying myself as "Chief Latin American Correspondent" (if you're going to be the *only* Latin American Correspondent, I figured, why not be chief?) and sent Blair Clark a cable ten days after our lunch in New York: "COLNEWS RIO OPEN FOR BUSINESS."

But it was pretty primitive business. The office had a cameraman, Mario Biasetti, who had come down from Boston to join me, and a secretary, a Lebanese emigré named Mireille, who had answered my ad in *Jornal do Brasil.*

But the office didn't have a telephone; there was a two-year wait for telephones in Rio. I hired a telephone expediter to try to speed things up.

The office didn't have a business license. When an inspector came by one afternoon demanding my business license, I tried to explain that CBS News was not a business: We manufactured nothing, we sold nothing. We were an organization of the highest principles. We did not make money; we only spent money. He smiled, unpersuaded, and said I must close the doors of my business until I obtained a business license. I hired a lawyer to try to straighten this out.

The office also didn't have any camera gear. In spite of arrangements carefully made with the Brazilian Consulate in New York, our lights, cameras and sound equipment resided in the Rio airport customs shed awaiting the payment of $40,000 duty. But we have an import permit, I said, displaying this document. We are not going to sell the equipment, I explained, merely use it in the free exercise of our newsgathering responsibility, don't you see? The customs officials did not see. I remembered the intransigence of the immigration officers who had put Phil Scheffler on that plane bound for Africa. I hired a customs broker to try to cut the red tape.

If you really want to learn about a country, work there. Slowly, I learned. Things could not be speeded up or straightened out in Brazil, and red tape could not be cut. Everything, however, could be, with patience, sidestepped. Brazilians have a word, *jeito*, untranslatable into English, which has no such word or concept. *Jeito* combines the meanings of a favor, a boon, a detour around difficulty, a solution for the insoluble. A *jeito* may involve a bribe, but is more likely to consist of a kindness. The telephone expediter, the lawyer, the customs broker, all came to my office and explained that they were seeking, and would surely find, a *jeito*. I grumbled that they seemed to be taking their own sweet time.

"We are being rude, Charles," said Mireille, the secretary. "You talk too fast when people come to the office, you press too hard, and you do not offer them coffee."

We bought a coffeepot. I learned to offer office guests, even guests who made me impatient, several small, sweet *cafèzinhos* before getting around to whatever we were to talk about. And whatever it was, I forced myself to talk slower. Mireille had a mastery of Arabic, which was useless to me, and only a fair knowledge of Portuguese, Spanish and English, the languages I'd hired her for, but she knew the conventions of the country. I learned to ask her questions, sometimes before making a fool of myself.

When a telephone finally was installed, it proved to be useless, except for calling around the city. Long distance calls often took hours to complete, and calls out of the country were out of the question. To talk to my bosses in New York, I had to book a radio transmission with the RCA office down the street and around the corner, enter a broom closet in the back of the building, put on a headset and shout into an ancient microphone. I wondered why I had ever wanted a telephone in the first place.

When at last we were able to spring the camera gear from customs and shoot our first story, a report on the building of Brasília, the new capital in the middle of nowhere, we found we were unable to ship our film. Brazilian law required that motion picture film be processed and viewed by censors before it could be forwarded legally. So I forwarded it illegally. Every time we finished shooting a story in Rio, I caught a taxi to the airport before a Pan Am flight was scheduled to depart for Miami, wandered innocently among the passengers until I found one with an honest face, and asked if he'd mind carrying a package for me. "It's a present for my cousin in Florida," I'd say. "Just hand it to the first U.S. Customs agent you see and my cousin will pick it up." Then I'd go back to town and send a cable to the CBS News traffic desk: "PACKAGE FOR COUSIN ARRIVING MIAMI PAN AM 301 0830 THURS." Not one shipment ever was lost.

I learned that everything could be done in Rio, though not today, and probably not tomorrow, and perhaps not according to the letter of the law. The lawyer came by to report, after a few cups of coffee, that we wouldn't be having any more trouble with the business license inspector.

"Did it cost you a trip to court?" I asked.

"No, Senhor," he said, "it cost me a trip to the liquor store."

I learned that I, who had lectured the government inspector on the lofty ethical principles of the organization I represented, had just bought him off with a case of Chivas Regal.

Not that the whisky cost very much. Great luxuries could be had in Brazil in those days for a few cents, provided only that one's income was paid in U.S. dollars. Brazil was suffering through one of the prodigious inflations in the history of the world, amounting to several hundred percent per year. Every day, the cruzeiro was worth considerably less than the day before. No matter how fast prices and wages were raised, they could not keep pace with the shrinking value of the currency. I felt profoundly sorry for people with savings accounts, some of whom did not understand what was happening until they withdrew their deposits and discovered that the money they had been counting on for retirement was now hardly enough to buy a good meal. All notions of the virtues of thrift were turned upside down; children were urged *not* to save, not even for a day, but to go out and *buy* something. I bought a used MG motorcar. The seller wanted cash. I filled a big suitcase with 1,000-cruzeiro notes, the largest denomination, and threw in the suitcase as part of the deal. He riffled through the contents to make sure there was nothing but currency in there and handed over the keys without bothering to count it. The day I bought the car, it cost the equivalent of $800. A few months later, that suitcase full of money wouldn't have paid for an oil change.

Newsgathering in Rio provided a puzzle almost as mind-bending as currency transactions. Where was I to find out what was going on? The newsstand on the corner sold about thirty daily newspapers, which I could read only with the greatest difficulty, and even after I succeeded in understanding what was printed on their front pages, I found I couldn't believe much of it. Nearly every paper represented a different shade of the arching rainbow of Brazilian political opinion, from the Communist daily on the left (actually, I think there were one or two papers to the *left* of the Communists) to the raving imaginings of the fascist right. If the police shot someone at a land reform demonstration in the northeast, the event became a screaming example of police brutality in one newspaper, and a triumph of law over terrorism in another.

To conquer my handicap with the language, I studied Portuguese every night after dinner in the dimly lighted sitting room of a penurious retired professor. This instruction was in the classical language of Lisbon, not in the colorful Carioca idiom I heard in the streets, but the professor's scholarly ministrations helped me cipher out the prejudices of the newspapers. To overcome my failures of understanding, I relied on the few resident American reporters, especially Juan de Onis of *The New York Times* and his deputy, Henry Johnston, who were generous with explanations of the arcane politics of Brazil. Hank Johnston took me under his wing, introducing me to all the most interesting politicians, tycoons, spies, models, musicians, money-changers, barflies and fellow expatriates of the city. Rio de Janeiro so intrigued Hank Johnston that when he was mustered out of the U.S. Navy in Rio in 1945, he never bothered to go home again.

I wandered out into the vast country to report stories. I traveled up to the northeast coast and inland to the Amazon headwaters and down to São

Paulo, a bustling, overgrown Chicago. Brazil is larger than the mainland United States, and was a lot harder to get around in.

I reported trouble, or rumors of trouble, in Chile, Argentina, Ecuador, Bolivia, Peru, traveling on perilous mountain roads, sometimes even on horseback. I was on hand when President Kennedy, carrying the torch for the Alliance for Progress, showed up in Mexico, Costa Rica and Colombia. I "lived" in Brazil, but I never bothered to get a visa to live there; the airlines issued thirty-day tourist cards, and I was so steadily on the move around the continent that I never overstayed the thirty days.

But it was always lovely to come back to Rio for a week or so, to return to my room in the Excelsior Hotel with its view of the soft curve of Copacabana Beach, and to the cramped office on Rua Mexico, with windows on Guanabara Bay. Nearly every person who lives in Rio enjoys an expansive view of water, and the poor people of the *favelas*, the wretched slums high in the hills, have one thing, at least—the best views of all. It was easy to decide that Rio de Janeiro, clinging to the narrow littoral between the mountains and the bay, was the world's most beautiful city.

The people were beautiful, too, I thought, a cheerful mixture of races and religions (around many a Carioca neck, a voodoo fetish and a Catholic cross hang on the same chain) with an agreeable mixture of tolerance and impartiality. When I sought to ask them, in earnest man-on-the-street interviews, about the struggle between the United States and Fidel Castro, they merely shrugged. A grinning shoeshine man tried a locution on me, delivering it in heavily accented English: "Make love," he said, "not war." In Rio, people were geographically thousands of miles below the fight, and geopolitically, far above it. About Cold War confrontation, most Cariocas gave not a damn.

They cared about music. As the time approached for *Carnaval*, the samba beat was everywhere in the streets. Bands hired by competing composers walked about in every block playing songs that were contending for official *Carnaval* theme song. During January and February, you could close all your windows and all your doors, and go into the innermost room of your house, and enter the closet, and stand there and hear that beat from the street. The sound of the drums and horns intensified for weeks until finally, in the days of *Carnaval*, it became a ceaseless din, a pandemonium. Mardi Gras days in Rio are not merely, as in New Orleans or Mobile, a lot of parades and parties. *Carnaval* is like nothing else on earth, an explosion of joy.

The other great passion of the city was soccer. *Carnaval* came once a year, but soccer went on forever. Every midafternoon when the sun dropped behind the tall buildings of Copacabana and the sunbathers on the beach went in, the soccer players came out. The beach was the scene of dozens of games, played by boys as young as five or six who could do to a round ball uncanny things with their heads and feet. Soccer was played all day and year-round in all the playgrounds and vacant lots of the city, and when the young Pelé and his team from Santos came to Rio to play an ordinary club match, it was routine for 200,000 spectators to crowd into Maracaña Stadium, standing and shouting the whole game through.

Brazil's national team dominated international competition in those days, and I could see why: The team had nearly the entire male population of the country from which to choose its players. During the World Cup matches of 1962, the rest of the country might as well have been on the team, too. That's how great the fervor was.

During a Brazilian game against Argentina during the Cup finals, with all of Rio indoors listening on the radio, I walked past the American Embassy on some errand. It was a Sunday afternoon. Only the U.S. Marine guard was on duty.

"How's the game going?" he asked, with a worried look.

I said, "Brazil was ahead by a goal last I heard."

He said, "I sure hope they win."

"You a big soccer fan?" I asked.

"Not really," he said. "But you know how everything bad gets blamed on the United States. If Argentina beats Brazil, I'm afraid everybody will come down here and break all the windows."

The guard needn't have worried. Nobody beat Brazil that year. When Brazil won the Cup, I happened to be in a downtown bank. Clerks shouted for joy and threw handfuls of money in the air. Elsewhere in the city at that moment, a man incautiously leapt through the window of a skyscraper, and out in the country somewhere, another man jumped into the air, forgetting that he was on the platform of a moving train. Both died in paroxysms of ecstasy. After experiencing the World Cup of 1962, the Super Bowl and the World Series have always seemed a little tame to me.

Not even rainstorms stopped the soccer games on Copacabana Beach. And on the day when the army tanks came rolling down the beach, the soccer players didn't even stop their games to notice.

The tanks were sent by the Minister of War to make a political point. I was having a drink at a beachfront bar when I looked up and saw them rumbling along, trying to avoid the soccer games. I was getting used to Brazilian incongruity by this time but I thought, *now* what the hell? I made a phone call and found out President Jânio Quadros had resigned.

Quadros, a slight man with a great bushy moustache, had been elected only a few months before with more votes than had ever before been cast for a Presidential candidate in Brazil. His election was hailed as the start of a new era, a break with the dictatorial past. But he proved an odd, quixotic man, ill at ease amid the trappings of power. He tried to avoid the gleaming new Presidential Palace in faraway Brasília, preferring to drive himself around Rio in his old Volkswagen. He had a few ideas for reforming the country and reducing inflation, but the Congress wouldn't go along with any of them. So Quadros decided one morning that he had had enough. He quit, and he disappeared. One moment, he was President. The next moment, he wasn't, and he was gone, nobody knew where.

Quadros's constitutional successor was his sworn enemy, Vice President João Goulart, a leftist hack who was at the moment on a state visit to China. The tanks on Copacabana were the Army's way of saying it had no intention of letting Goulart return to rule the country. But already, I was told on the telephone, there were reports that military units away to the south in Rio Grande do Sul Province, where Goulart came from and had his power base, were disobeying orders and preparing to defend his claim to the Presidency.

This was Brazil. Make love, not war. I was pretty sure there wasn't going to be a civil war, not with the sun shining and the soccer players ignoring the tanks. But I paid for my drink, grabbed a taxi for the airport and caught the first plane to Pôrto Alegre, Goulart's hometown. It was good I didn't stop to pack a bag. That was the last plane into Pôrto Alegre for days, except for the one that brought João Goulart—President Goulart, he now called himself—home from China. The local army and air force commanders, rebelling against headquarters in Brasília, had barrels rolled out onto the runways at the airport, sank a scow at the entrance of the harbor to prevent entrance from the sea and barricaded themselves behind sandbags in the Governor's Palace in Pôrto Alegre. I found myself inside a blockaded city without even a toothbrush, and more important, without any means of getting the story out, since cable and wireless connections to Pôrto Alegre had been cut from the other side.

Not wishing a most un-Brazilian shooting war, both sides commenced a war of nerves. Back in Brasília, the War Minister demanded that Congress declare the office of vice president vacant and arrange for new elections. The Congress refused. The Congress demanded that the War Minister read the constitution, especially the part about legal succession, and permit Goulart to take office. The War Minister refused. The War Minister sent tanks toward the border of Rio Grande do Sul. The commanders in Rio Grande hauled artillery up toward the border to meet them.

In the basement of the sandbagged Governor's Palace in Pôrto Alegre, the pro-Goulart forces set up a shortwave radio station to try to broadcast their message to the rest of the country. They gave it an important-sounding name, Radio Legalidade, but the transmitter was an ancient model with glowing vacuum tubes and the antenna was a copper wire leading to the chimney on the roof. I regarded this rig with grave doubt, but it was the only link with the outside world. I made myself presentable and paid a call on the Colonel who had command of the building.

"The world press is in Rio reporting the news from the other side," I said.

The Colonel agreed, gloomily.

"But I am here," I said. "I would like to report the news from this side."

"What do you want?" he asked.

"Ten minutes on your radio station every morning," I said, "and another ten minutes in the evening."

The Colonel, who had no idea whether his radio station was getting out past the city limits, thought about this for a minute and then nodded his assent.

I had my air time. I could broadcast to the world. The only problem was that nobody in the world would be listening.

I scribbled a cable to Ralph Paskman in New York, giving the frequency of Radio Legalidade and telling him I'd be up on that frequency every day at ten A.M. and six P.M. New York time. I could see Paskman rolling his eyes and muttering about that kid Kuralt wasting CBS's money again. Then I really wasted some of his money. I found a cabdriver in the street, presented him a thick wad of cash, handed him the cable and instructed him to send it from the nearest possible place—Uruguay, 200 miles away.

"Give it to the first telegraph office you come to, and stay there until it is sent," I said. "Can I trust you?"

"You can trust me," he said.

"It is very important," I said.

"I am a gaucho," he said.

All the men of Rio Grande do Sul call themselves gauchos, after the gallant cowboys of the pampas. Gauchos have a well-known code of honor. A gaucho's word is his bond, and there are stories about gauchos drawing their daggers and killing those who question their integrity. So I didn't question my gaucho, whose steed was an old but polished Packard. I watched him ride off into the sunset toward the Uruguayan frontier.

I saw him again two days later. The Packard was covered with dust. He said simply, "Your message has been sent." But he asked for a little more money for fuel. He had crossed into Uruguay with no difficulty, but found there were no cable offices in any of the border towns. So after his 200-mile journey, he kept going. He kept going *another* 200 miles. He had sent my cable from Montevideo. The man standing before me had just returned from an 800-mile round trip to send a telegram! I felt like hugging him, but something told me you don't hug gauchos.

I had already discovered that I didn't like the competitive pressure of being CBS's only correspondent in South America. NBC always had at least three good reporters working against me, Richard Valeriani and the husband-wife team of Wilson and Lee Hall, and the chances were good that one of them would beat me to any given breaking story. I was forever getting cables from Paskman: "NBC HAD SIX HOUR BEAT ON CHILE EARTH-QUAKE. WHERE YOU?"

But the only other American reporter I ran into in Pôrto Alegre was Morris Rosenberg of the Associated Press, who had made his way across the river from Uruguay. NBC wasn't there and probably couldn't get there, so for once I had a page-one story to myself—if, that is, Radio Legalidade had a strong enough shortwave signal to reach New York.

Each evening, the makeshift station interrupted its routine of propaganda and martial music for a few minutes. An announcer shouted into the microphone in impassioned Portuguese, "And now, Radio Legality pauses in its regular transmissions of candor and veracity to permit the truth to be broadcast to the world in the English language!" Whereupon, I would slide into the chair and say, "Hello, New York, hello, New York. This is Kuralt talking up for CBS News, New York. I will begin in sixty seconds. . . ." And so on, to a countdown, "Five . . . four . . . three . . . two . . ." Then, I'd deliver my report on the political declarations and troop movements of the day in the cutoff and beleaguered provincial capital, repeating the reading a couple of times and signing off, "Charles Kuralt, CBS News, Pôrto Alegre, Brazil." I felt frustrated after each of these exercises, unsure whether I was triumphing over the opposition with reports they couldn't possibly have or making an ass of myself by talking into thin air.

At length, the opposing forces in the political impasse reached a compromise, found a *jeito:* The army would permit Goulart to assume the Presidency, but, at least for the time being, without most of the Presidential powers. In Pôrto Alegre, cheers went up, barriers came down, and a couple of ancient airliners showed up at the airport to conduct Goulart and the press to Brasília for the swearing-in.

"Pistola, pistola?" inquired a functionary at the door of the press plane, collecting the pistols of the reporters, all of them Goulart partisans in a celebratory mood. Each man dropped his pistol into a basket after

inserting a rolled-up business card in the barrel to facilitate the weapon's return upon landing. Morris Rosenberg and I, the only unarmed reporters on the plane, were glad to see the pistols locked away in the cockpit, since the *cachaça* was *not* confiscated. Each man brought aboard a bottle or two of the potent Brazilian white lightning with labels like "Black Cat" and "Bad Saturday Night" and all through the long night on the way to Brasília, the reporters argued, laughed, sang old campaign songs and rolled empties down the aisle. The press was poured out of the plane at the end of the trip, collected its weaponry and went weaving off into the city, a small army of drunks with pistols in their pockets.

I covered Goulart's inauguration and flew home to Rio to find a stack of cables from the radio editors in New York. They said things like "ALL YOUR PORTO ALEGRE TRANSMISSIONS RECEIVED" and "YOU WERE WORLD NEWS ROUNDUP LEAD FOUR DAYS IN ROW" and "CONGRATULATIONS YOUR INITIATIVE." There was also a cable from Ralph Paskman: "NBC HAD GOOD COVERAGE ARMY SIDE OF CONFLICT. WHERE YOU?"

I tried and tried to think of a response to this incredible message, but the words wouldn't come. I had a souvenir in my baggage, a gaucho dagger. I wrapped it carefully, addressed it to Paskman, went down to the post office and sent it off, airmail. Then I went to my hotel room and slept the sleep of the just.

8

EQUATOR CROSSINGS

*R*alph Paskman, my friend, my boss, my nemesis in faraway New York, thought it ought to be easy to commute back and forth between Pôrto Alegre and Rio, something like catching the air shuttle from New York to Washington. He never understood the distances in Latin America. He dashed off cables saying "THINK YOU BETTER HOP OVER TO MEXICO CITY" without the slightest idea that he was speaking of a 5,000-mile hop. He thought—for all I know, the CBS News Foreign Editor still thinks—that Rio de Janeiro is down there near Tegucigalpa somewhere, that Latin Americans all wear sombreros and take siestas under palm trees, that the countries are all pretty much alike. I began to appreciate the differences, as great as among the countries of Europe, and to find favorites among the cities.

I liked Buenos Aires for its tree-lined boulevards and good wine and European flair—if not for its people, who struck me as often cold and intolerant; Punta del Este, Uruguay, for its *dolce vita* sophistication; Quito, Ecuador, and La Paz, Bolivia, for the opposite of sophistication, an appealing Andean simplicity. In spite of an aura of violence which was even then in the air, I liked Bogotá, Colombia, for its intellectuality and fine use of language; most of the statues in Bogotá are of poets, not generals. I liked San José, Costa Rica, for its air of freedom, its dislike of dictators and its painted horse carts.

I did not much like Asunción, Paraguay; the people were cautiously friendly but meek under the authoritarian thumb, as if they remembered Francisco Solano López. He was the nineteenth-century dictator who came unhinged and insanely declared war on Brazil, Uruguay and Argentina all at once, resulting in the death by warfare, famine and disease of 225,000 Paraguayans, more than half the population of the country. Ninety years had passed since then, and the current dictator was named Stroessner. He seemed never to be criticized, not even in whispers. Paraguayans had heard from their grandparents what a dictator could do to them when vexed.

I never could bring myself to like Lima, Peru, city of vile poverty, bad smells and colonial relics, chief among the latter cruel Pizarro himself, a shrinking mummy under glass in the cathedral. I usually went to Lima during times of trouble in the streets; three times I was caught in tear gas attacks in the Plaza Bolivar. I associate Lima with choking and gasping for breath.

Rural Chile was beautiful and invigorating, but I could not love the capital, Santiago, all cold stones, dark clothing, goose-stepping soldiers and scowling faces. Once, leaving a cafe after lunch with a Chilean newspaperman whom I regarded as friendly, I dropped a coin into the cup of an old man in Indian garb who was standing on the sidewalk. "No!" shouted the newspaperman. He rushed over, retrieved the coin and gave the beggar a furious shove into the street. *"¡No es chileno!"* he exclaimed, "He's not a Chilean!" Meaning, I suppose, that Chileans are too proud to beg. My own thought was that maybe Chileans were too proud, period.

I dreaded my trips to Managua, Nicaragua, a hot, brutal place, tubercular and corrupt. Lake Nicaragua is the only freshwater lake I've ever heard of that is full of sharks, and Managua was full of sharks, too, Somozas, father and sons, nephews and cousins, all feeding on the people.

It didn't do anything for my Yankee self-respect to reflect that many of Nicaragua's woes were the fault of my own country. Starting back in the 1850s when a mountebank from Tennessee named William Walker actually established himself as President of Nicaragua for a couple of years, the United States has treated Nicaraguans as wayward children in need of frequent chastising. President William Howard Taft chastised them with the United States Marines, and the Marines stayed on right into the 1930s. I remembered the old-time sergeants at the tent camp down the road from my grandparents' farm in North Carolina who had earlier known, and presumably hated, Managua. The Marines didn't leave until they found somebody they could trust to run the country their way, Anastasio Somoza García. "He's a bastard," they used to say of Somoza in Washington, "but he's *our* bastard." After twenty years, having learned all the tricks of fraud and torture, one of Somoza's sons took over. With Washington's approval, this younger Anastasio Somoza set out to screw the lid on the country even tighter. I went to Nicaragua for the first time in 1961, nosed around for a few days and sent a series of stories back to New York warning that the Somoza lid might be about to blow off. Who cared? Most of the stories never even made it to the air. The Sandinista guerrilla movement started in 1962.

I was always uneasy in Managua, worried about something that hadn't happened yet. Little earthquakes would come in the night and I would lie awake waiting for the big one. (I wasn't there when the big one came. It killed 6,000 people in 1972 and left the city in rubble.) Little incidents in the street had a way of flaring unexpectedly into violence.

There was a bell tower overlooking a plaza in Managua. During one of Somoza's staged "elections," I wanted to start a story with a picture of the clock in the tower and the sound of the bells ringing out the hour of twelve—probably to be accompanied by a line of narration about "high noon in Nicaraguan politics" or some such trite expression. I was working with Wendell Hoffman again. We arrived at eleven-thirty A.M. or so and set up the camera in the empty plaza to wait for noon. As we stood there, a couple of people walked across the plaza to see what was going on.

"*¿Qué pasa?*" one of them asked.

"*Nada,*" I said. "Nothing's going on. We're just waiting to take a picture of the tower."

Curious, these two people waited with us. Seeing them there, several other people strolled over with the same question, "*¿Qué pasa?*"

"*Nada,*" I said. "*Esperamos el mediodía.*" These people, too, decided to stick around to see what was going to happen at noon. Still others arrived. By eleven forty-five, we had a pretty good-sized crowd standing around us.

I felt silly. I made a little speech in my most plaintive Spanish. "Look, *nothing* is going to happen. We are going to take a picture of the tower at twelve o'clock, that's all!" But nobody left.

A van full of anti-Somoza youths happened to pass by the plaza just then. Seeing the crowd and the camera, they stopped, jumped out of the van and came running over to us unfurling a banner and chanting political slogans.

I said to Wendell, "Well, let's forget it. They're making such a racket we'll never be able to hear the bells anyway." He removed the camera from the tripod and we started packing to leave. Twelve o'clock came and went. We had missed our shot, and we weren't about to film a demonstration that was being put on just for us.

The demonstrators had lost the camera, but they still had the crowd; they chanted louder and began a march around the square with most of the throng following. Wendell and I, disgusted, were walking back toward our hotel when we heard sirens approaching. Police cars roared into the plaza. Cops got out and waded into the marchers, swinging clubs. An NBC camera crew came huffing and puffing around a corner. Tear gas was fired and rose from the scene in thick clouds. A couple of the demonstrators, fighting back, were clubbed to the ground. A shotgun went off and a man, wounded in the legs, was hurried away to the hospital in the back of a panel truck.

Wendell and I watched all this in amazement. The next day, of course, one of Paskman's cables arrived: "NBC HAD GOOD COVERAGE RIOT. WHERE YOU?"

I was always glad to get out of Managua. Many years later, when the Sandinistas chased the Somozas into exile in Florida, I rejoiced inwardly that relief had come to Nicaragua at last. But the Sandinista leaders turned out to be swaggering young incompetents, more interested in power than in reform. Most of the non-Communists among the revolutionaries defected. And the United States, as always, was ready with a machination. President Ronald Reagan, vividly imagining an army of Red Nicaraguans marching into Brownsville, Texas, organized a huge armed band of Contras to bring the Sandinistas down. What the marauding Contras couldn't accomplish, the Nicaraguan voters finally did in 1990, thirty hellish years after my first visit to the country. Maybe the people there will have a taste of peace now, and a taste of liberty. I hope so, but since they live in Nicaragua, I would never bet on it. "Nicaragua needs our help," Ronald Reagan used to say, meaning the sort of "help" we have been giving that forlorn little country for most of the century. What Nicaragua needs are our prayers.

Eric Sevareid, the best of the thinkers and writers among the CBS News Correspondents, said on the air one time, "Modern revolutions do not make people freer. Revolutions always make them less free." I thought at the time that it was an odd and reactionary remark, but then I thought of the outcome of the Bolshevik Revolution, of the one in China, and of the two Latin American upheavals of my own experience that qualify as genuine revolutions, the Nicaraguan one, and before that, Fidel Castro's Cuban Revolution, and I realized that Sevareid was on to something there. One trip to Cuba is enough to break your heart. I made a lot of trips to Cuba.

I didn't like Havana. I didn't like the depraved Havana of the dictator Fulgencio Batista, which was Miami but moreso, swarming with prostitutes and high rollers, American mobsters and the rich relatives of Batista generals on the make. It took me a while—having seen plenty of right-wing regimes in Latin America, I thought maybe a left-wing revolutionary ought to be given the benefit of the doubt—but finally I came to be even more appalled by what Havana was becoming under Fidel Castro, the capital of a preposterous, regimented police state, a kind of tropical Bulgaria.

My disillusionment became complete in the spring of 1962 when the Castro revolution was three and a half years old. A year had gone by since the American-sponsored invasion at the Bay of Pigs had ended in debacle. During that year, U.S. reporters were effectively barred from Cuba. I applied for visas, I wrote to officials in Havana asking them to intercede, I stopped at Cuban embassies in other countries to appeal for entry, I even became friendly with the Soviet *chargé d'affaires* in Rio, thinking he might be able to help. Nobody ever said no, but nothing happened. I was beginning to think I'd never get into Cuba again.

One day in April 1962, a clerk at the Cuban Consulate in Rio called on the telephone.

"When would you like to pick up your visa?" he asked.

"What visa?"

"Your name is Kuralt?"

"Yep."

"I have instructions from Havana to issue you a onetime admission to Cuba. You may enter from Mexico."

I didn't ask any questions. The next morning, I was on a plane to Mexico City with a thirty-day Cuban visa stamped on a page of my passport. The immigration officer at the Havana airport looked doubtful and checked my face against the passport photo a couple of times, but finally waved me into the country. At the airport curb, I recognized an old acquaintance among the cabdrivers and fell into the front seat of his rattling '52 Cadillac.

"How's it going?" I asked him on the way into town.

"*Horriblemente,*" he said. "*A más no podemos.* There's nothing we can do about it."

We drove straight to the Foreign Ministry, where visiting reporters had to be accredited. On the stairway, I ran into Carlos Rafael Rodríguez, an old Communist intellectual in the underground days, now a bureaucrat wrestling with Castro's agricultural reform.

"What the hell are you doing here?" he asked.

"Special invitation from the first Socialist Republic in the Western Hemisphere," I said cheerfully.

"Come with me," he said. He led me into the press office.

"Give me your passport," he said. "Sit there." He disappeared into a back room. Functionaries unused to visits from a government minister bustled in behind him.

After a few minutes, he emerged laughing and shaking his head. "You are not supposed to be here," he said. "They thought you were a goddamn Brazilian. You must leave on the next plane that has space for you."

My heart sank.

"However," he added, giving me back my passport, "there is no space on any planes for at least three weeks."

I walked down the stairs with him. "Don't get smart and try to leave the capital without permission," he said. "I will send one of my guys with you if you want to see the countryside. We will show you some of the good things we've done."

"I want to see the bad things you've done," I said.

"I know," he said. "That's why you must have an escort."

"How about lining me up an interview with the Maximum Leader?" I asked.

"Go to hell," Carlos Rafael Rodríguez said.

In the streets, martial music played from loudspeakers. Giant portraits of Fidel Castro towered over the city. "This is Radio Havana, Cuba," the radio announced every half hour, "Free Territory of the Americas."

The next day was May Day and there was a workers' and peasants' parade. Since I was working without a camera crew, I enlisted a teenager from the crowd on the curb to carry my tape recorder and point the microphone at the parade while I did the filming. Through the viewfinder, I watched lines of cane cutters march by with their machetes at right shoulder-arms, columns of children in uniform holding up their schoolbooks, marching nurses with stethoscopes. Banners said "*¡VENCEREMOS!*" "We Will Win!" and "Remember the Bay of Pigs!" and "Do Your Fisminutos!"—daily exercises beside your desk or machine—and "Forward, Comrades of the Defense Committees!" The Defense Committees were block-by-block organizations which had been set up for the purpose of spying on the neighbors. The May Day parade was earnest and humorless, a bad dream out of Orwell. The Defense Committee members marched past holding up hundreds of pictures of Big Brother, Fidel Castro. They sang "The Internationale" in Spanish.

When the parade was over, the marchers stuck around to hear a speech by Castro, who appeared on a bandstand in the late afternoon. "*¡Viva nuestra revolución socialista!*" he shouted, and the crowd answered, a little mechanically, I thought, "*¡Viva!*" Dusk came on, and dark of night, and still Fidel went on, blustering at the top of his voice, drunk, so he seemed to me, on his own rhetoric. *"¡Cuba sí, Yanqui no!"* he thundered, and the crowd took up the refrain, *"¡Cuba sí, Yanqui no!"* so vehemently that I began to get edgy. A man waving a big Cuban flag stopped long enough to grin at me and say in English, "Don't worry. We don't mean you."

The next day, I went for a walk with the camera. On a corner where a Chevrolet agency had stood, I found the House of Czechoslovakian Culture. On a former shopping street, there were few shops and no shoppers, but there was a Hungarian exposition featuring a display of machine tools. The Soviet flag hung beside the Cuban one all over town. The American Embassy was boarded up and empty, with a Swiss flag flying over it for protection.

I stopped in a poor residential neighborhood to take pictures of a food store with almost no food in it. The ration in the cities was down to five eggs per person per month and three-quarters of a pound of meat per week. Even rice and beans were in short supply. As I aimed the camera at the food store, a woman came running out of a house across the street shouting, *"¡No puede filmar!* You can't take pictures here!" She held up her hand to block the camera lens. I had run afoul of a comrade of the Defense Committees.

I was polite. I showed her my credentials from the Foreign Ministry. She said the Foreign Ministry didn't decide things on this block, the Defense Committee did. She shouted for a cop at the top of her voice. I smiled, nodded good-bye and made a fast getaway, leaving her there shouting on the sidewalk.

At night when I returned to my hotel room, I found my belongings slightly rearranged, papers in my briefcase in a different order than I had left them, even the drawer in which I'd put my socks and underwear freshly disheveled. Somebody had searched the room, without bothering very hard to hide the fact. This became routine. I left a note in the underwear drawer: "No secrets here, just underwear." Whoever it was made off with the note. Clicks were heard on the telephone when I tried to use it. It was surveillance, but of a particularly clumsy sort. I thought the Cubans were going to have to get better at this if they aspired to a world-class despotism.

They were more successful at teaching children, some of whom had never before been to school. All over Havana, I found school kids wearing neat uniforms and living in luxurious buildings that had been yacht clubs a couple of years before, or the mansions of the rich. The gaudy old Hotel Nacional, in whose casino I had once lost a few dollars at roulette, was being put to a more constructive use: it housed 1,200 former domestic servants studying mathematics, grammar, penmanship, shorthand, typing and "revolutionary instruction"—how to overcome the servant mentality. Education in the new Cuba was pervasive, and touching, even inspiring, to witness.

But nearly everything else was in a terrible muddle. By 1962, Che Guevara had told me two years before, Cuba would be producing steel and starting a shipbuilding industry. Cuba would manufacture its own radios, sewing machines and typewriters. A $250 million nickel plant was in the works, he had said. Now it was 1962, and the only new undertakings I could discover were a cement works, a tomato canning plant and a pencil factory. (There were also missile launching pads under construction, but I didn't find out about those. The world found out about them a few months later when the Cuban missile crisis occurred. The first thing I thought of then was Carlos Rafael Rodríguez's warning to me not to go poking around in the countryside.) Che Guevara had boasted that Cuba would be manufacturing trucks and buses by 1962. In vacant lots all over Havana, I saw collections of broken-down American buses. Cuba didn't even make spark plugs or fuel pumps to keep them on the road.

There was plenty of aid from the Soviets. I counted 750 big Zovod trucks on a Havana dock. A dockworker told me they had been sitting there for seven months. The Cubans couldn't think of any use for them. The warehouses at the docks also held thousands of cases of lathes and drills and electronic instruments from China, Czechoslovakia and East Germany, equipment hardly anybody in Cuba was trained to use. I counted boxes containing 200 electron microscopes; Cuba might have needed eight or ten. The same building held 50,000 Chinese voltmeters; the order had been for 500, I was told, but somebody had misread it. I took a certain satisfaction in noting the awful mess the Communist world was making of aid to Cuba. I had been traveling all over Latin America finding examples of waste and inefficiency in the U.S. Alliance for

Progress program. But not even the United States would have shipped a country 750 useless heavy trucks or 49,500 too many voltmeters.

Even more conspicuous than the failure of industry was the failure of collectivized agriculture. One of Rodríguez's land reformers took me out to see an exhibition dairy farm. Canadian milk cows, purchased with scarce dollars, were milked by former sugarcane cutters, *guajiros*, the impoverished field hands of the old Cuban society, now earning three times their former pay, with free housing and paid vacations. The cattle were beautiful and the workers were happy, but the manager of the collective farm admitted the farm didn't produce enough milk to pay the workers' wages, let alone to become profitable.

With the cane cutters promoted to other jobs in Castro's classless society, somebody had to harvest the sugarcane upon which everything else in the Cuban economy depended. That became the job of "volunteers" from the city. I found schoolteachers swinging machetes, sweating and grousing in the cane fields of Las Villas Province while a brigade of workers loaded the cane into trucks. One man's straw hat proclaimed him a "distinguished worker." I stopped to talk to him and found that he was a distinguished *electrical* worker. The amateurs in the fields were bringing in a harvest down 25 percent from the year before. They were subsidizing with their labor the new houses and schools that Castro aimed to provide for 300,000 rural families, formerly the poorest of the Cuban poor, now the core of support for the revolution. But after listening to the grumbling among the teachers and electrical workers in the cane fields, I thought I saw some counterrevolutionaries being created, too.

"Gusanos," they were called, "worms," who complained too much about the way things were going. They included almost all of the former shopkeepers, professionals and small business people, the old middle classes of the country. By the hundreds every day, the *gusanos* were leaving Cuba, leaving everything they owned behind. At last, the day came for me to join a planeload of them for the flight to Miami. A dentist was stationed at the airport to remove gold inlays. An old woman, weeping, was forced to give up her wedding ring. A guard opened my camera case and confiscated all my film. I put up a big argument, but it was just for show. The film was blank; I had talked an acquaintance at the

Mexican embassy into shipping my precious exposed film, the first American views of Cuba in more than a year, by diplomatic pouch to Mexico City.

The Pan Am flight taxied to the end of the runway—then was called back. It was a bit of spiteful theater, preplanned vengefulness. Policemen came aboard, seized a passenger who had thought he was safely away, handcuffed him and marched him off the plane while everyone else sat frozen in silence. The silence continued as the plane left the gate again, reached the end of the runway again, took off and climbed away from the island, the passengers united in mute tension.

The silence was not broken until the voice of the pilot was heard. He said in Spanish, "We have left Cuban airspace and will be landing in twenty-five minutes."

A great cheer went up. People broke into tears and clapped one another on the back. The plane began to descend, and the passengers, all talking excitedly at once, peered through the windows for the first glimpse of land.

"Welcome to Miami, Florida," the pilot said, "*Free* Territory of the Americas." They cheered again, even louder than before.

To my surprise, I felt like cheering, too. I had been in Cuba only twenty-three days and unaware of any great pressure, but what lifted from my shoulders in that moment was a very heavy weight. The busybody comrades of the Defense Committees, the dresser drawer-rifling secret police, the marches blaring from loudspeakers, the Big Brother slogans, the sense of menace were all behind me, and America was just ahead.

I was to have the same feeling again in years to come—on taking off from Saigon and escaping the war in Vietnam, and on getting out of pre-*glasnost* Russia, and on leaving brutal China behind me in the midst of the Tiananmen Square uprising. The peace of the twenty-third Psalm settled upon me, the part about still waters and green pastures and the soul restored.

I felt released. I felt light as air.

9

HOLLYWOOD

Sory and I were divorced in a courtroom in Hillsborough, North Carolina. I didn't have to be there, for which I was grateful. She was planning to remarry, Lisa and Susan were doing well, so Sory and I both had what we had wanted. She had a close family, and I had a thick passport.

But now I found I was lonely. My old pal Reasoner was becoming a television star on a daily morning program called *Calendar* (with Andy Rooney as chief writer and Mary Fickett as costar, perhaps the best series CBS News ever put on the air). My old pal Phil Scheffler was becoming an important producer. And I was thousands of miles away in Rio, working on stories nobody much cared about but me. I needed somebody to have a drink with once in a while, and tell my troubles to.

On rare trips back to New York, I always had a drink with Petie Baird, the beautiful secretary who used to run along the Grand Central catwalk with me, arranging Doug Edwards's scripts. She was a reader of books, all books, Thurber, Steinbeck, Faulkner, Bruce Catton, Rex Stout, Alexander Pope. She was always able to tell me things I didn't know. One night, she overcooked a pork chop for me at her walk-up apartment in Greenwich Village.

"You are a terrible cook," I said. "I don't suppose you'd like to marry me?"

"Maybe, someday," she said.

I reminded her of this remark now and then in letters from Rio. When I came to New York to make a half-hour documentary of the footage from Cuba, I took her to dinner and asked, "Why not now?"

She said, "All right. Now."

"I'll be traveling all the time."

"I'm used to being alone."

"I'm not kidding. I'll never have a nine-to-five job."

"I couldn't stand having somebody always around the house from five to nine."

I called the Moore-McCormack Line, which ran steamships to Rio, and booked passage for the next week. I asked whether the ship's captain really could perform weddings at sea. Of course, I was told. Petie and I sent our bags down to the docks. She quietly resigned her job, explaining, and actually making everybody believe, that she had come into an unexpected inheritance. We knew our marriage would create a stir in the office, we had friends who ought to be invited, and we knew we didn't want to go through all that. I raced to finish the Cuba documentary before the sailing date of the SS *Argentina*.

An American in Cuba was broadcast May 25, 1962. It expressed my conviction that the Cuban Revolution was a disorganized flop and that Cuba was becoming a police state, but the program still caused a considerable fuss in Miami. The fiercely anti-Castro exiles were upset by the part about good schools and decent housing. "Lies!" they said in telegrams and phone calls. "CBS is a dupe of the Communists!" Most people, I was discovering, don't want to hear the truth of controversial subjects, they want to hear the truth as they wish it were or imagine it to be. A Florida congressman demanded that I appear before an Un-American Activities subcommittee.

I figured I couldn't be subpoenaed if I was on a ship at sea. I called the shipping line to reconfirm the reservations. I asked again, "And the captain can perform weddings, right?" The woman on the phone said, "Yes, the captain can perform weddings, but not on this particular ship. The sailing was cancelled this morning. There has been a seamen's strike."

I went down to the docks and had all our suitcases transferred to Idlewild Airport. I called Harry Reasoner and asked if he would like to be best man at a City Hall wedding. The next day happened to be the first of June. While Petie and I waited on a bench for Harry to arrive, a reporter named Tom Costigan, an old friend from the assignment desk, showed up with a camera crew. He was doing a feature on June brides.

"I thought I was assigned to this," he said.

"I am not here to do a story," I said. "I am here to get married. Kindly point that lens in another direction."

He kindly did. There was a time clock on the desk of the clerk who performed the ceremony which went "chunk" once every sixty seconds. It only chunked once while we were in there. We were married in less than two minutes. We went out to the airport and caught the Pan Am flight to Rio.

I suppose we haven't spent more than a week at a time together from that day to this. Petie has not minded this much. People ask, "And what does your wife do while you're away?" I say, "She reads, and when I come home, she tells me things I don't know."

I kept wandering around the hemisphere, trying to work Fidel Castro's name into every lead so they'd use the story on the news back home. I developed pretty good sources in most of the capitals of Latin America, set up a network of stringer reporters and cameramen who could keep me informed about stories coming up in their countries and polished my Spanish and Portuguese. Just as I was beginning to get good at my job, I was told I was being transferred back to the United States.

Naturally. Correspondents at CBS get used to being whisked away from jobs they're good at on the whim of some executive. Only the great Winston Burdett resisted successfully, by explaining calmly that if ever transferred from Rome, he would resign. He spent his whole career there, outlasting several Popes. I was no Burdett, either in ability or clout. I resisted briefly and gave in. "You'll get on the air more often if you're in the States," I was told.

I was given a choice of two assignments, the White House or the new Los Angeles bureau. I knew I'd be number two man to Bob Pierpoint at the White House and that I'd never get to travel, except as part of the pack on the press plane. I knew nothing at all about the alternative, except that the job called for keeping track of the news in places I liked, California, Oregon, Washington and the mountain states east to the Rockies. Petie and I had acquired some furniture by now. I pasted Los Angeles stickers on the packing crates.

Before long, we were lying awake listening to that heavy furniture from humid Brazil splitting along the grain in the dry California night in sudden contractions that sounded like pistol shots. The house was in the Hollywood hills above Sunset Boulevard. About eight inches of the house was on solid ground. The rest of it was cantilevered perilously over a canyon; to stand at the edge of the sun deck was to experience the giddy sensation of the high diver at the end of the board. Eartha Kitt's backyard swimming pool was down there a couple hundred feet below.

Like the furniture, I had trouble adapting to southern California. I tried. I bought sunglasses, and a white convertible to go with them, and drove down the hill to Television City with the top down. ("Mr. Kuralt" it said at my parking place near the artists' entrance.) I got introduced around town by Bill Stout, the most knowledgeable reporter in Los Angeles, temporarily working for a rival independent television station between long stints at CBS. I nodded to Judy Garland and Sammy Davis, Jr., when I chanced to meet them in the halls. I tapped my toe in time with the music that filtered into the office from the rehearsal hall next door. I became known to the *maître d' hôtel* at Chasen's Restaurant. All the time, I was aware of playing a role, and I felt miscast—awkward country boy as Hollywood man-about-town.

The bad telephone circuits between New York and Latin America had meant I was usually free to choose my own assignments while based in Rio. Now, though I was called the West Coast Bureau Manager, I was under the thumb of the New York assignment desk whenever an important story came along, and New York had some odd ideas about what constituted an important story. As long as I was at my desk in Los Angeles, I was vulnerable to telephone calls sending me off to pointless stakeouts at the Governor's Mansion in Sacramento or to interviews with movie stars.

To escape, I found as many stories as possible in places where I could make myself hard to reach, the Willamette Valley of Oregon, the

Cascades, the Sierra, small-town Nevada and the Grand Canyon country. I gloried in the landscape of the rural west, loved working alone with a camera crew out in the country, and always resented it when real news came along that demanded my presence on the scene.

It seemed to me that everything of genuine importance happened on somebody else's beat, anyway. That was all right with me. I had done a typical California bureau story, a report on Chatty Cathy, the first talking doll, a pretty good story, I thought. I had shipped it to New York, where it languished on the shelf, so before heading to the office one November morning, I called Don Hewitt in New York, thinking I'd remind him about Chatty Cathy.

"He can't come to the phone right now," said the young woman who answered. "Everybody's over at the wire machines. Something about President Kennedy being shot."

I turned on the radio in time to hear the first bulletin. After that, all I could do was watch and listen as a newly hired correspondent named Dan Rather told the story from Dallas, coolly and accurately. I was aware that I was witnessing a prodigious job of reporting. Without raising his voice, Rather scooped the world by many minutes on the fact of the President's death. I sat in my living room in West Hollywood dry-mouthed, paralyzed by the enormity of the news. I remember thinking, thank God I'm not there. I knew I could never do what Rather was doing. It took all my willpower to get myself to the corner of Hollywood and Vine for a live man-on-the-street interview as the news spread through the city.

I had a drink that night with Bill Stout. I confessed that my unprofessional shock and dismay had overwhelmed all my reportorial instincts. He put a hand on my shoulder.

"Look," he said, "there's nothing you could have done anyway. It's not exactly a Hollywood story."

When Hollywood stories did come along, I had a way of blowing them. Frank Sinatra, Jr., was kidnapped, an abduction that held the country's attention for days. I reluctantly abandoned a story about Basque sheepherders in Nevada to send daily reports to the network from Lake Tahoe, scene of the kidnapping. I was still working all the Tahoe angles when young Sinatra was released—at an exit of the San Diego Freeway back in Los Angeles. I had missed another one. Nothing to do but shrug and rejoin the Basques, whom I found far more interesting. But the feeling was growing in New York that the West Coast Bureau Manager was not exactly a news hawk when it came to breaking stories.

Fred Friendly had become the President of CBS News. He was an active volcano. When he erupted on the telephone, hot coals and lava burned the wire from New York to California. He called me to say that he did not give a hoot in hell about Basque shepherds or Basque sheep. Would I please start covering the news?

I did the best I could, but kept getting diverted. California was a big prize in the 1964 Republican Presidential primary. Nelson Rockefeller, all reasonableness, and Barry Goldwater, all bluster, made repeated sweeps through the state. I dutifully covered them while steadily losing interest in them. When the Goldwater campaign branched out one day to Reno, Nevada, Robert MacNeil, a reporter for NBC News in those long ago pre-*MacNeil/Lehrer* days, mentioned to me that he had never visited a gambling casino. We asked some other reporter to cover for us at a luncheon at the old Riverside Hotel in case Goldwater varied the speech we both had heard a dozen times or more, and while the rest of the press corps went to the lunch, MacNeil and I went to the roulette table.

"It's a child's game, Robin," I said, out of my vast experience in Latin American gambling hells. "You just put a couple of chips on 27, the red, and wait for the little white ball to drop into the 27 on the wheel."

We both did, and I'll be damned if it didn't.

We stood there half an hour, plunging—at least as working stiffs understand the word. Neither of us could lose. By the time Goldwater had finished his speech, I had won $1,600 and MacNeil nearly $1,000. At the cashier's desk, MacNeil said, "Nothing to it! I can't wait to try this again!"

He has since told me that those thirty minutes in Reno proved expensive in later life, and that he blames me. At the time, a good deal richer, we both had to hurry to catch up with the motorcade and file our stories on Senator Goldwater's stirring speech in Reno.

Then came the earthquake.

Most people don't remember earthquakes, even the big ones, unless they were there. They don't remember the one in the Peruvian Andes that buried alive 67,000 people, some of them people I knew, in 1970. Or the one that killed more than 22,000 in Guatemala early in 1976. Even if you ask them about the earthquake in the summer of '76 in which as many as 800,000 people may have perished in China, a calamity almost beyond imagining, they look blank. The Alaska earthquake of 1964 is mostly forgotten now. Except by me.

It struck on March 27 with a force of 8.5 on the Richter scale, the most powerful earthquake ever recorded in North America. Within seconds after the bulletin appeared on the wire service machines in our Los Angeles office, I was on the phone to Alaska, only to discover, as I had feared, that suddenly there were no working telephones in Alaska. I called Seattle and found that the Navy was summoning doctors and collecting medical supplies for a relief flight which would leave for Anchorage within hours. I wangled a space on the plane for a Seattle cameraman. Then I called New York to tell the assignment desk I was off to Seattle to try to get aboard the Navy plane myself.

"Don't go," I was told. "We're not even sure there's a usable runway in Anchorage. This is going to take days to sort out and somebody is going to have to give us reports from Los Angeles in the meantime. Anybody else you can send?"

I looked around the office. My eye fell on Terry Drinkwater, a young election researcher who had never done a television story in his life. But I knew he wanted to be a reporter.

"Go to Seattle right now," I said. "Call me as soon as you get there. I might be able to get you on the first plane into Alaska."

Terry Drinkwater made the plane. So did a reporter from NBC. Terry did his first quick report from Alaska right at the Anchorage airport showing the damage there. So did the reporter from NBC. Terry alertly shipped the film back to Seattle on the plane he'd come in on, which had been converted to a medical evacuation flight for some of those injured in the quake. The NBC reporter got his film on the plane, too. With no way of knowing any of this, I had a motorcycle courier I'd relied on in the past stand by at the Seattle airport. NBC had a courier, too. I gave mine instructions to call me at any hour of the night or day when he found a flight was expected from Alaska. He called. The navy plane was returning, expected to arrive in one hour. I alerted New York and made sure the CBS station in Seattle was ready to feed film instantly to the network. The plane landed. The CBS film and the NBC film came off the same plane at the same time. Both motorcycle couriers, mine and NBC's, roared off toward the city.

Mine ran out of gas.

NBC went on the air with the first film of the Alaska earthquake, beating CBS by twenty-six minutes.

Fred Friendly called it his "Bay of Pigs." He convened a formal court of inquiry a few days later to discover how this humiliation could have occurred, with all of his executives in attendance in his office and I testifying by telephone. When I got to the part about the motorcycle running out of gas, I tried a euphemism to protect the courier's job, if not his life.

"He ran into logistical difficulties," I said.

The volcano rumbled and blew.

"And by the way," Friendly roared, "why didn't *you* go to Alaska?"

"The desk in New York told me not to."

There was a pause while Friendly verified this with the others in the room. Then he came back on the line.

"The next time the desk tells you not to go to Alaska," he bellowed, *"go to Alaska!"*

He slammed down the phone.

Terry Drinkwater went on to become a CBS News Correspondent on the basis of his good reporting of the Alaska earthquake.

I got recalled to New York on the basis of an empty gas tank.

10

NINETY DEGREES NORTH

*H*aving decided that I was a washout as a reporter of breaking stories, my bosses assigned me to work on documentaries.

I should explain to the young: We made documentaries back then, programs of thirty minutes or an hour on single subjects. We did not do this because we thought they would attract large audiences or beat the other networks in the ratings. We did it because the management thought we ought to.

The management of CBS News passed from Fred Friendly to Richard S. Salant. Fred's inner Mount Etna went off in a dispute about news coverage with the management across town. He resigned. Salant was a company lawyer with no background in journalism. Never mind his background; Salant was the best leader we ever had. Almost alone among CBS News Presidents, he represented the news staff to the CBS corporation, rather than the other way around. Salant's idea was that he would worry about sponsors and ratings and air time, leaving the rest of us to worry about telling people the news. Salant had high principles and expected us to live up to them. With the advice of two able deputies, Bill Leonard and Gordon Manning—also the best we ever had—he codified all the unwritten ethical rules of broadcast journalism into a thick white book with a plastic cover, *CBS News Standards and Practices.* He made it a loose-leaf book so that he could add new rules as he thought of them.

Among the first documentaries I worked on was a one-hour study of the labor union movement, *The State of the Unions*, produced by Joe Wershba, one of the most gifted of Ed Murrow's former producers. Our program was a comparison of an old, powerful union, Walter Reuther's United Auto Workers, with the young, weak one Cesar Chavez was organizing among California farm workers. For the sake of a little historical background, we filmed the opening in Chicago at the site of the 1937 Republic Steel massacre. "The strikers were here," I said, "the police ranks were over there. . . ." A public relations man from Republic Steel wandered out of the building to listen to this speech. He must have reported it to his superiors because a few days later in the interoffice mail Joe Wershba and I received copies of some correspondence. The President of Republic Steel had written a sharp letter to Frank Stanton, President of CBS, saying Republic Steel did not appreciate CBS News dredging up ancient history this way and reminding Stanton that Republic Steel was sponsoring certain entertainment programs on the network. Stanton had passed the letter to Dick Salant for a reply. Salant's reply said, "I assume this filming was done for a broadcast we are preparing called *The State of the Unions*. . . ." He went on to tell the President of Republic Steel when and where he could see this program if he wanted to, and signed the letter, "Very truly yours . . ." Salant sent copies of these letters to Joe Wershba and me without comment. He never even asked us what we had done outside the Republic Steel property. His letter said unmistakably to this big sponsor that *whatever* we had done was going on the air just as we had done it. And it did.

The reporter is a stone skipping on a pond, taking an instant to tell one story and ricocheting to the next, covering a lot of water while only skimming the surface. But in those years of the mid-sixties, I got good and wet. I spent several weeks in one block of Harlem working on a documentary that tried to explain the grievances of people who were black and poor, *117th Street, New York, New York*. With another of Murrow's old producers, Jack Beck, I worked on an hour-long broadcast about Mexico, and with still another, David Lowe, I delved into the ugly mysteries of the Ku Klux Klan.

I spent nearly all of December 1964 in the dreary hollows of

Letcher County, Kentucky, with a friend from *Eyewitness* days, Bernie Birnbaum, and a skilled cameraman, Walter Dombrow. The resulting broadcast, describing a dark and silent *Christmas in Appalachia*, shocked viewers with pictures of children thin and pale and dying of hunger in the richest country in the world. I was shocked, too. I kept returning to eastern Kentucky and West Virginia to make sure nobody missed the point that half a million of their fellow citizens were living in tar paper shacks without electricity or running water, families of six subsisting on nothing but $56 a month in food stamps. I am not sure those stories did any good. I'm pretty sure they didn't. But they were stories, perhaps the only ones, ever, I felt I had to do.

Bernie Birnbaum and I looked around again the next year for the most miserable possible place to spend Christmas. We settled on Vietnam. We picked a First Division infantry squad fighting a war against snipers and booby traps at a place called Lai Khe. We were there long enough to get to know every man in the squad and to take it personally when incoming bullets and mortar rounds started picking them off one at a time. A mine exploded in the brush one day while two of Sergeant Ralph Bosalet's men, Bill Floyd and José Dueñas, were creeping around in there. Our cameraman, a brave man named Jerry Sims, stopped filming to help the badly wounded Floyd into a truck. His assistant cameraman wrapped a tourniquet around Floyd's leg to stop the bleeding. Then, while I twisted the tourniquet and held it tight, Sims filmed the wild ride to the aid station and the attempt to save Floyd's life, muttering as he worked, "Goddamn this war, goddamn this war . . ." You can hear him murmuring this phrase in the background of the film's sound track. I was feeling the same way. Floyd lost his leg. We visited him at the army hospital in Denver when he got home, and again when he was married. Years later, we found him still trying to adjust to his artificial leg at his home in Florida.

There was nothing we could do for Dueñas but pay our respects to his family. Dueñas was killed when the mine went off. *Christmas in Vietnam* ended with a picture of the squad leader, Ralph Bosalet, a spirited and animated man, sitting on an ammunition box beside an outdoor Christmas tree, lost in grief.

I came back to America persuaded that I had had enough of death and danger. It always has been a mistake to walk around the halls of 524 West 57th Street where your bosses can see you. One day late in 1966, I ran into Bill Leonard in the hall. He was the vice president in charge of documentaries.

"Yes!" he said. "You're the one!"

"I'm the what?" I asked.

"Come into my office," he said. "Sit down."

He poured me a cup of coffee. This was more hospitable treatment than I was used to from my superiors.

"Next spring," he said, "a bunch of Minnesotans are going to try to drive snowmobiles to the North Pole."

I felt an icy premonition down my spine.

"We're going to do a one-hour documentary. Bob Clemens is going to shoot it. Dick Wiggins and Bob Mingalone are going along as soundman and assistant. Palmer Williams will be the producer in New York. I've been trying to think of a correspondent we can spare for a couple of months."

"And?"

"And you're the one. Stop looking so worried. You're going to love it." He wrote a name and telephone number on a piece of paper and handed it to me.

That's how I met Ralph Plaisted. He was not a professional explorer. He was a former door-to-door peddler of spices, extracts, fly spray and cattle vitamins around Askov, Minnesota, Rutabaga Capital of the World. Now, at thirty-eight, he had graduated to selling insurance in White Bear Lake. He was an outdoorsman, like so many others who live on the rim of the Great Lakes, always seeking some new strenuous adventure. The winter before, he had wondered how long it would take him to drive a snowmobile to St. Paul from his summer cabin at Ely, 250 miles away. It took him thirteen hours and fifty-two minutes nonstop in thirty-below-zero temperatures. He started looking around for some other place to go on a snowmobile. He settled on the North Pole.

The National Geographic Society disdainfully declined to sponsor him. Ralph was a little rough-hewn for the gentleman-explorer establishment. At a luncheon in the society's inner sanctum in Washington ("Six pieces of silverware on each side of the plate. Real dainty food. Nothing to drink"), he was told that he would never make it to the Pole. He told the society bigwigs they could just sit there and watch him.

He rounded up some of his pals, a doctor, a high school geography teacher, a dentist, a computer engineer and others, and talked them into going along. He used his flair as a salesman to collect donated supplies— ten snowmobiles, 250 pounds of soup, forty-five pounds of mixed nuts, tents, pickaxes, candy bars, sleeping bags, caribou hides, medical supplies, sleds, dried milk, canned beef, radios, nylon cable, pots and pans, thermal underwear and cheese in wheels and tubes and boxes which came with a flag to be raised at the North Pole emblazoned: "3110 Miles to the White Bear Lake Cheese Shop."

By mail, Ralph sent me my uniform. There was an inner parka, knee-length, made of poplin and lined with Sherpa cloth, its hood encircled by wolverine fur. This garment alone would have sent any Eskimo into raptures, and it was only the *inner* parka. The outer parka was made in layers of windproof canvas duck and quilted spun nylon with hand-stitched hem, cuffs and hood lined with arctic wolf fur and the finished article dyed a bright color for easy identification on the trail. Mine was bright red. The trousers, of matching, thickly insulated duck, were held up by gaudy suspenders and tied at the bottom between knee and ankle with rawhide thongs. The boots were most impressive of all. They were Eskimo-style *mukluks* of smoked moosehide, lined with seamless Finn boots made of raw carded wool with soles of plastic mesh and felt, designed to be removed and dried at the end of the day.

I put on all this gear in my apartment in New York and looked at myself in the mirror. My Plaisted Polar Expedition patch blazed back at me from the breast of my crimson parka. The wolverine fur bravely circled my face. I was Nanook, or Peary, or Roald Amundsen. I took all that stuff off before somebody came to the door and caught me wearing it.

Self-conscious rehearsals were staged on the ice of Mille Lacs in northern Minnesota, a smooth, glassy surface as different from the Arctic Ocean as a millpond from a rapids. Little crowds of people began showing up on the lake to see what polar explorers looked like. Bumps Woolsey, Ralph Plaisted's dentist, opened the flap of the tent out there one Saturday afternoon in February and peered back at the people.

"You know, Ralph," he said, "if we keep talking about going to the North Pole like this, we're really going to have to go."

We really went.

We assembled at the Queen Elizabeth Hotel in Montreal on Good Friday, March 24, 1967. The waitress in the coffee shop, who could hardly overlook our colorful wind jackets, asked where we were going.

"The North Pole," we answered.

"What are you running away from?" she asked.

We flew north in a Royal Canadian Air Force C-130 Hercules—also donated—with our knees rubbing against a towering twelve-ton mound of cargo. Montreal is about 2,200 miles from Canada's most northerly regions. Canada is approximately as tall as it is wide. You have to make the trip in a metal bucket seat to appreciate the fact. On the way, I read Vilhjalmur Stefansson's classic books on the Arctic and other cold-weather advice: "If your hand freezes to your ax blade at 50 below, urinate on it. If *both* hands freeze to your ax blade, you'd better have a friend along."

We made an overnight stop at Thule Air Base in Greenland and took off in the following dawn for Eureka, a nine-man U.S.–Canadian weather station on Ellesmere Island, where an unused building was to serve as the expedition's base camp. I stepped out of the aircraft into blowing snow to see three animals racing toward me with bared fangs. I thought, my God, wolves! and took an involuntary step back toward the door before I noticed their tails were wagging. They were the weather station huskies.

The insulated tin buildings of Eureka, the only habitations ever constructed in that part of the Arctic, sit squarely on latitude 80 degrees north—100 miles down Nansen Sound from the edge of the Arctic Ocean and exactly 600 nautical miles from the Pole. The Plaisted Polar Expedition set out three days after our arrival on snowmobiles towing sleds top-heavy with spare parts, charts, chain saws, rifles, ice axes, duffel bags, radios, camera gear, tents, sleeping bags and food. One sled carried a 450-pound drum of gasoline. Never having been on a polar expedition, nobody knew exactly what to take on a polar expedition—so they took everything they could pack.

Bob Clemens rode with the lead snowmobiles. The plan was for Wiggins, Mingalone and me to shuttle back and forth to the expedition by plane. So it was Mingalone who filmed the departure in the frigid morning as Plaisted, at the head of the column, raised his arm, circled his mittened hand in the air and pointed north. One by one, the bright yellow machines followed, the overloaded sleds wobbling precariously behind. We followed them with the long lens of the camera until they disappeared into the cold mist. It was a great scene. Mingalone and I went inside to reload the camera. When we opened the camera door, thousands of little film chips spurted out at us. The film had frozen and shredded into confetti.

Bob Clemens wasn't having any better luck. His sled tipped over in the first mile; as he righted it, all he could think of were the 599 miles to go. The lens of his camera became ice-covered. The tripod head affixed to his snowmobile froze up and wouldn't move.

And the rest of the expedition was encountering even worse troubles, straying in wrong directions. Compasses are useless at that latitude, the Magnetic North Pole lying, as it does, away to the *south*, so Plaisted relied on the direction of the sun, which circled the sky above the horizon, neither rising nor setting in the early spring. Jerry Pitzl, the navigator, had a sextant for taking sun shots, but in the whiteouts, it sometimes took close study of Bob Clemens's photographic light meter to find the location of the sun. The comparatively simple trip up Nansen Sound to the edge of the Arctic Ocean took the expedition long, miserable days to accomplish.

Back at the base camp, we fought off cabin fever by playing chess, teaching one another Morse code, or walking up to the weather station to watch the weathermen send up their meteorological balloons (special fun on windy days).

The building where we slept was insulated and warm but the toilet was an unheated outhouse. Since temperatures there remained below zero, the old two-holer had to be approached with a kind of daily heroism. "The only true happiness in the Arctic," Bob Clemens said, "is pulling your pants back up."

Water for bathing and drinking came from a handy iceberg frozen into the fjord a mile or so away. Somebody had to take a Ski-Doo out there every morning, chip off a sledload of ice and haul it in to melt on the cookstove, a woodburning relic off some ancient schooner which a whimsical mechanic had converted to oil. The stove burned with a hellish roar, and there being no way to regulate the heat, it cooked capriciously. A ham came out burned to the core after a few minutes in the oven; a cheesecake, after cooking for hours, remained a flabby pudding. We all lost weight at base camp.

One day, on an ice-collecting and exploring trip, Dick Wiggins and I took snowmobiles miles across the hills of Ellesmere. The little cluster of weather buildings vanished in the distance. The impression came upon us that we were the only men who had ever ventured into this wilderness. It was a beautiful subzero day. We came across snowy fields full of arctic hares, entirely white except for the black tips of their ears, and so unafraid of human beings that they permitted us to walk almost close enough to touch them. They communicated with one another by shadowboxing, each flurry of boxing in the air followed by quick hops toward fresh patches of sparse brown grass growing up through the snow. They pawed and nibbled and boxed for two hours or more as we stood among them, fascinated.

Then we spotted a herd of musk-oxen and gave chase. At first, the great shaggy animals ran from us, but when we caught up to them, they formed their characteristic circle of defense, old bulls shoulder to shoulder on the outside of the circle, horns lowered, with cows and calves herded into the center. It is a strategy musk-oxen must have learned in the Ice Age as a defense against wolves, a tactic copied by covered wagoneers on the western prairie and by British grenadiers in battle against Zulus. We made pictures, but the fixed look of a formation of stomping, snorting musk-oxen has a certain forcefulness which restrained us from moving in for close-ups.

The Arctic Ocean ice is constantly in motion. The floes, shifted by wind and current, break apart, creating "leads" of open water, and grind together, forming jumbled pressure ridges. Both leads and ridges slowed the Plaisted Expedition, which was forced to camp frequently to wait for wide leads to freeze over or to spend hours chopping rough paths through towering barriers of ice. Sleds turned over and broke apart in the rough going, skis separated from the machines and went flying. When at last it was time to camp, sleep was hindered by condensed moisture dripping from the walls of the tents, often by loud cracks as the floes chosen as campsites began to break up, once by a fire when a catalytic heater tipped over, once by the arrival of a curious polar bear.

They knew they must reach the Pole by early May when the arctic storms begin and create huge channels in the ocean ice. Mid-April found them in a region of jumbled ice Bumps Woolsey called "the Rock Quarry," through which they had to cut a path for every inch of progress. After that came a monstrous pressure ridge which forced them to rope machines and sleds up one side and down the other. The cold and the exertion induced a profound weariness none of them had ever experienced before. The vigorous doctor of the expedition, Art Aufderheide, wrote in his diary one night: "This could turn out to be too much for a 45-year-old man."

I took a turn on the ice to spell Bob Clemens for a few days. The first morning was a fast, easy floe-hopping operation. I rode standing on Woolsey's sled. I had to bury my face in the fur lining of my parka hood to escape the icy draft our speed created. In the afternoon, we entered an area of broken ice, first jagged cracks two or three feet wide that lent themselves to thrilling snowmobile jumps, then wider leads that required us to dismount and test the thickness of the ice crusts before crossing. It was hard not to think of the ice as "land" and the cracks as "streams"— but those streams were hundreds of fathoms deep. To reach the Pole in time, we needed an average daily advance of eleven miles. That day, we made ten.

The next day, we made at least thirteen, and the next day twenty, in a bracing, exciting scramble through a gathering fog. The plane came out, guided now by a tracking beacon, landed and took me back to base camp with the film I had shot out there. As we took off from the ice, all I could see to the north was a broad, smooth expanse leading straight toward the Pole. It looked as though the Plaisted Polar Expedition had gone and got lucky.

That night, the wind came up as the men on the ice were pitching their tents. Aufderheide suggested it might be a good idea to build a snow wall around the tents and they did. Jerry Pitzl brought out his anemometer. It showed a wind speed of 1,500 feet per minute, about eighteen miles per hour. Nothing to worry about. Then he checked his other instruments. The barometer read 29.5. It was falling fast. The thermometer read +2° F. It was the first time the mercury had risen above zero. These readings were a classic indication of the approach of an arctic spring storm. They all knew it. They just didn't want to believe it.

That night, high winds were blowing from every point of the compass over half the Arctic Basin, attracted by the vacuum effect of a monstrous low-pressure system moving across the North Pole from Siberia. As the storm approached the men on the ice, its winds, backing clockwise in a 500-mile diameter, reached a speed of sixty miles per hour. This wind hit their light tents after midnight. They heard a series of loud concussions over the roar of the flapping tent walls. That was the ice breaking up around them.

Their two tents were fifteen feet apart. In the blowing snow of the morning, they couldn't see from one tent to the other. They had no choice but to stay where they were and hope their floe outlasted the storm.

On the third day of the big blow, Ralph Plaisted realized he had stopped thinking about taking these men to the Pole. He was thinking only about keeping them alive. He decided that if they were alive when the storm ended, he would end the expedition there and take the men home.

If a tent had blown away, if the floe had cracked beneath them, they would have perished. But on the afternoon of the seventh day, the wind stopped.

It stopped. It did not slowly diminish, the way wind usually does. It dropped in fifteen minutes from a gale to a dead calm. The sky cleared, except for streaks of black cloud trailing back from the southeast, and within an hour, even they had disappeared.

It was over.

Back at the base camp, I happened to be passing the radio room. I heard a small voice coming through the static we had been monitoring for a week. I pressed the mike button and said, "Go ahead."

It was Jerry Pitzl's voice. "I have to talk fast because the generator is sputtering. Our position is 83-34 north, 89-32 west. Send out the plane."

The Plaisted Polar Expedition of 1967 ended there, in failure, 384 nautical miles short of the North Pole. The exhausted men, glad to have survived the storm, crossed their last lead on May 4 to reach a floe big enough for the plane to land on. It was a fresh crack, four feet wide. They bridged it with the slender poles of the radio antenna and drove recklessly across. The crack widened while they were crossing. The last sled across knocked the poles into the ocean.

After the plane landed, they loaded one snowmobile, one tent and their sleeping bags. All the rest of the equipment they were forced to leave on the ice. It is still floating there, I imagine. Someday, if the floe drifts down into the North Atlantic, a passing mariner may be startled by what he sees through his binoculars: bright-yellow snowmobiles and toboggans, food boxes, stoves and axes and caribou hides. More likely, the floe will break up in some future storm—as it almost did during the big blow of April and May 1967—and these last remnants of the Plaisted Polar Expedition will drop to the bottom of the sea.

When the plane landed at the Eureka airstrip, Jerry Pitzl was the first to step upon solid ground.

"It was just a shame," he said, "just a damn shame. I've got to tell you. We could have run and run and run. I climbed up on a big ridge just before the plane came in, and for miles to the north was good going, nothing but good ice as far as I could see. . . ."

He put a finger under his sunglasses to wipe tears away.

That night, we opened the champagne we had hoped to drink at the Pole and drank it all. What Plaisted, Pitzl, Aufderheide and some of the others talked about that night were the mistakes they had made, the lessons they had learned—and their next attempt to reach the Pole.

I was proud of them. There have always been a few people who, with no visible motive, background of experience or likelihood of gain, have strained for the ends of the earth. I put Ralph Plaisted and his buddies in that company.

The next year, with some of the same men, Plaisted returned to Ellesmere, set out earlier, traveled lighter, left his fears behind him and reached the North Pole. I wasn't along. I was in Cedar Rapids, Iowa, where Collins Radio had set up a shortwave link to the new expedition.

I asked, "What's your location, Ralph?"

His shout filled the room in Cedar Rapids.

"Ninety north! Ninety north!"

A U.S. Air Force plane flew over and confirmed it. Ralph Plaisted was camped at the North Pole.

Except for the officers of the National Geographic Society, which sponsored Commander Robert E. Peary's attempt to reach the Pole in 1909, hardly any modern arctic expert believes Peary made it. At about 88 degrees north latitude, Peary sent his navigator and all other scholarly members of his party back toward land, continuing toward the Pole with Matthew Henson, his black assistant, and four Eskimos. On April 6, Peary abruptly announced to Matt Henson that this was to be their final camp. He started for land the next day. At this point, his speed miraculously doubled. A close examination of Peary's diary shows that after leaving the "North Pole" he made 150 miles in two days, walking all the way. When later challenged on this distance by Congress, he was able to walk only thirty miles per day on the roads around Washington.

I reviewed the Peary diaries and the testimony of Peary and others for a month or more on returning to the United States, and what I believe is this: that Peary, who left with great fanfare on his ninth arctic expedition, which he knew must be his last (a fleet of yachts and a cheering crowd attended his departure from New York, and President Theodore Roosevelt, wringing his hand, said, "I believe in you, Peary, and I believe in your success if it is within the possibility of man") was determined not to return this time without the prize; that after thirty-seven days of hard travel northward, his observations showed that the Pole was still beyond the farthest ice ridges; that there in the wasteland of ice, his crippled feet tormenting him, his years telling on him, he was overcome by the uselessness of going on toward an abstract Pole no different from the rest of the ice pack; that he raised his flags and took his photographs, secure in the knowledge that nobody on earth could successfully dispute his claim.

In his own account, Matt Henson reported that when Peary took his last sextant observation, "I was sure that he was satisfied. Feeling that the time had come, I ungloved my right hand and went forward to congratulate him."

But Peary did not take Henson's extended hand. He only covered his eyes, murmured that he was tired and entered his igloo to sleep.

I believe Robert E. Peary did not cross the ice to the North Pole.

If he didn't, then the first who did was Ralph Plaisted, an insurance man from White Bear Lake, Minnesota.

BOXES ON WHEELS

*I*n early fall 1967, Jim Wilson and I were flying to Cleveland. And drinking, the way people do on airplanes, and looking out the window. It was one of those cool, clear nights when you can see the lights of all the small towns from 30,000 feet. We had enough airline whisky in us to make us maudlin.

"Look down there," Jim Wilson said. "Every one of those lights has a story to tell."

"Yep," I agreed mushily. "Damn right."

"Here we are, flying to a story," Wilson said, "and flying right over *ten thousand* stories!"

"A *hundred* thousand!" I exclaimed. I recalled for Wilson the joy of my driving trips through the Great Plains with Wendell Hoffman years before. "By God," I said, "next time we go somewhere, we ought to drive and find out what's really going on in this country!"

The next morning, we were both perfectly sober. The tipsy idea of the night before still seemed a good one. Wilson was a temperamental cameraman with a bit of the artist in him. He was trying to get out of the lock-step routine of hard news coverage. I had known from the beginning that I was better suited to feature stories than to wars, polar expeditions, politics and calamities. I had worked ten years for CBS News, often on assignments that taxed my physique and temperament. While I did not plan to say the word out loud, I felt I needed a vacation. When I got back to New York, I went to see Dick Salant.

I said, "Why don't you let me just wander for three months to see what I can find?"

He said, "What do you *think* you'll find?"

I waxed poetic. "Farmers bringing in their crops, first-graders starting school, county fairs, town meetings. Pulse of the country. You know."

President Salant was distracted by the pile of work on his desk.

"Okay," he said. "Try it. Keep the budget down."

I called Jim Wilson. I said, "We'll go in a couple of station wagons."

"No," he said, "let's go in a motor home."

I said, "What's a motor home?"

That's how long ago it was. Motor homes were still a novelty. I had never seen one. Many times in the next twenty years, I was to wish I *still* had never seen one. Of all the mixed blessings and curses of my life, I put motor homes at the top of the list.

Wilson explained that a motor home was a house trailer with a motor and steering wheel. A neighbor of his in Maryland, a *National Geographic* photographer, had just driven one to Alaska and back for a photo essay on the Alcan Highway. Wilson thought we could rent this very vehicle from the *National Geographic*. "It's parked in this guy's driveway," Wilson said. "Come down tomorrow and we'll have a look at it." Bob Funk, who volunteered to make the trip as our soundman, and Bill Lewis, who was to be our lighting man, came too.

What greeted my eyes was a tall, fiberglass box on wheels, originally painted beige, I believe, but bleached pink by the sun. I wondered whether I really wanted to traverse America in a pink box. But when Wilson showed us all the wonders inside—the refrigerator, the stove, the electric coffeepot, the combination shower room and toilet, the sofas that converted into beds, I was seized by the romance of it all. Why, we wouldn't even have to stop at motels for the night! We could pull off the road wherever we wished in all this fair land, and watch the sunset through our own picture window as we cooked our own steaks on our own broiler and washed them down with cold beer from our own electric icebox!

(We could also, I learned, sleep miserably on hard foam rubber bunks and rise grumpily, four grown men all trying to bathe and shave in cramped quarters at the same time, quarreling over whose turn it was to cook breakfast. We soon converted the convertible sofas into what we really needed, storage cabinets for the lights and cables and film supplies, and started looking for motels and cafes when the sun went down. Sleeping in the bus lasted about a week.)

We duly rented the pink box, and had a sign painter place the words "On The Road" in modest letters on the door, with the stylized CBS eye. I did not know at the time that I was making a deal with the devil: In return for the freedom of the road, I was going to have to spend the rest of my life in a motor home.

Motor home technology was primitive in the beginning and has not advanced very far since. The things are always breaking down. We've been through more than half a dozen "buses" as we call them. That first one, the one we rented, was a prototype Travco, a Dodge truck chassis perilously supporting a lofty fiberglass body. The pink box swayed alarmingly when under way, like a sailboat tacking into the wind. In the Travco, we learned to hang on to our coffee cups in the curves. When the stove stopped working, followed by the water pump and the propane system, we didn't even bother to have them fixed, figuring these were the landlord's problems, not ours.

When our allotted three months of travel were up, nobody at CBS said stop, so we pluckily kept going. We returned the rented Travco to the National Geographic Society much the worse for wear and bought a new one with CBS's money. We painted it white. Since then, we've painted all our buses white. Except for the paint job, the second Travco was not much improvement over the first. It would have been fine for family vacations, but it swooned under months of hard pounding. One day, as we labored along a dirt road near Stuttgart, Arkansas, a piston rod came flying through the roof of the engine compartment and landed greasily in Bob Funk's lap, persuading me that it was time to look around for a different model motor home.

Jim Wilson and his crew, having had enough of rusticity, now resigned to return to the comparative ease of jet airplanes and Hertz rental cars. Wilson's place was eventually taken by Isadore Bleckman, a congenial Chicago-based cameraman who had run a one-man sports car garage in his youth. Izzy prided himself on his mastery of mechanical matters. He volunteered to search out the state-of-the-art vehicle we could drive confidently into the future. His kitchen table in Evanston became heavy with brochures for this "Interstate Cruiser" and that "Land Yacht." The motor home, which I had never even heard of two or three years before, was becoming a national rage. Suddenly, there was such a thing as a Winnebago, and dozens of other makes to choose from. Izzy chose the Cortez.

Our love-hate affair with the Cortez lasted nearly a decade. Until one of those gas shortages of the '70s forced consumers to reconsider vehicles that got nine miles to the gallon on the open road, the Cortez was made, more or less by hand, in Kent, Ohio. It was better-engineered than the lumpy old Travco, but with a fatal flaw of its own: The metal body was way too heavy for the flimsy chassis and suspension system. In the Cortez, we winced at every pothole, knowing that what was a bump in the road to others was probably a blowout or broken wheel to us. From lonely crossroads stores, from the garages of baffled mechanics, from at least one farmhouse outside which our glamorous vehicle had sputtered and died, from a dozen remote and inconvenient places, and frequently from a mobile telephone we finally installed in our too-frequently-immobile bus, we called the Ohio factory for new wheels. Expressmen bearing Cortez wheels did a brisk business nationwide for a few years there.

The tires were a novel size made by Goodyear to fit only a certain obscure cattle trailer and the Cortez. Whenever we found a tire dealer with a supply of these tires, we bought them all and warehoused them in a compartment atop the bus, knowing we were going to need them. We experienced four spectacular blowouts in May 1974 alone, in California, Arizona, Missouri and finally, in Ohio, when both rear tires blew at once. The 11,000-pound Cortez descended upon its rear springs at sixty miles per hour, sending up a rooster tail of sparks for a quarter of a mile behind us before we could get the thing stopped.

Some of the troubles we had with the Cortez were our own fault. We drove it on rutted back roads where it was never meant to go, getting out to check the undersides of little country bridges before daring to drive across. Izzy pretty regularly used to knock the protruding side mirrors off on roadside signs and telephone poles. But it was the wheels and tires that drove us crazy.

Here are Izzy's notes for a four-month period in 1975:

Monday, July 7, Hannibal, Missouri, changed cracked wheel.

July 9, Topeka, repaired cracked gasket on generator.

July 12, Topeka to Wichita to Lincoln, replaced exhaust system.

July 16, Alliance, Nebraska, Sandoz ranch, replaced cracked wheel.

July 19, Des Moines, changed wheel.

Aug. 14, Grand Portage, Minnesota, new wheel.

Aug. 27, Duluth to Bismarck, changed cracked wheel.

Sept. 1, Billings, Labor Day, garages closed. Changed wheel, replaced muffler, adjusted brakes, greased suspension, changed plugs, adjusted torsion bar in motel parking lot.

Oct. 27, Detroit, Greenfield Village. Picked up two new wheels.

Nov. 8, Indianapolis. Changed two wheels, one cracked, one bent in blowout.

Nov. 13, Columbus, Ohio. Changed tires and one cracked wheel.

Nov. 17, Lower East Side, New York. Guy refused to fix air-conditioning coil, so Larry and I replaced it ourselves on the street. Guy then charged it with Freon and asked for one hundred bucks.

We never could have made it without Izzy. Driving along in the California redwood country one Sunday, I glanced into the rearview mirror to notice that we were trailing smoke and fire. I pulled off the road outside Boonville, where a kindly resident named Jack June let us prop the rear of the bus on a white oak stump in his front yard. The rear wheel bearings had welded themselves to the rear axles. Izzy chopped the bearings off the axle stubs with a cold chisel, used a thread file to reconstruct the threads and installed new bearings. It sounds easier than it was. The effort took all day, lacerated Izzy's knuckles and got grease all over his best Eddie Bauer safari shirt. When Mrs. June cooked us supper and served it on the kitchen table, blood from Izzy's knuckles dripped on her tablecloth.

The Cortez transmission had to be replaced in Seattle when we cracked it driving over some railroad tracks, and again in Evanston, Wyoming, after the oil cooler broke in a blizzard and dumped out all the transmission fluid. I say Evanston, Wyoming, because that's where it happened. There was nobody in Evanston who wanted to tackle the job, though, so we hired a wrecker to tow us back to Salt Lake City at the rate of one dollar a mile.

We took aboard one of those wheeled dollies mechanics use to hike themselves under cars without jacking them up. Izzy spent more time under the bus than in it. One time in the middle of a week of breakdowns, we pulled into a rest stop somewhere between Bartlesville and Ponca City so Izzy could see what was wrong with the transmission case this time. Mixed with the sound of mechanical clanging and banging coming from under the bus, I heard a different sound. It was Izzy under there crying.

We liked the way the Cortez looked and liked the way it rode. It was just that so much of the time, it wouldn't ride at all. After the second Cortez broke down irreparably, we discovered that the company had gone broke and was blessedly unable to provide a third.

We bought a brand-new Revcon, an elegantly appointed product of California. This was my idea. I liked the thick carpet. I liked the swivel chair and baronial desk the factory custom-built for me. I liked the expansive view from the big curtained window on the starboard side.

Izzy, bruised by the Cortez in body and mind, had his doubts.

"What do you think?" I asked him, after his first close inspection of our gleaming new bus.

"I think every moving part is going to break down," he said.

We bought it anyway. Every moving part broke down. We found that the big signs on the outskirts of cities that say "RV Repair" don't mean anything. When we pulled into the garages under the signs, there was always a guy who took one look at the Revcon and said, "Well, I dunno . . ." When he started scratching his head, we learned, it was time to get out of there. That guy wasn't going to be any help to us.

We switched to a ten-year-old used FMC we found on a motor home lot in Wisconsin. The salesman said, "An elderly doctor used it only once a summer to take his grandchildren to the place on the lake." I do not doubt that it served the old gentleman well. It must never have rained on these annual excursions, however, for the first time we turned on the windshield wipers, one of them flew off and vanished into the storm. When we switched on the auxiliary air conditioner, it blew the electrical fuses—not only the air conditioner fuse but also all the others. The FMC company no longer makes motor homes. I think they switched to making tanks for the Army.

This vehicle also came with its own mouse, a traveling companion who revealed himself in the first day of our ownership by leaving only crumbs and scraps of paper where there had been, in a cabinet, half a box of Ritz crackers. That night, while we settled on canned chili and beans for dinner, the mouse dined in our pantry on imported macaroons. After a few days of this, Larry Gianneschi, who had settled in as our permanent soundman, also appointed himself exterminator. He set a trap with Camembert cheese. The mouse enjoyed the cheese and left the trap unsprung. You may take it from me that a mouse will unwrap and eat an entire Bit-O-Honey candy bar. This one did. We chauffeured that Wisconsin mouse through Michigan and northern Pennsylvania, catering his meals and providing him with warm lodging, while never directly making his acquaintance.

Finally, there came a cold night outside Erie when the electrical line we used to keep the camera equipment warm worked itself loose and the interior of the bus suffered a deep chill. The camera gear came through unharmed, but the mouse must have been made uncomfortable. We never saw evidence of him again. Other motor homes were parked about the motel lot that night, and we figure he chose one of those in which to continue his journey. For his sake, I hope his new conveyance had a full pantry and was headed south. For a day or two there, we sort of missed our mouse.

The FMC was never intended for cold-weather travel, either by mice or men. Over the winters, we have gradually insulated it, using foam pads, bits of carpeting, rags and old underwear to caulk its many drafty seams, but the interior still feels like a wind tunnel when the bus is up to speed on a cold day. We dress for winter trips in down jackets and wool caps, and I keep a portable electric heater under my desk to keep my toes from freezing off and rattling around in my boots.

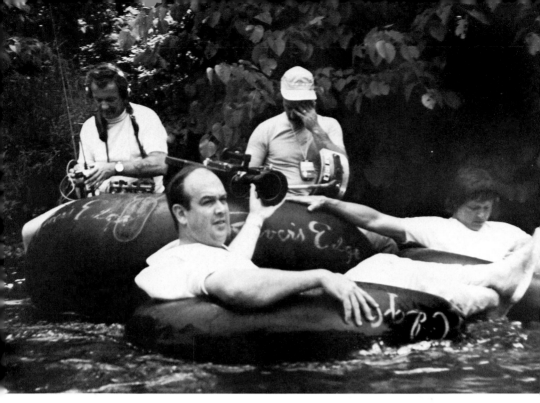

Tubin' on the Apple.

Morning on the road.

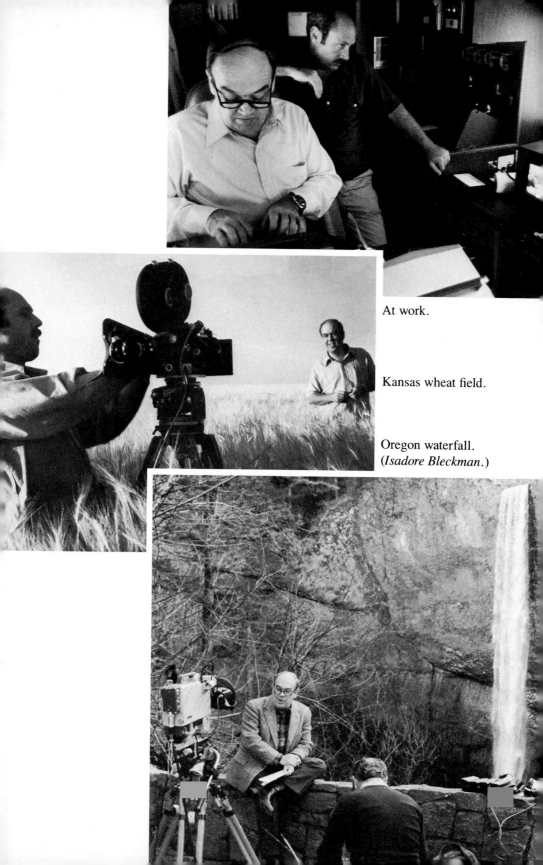

At work.

Kansas wheat field.

Oregon waterfall.
(*Isadore Bleckman.*)

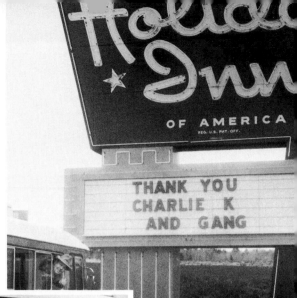

Celebrity. (*Isadore Bleckman.*)

Celebrity. (*Isadore Bleckman.*)

Fair warning. (*Isadore Bleckman.*)

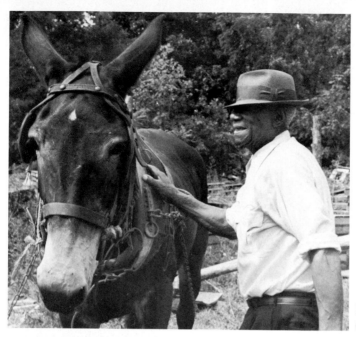

Mr. Black and his mule. (*Isadore Bleckman.*)

Mr. Black in the Oval Office. At extreme left: Harvey J. Witherell.

Odd Fellows Hall in Kansas. (*Isadore Bleckman.*)

Calling the office from Wahoo, Nebraska. (*Isadore Bleckman.*)

With Father Ron on the slopes of Mount McKinley. (*Isadore Bleckman.*)

In Andrew Wyeth's museum, Chadds Ford, Pennsylvania.

In Vladimir Horowitz's living room.
(*CBS News.*)

Alf Landon on his front porch, Topeka,
Kansas. (*Isadore Bleckman.*)

In the Bamboo Room with Senator
Howard Baker.

Dr. Aseyev remembers. A park
bench in Moscow, 1988.

A tourist in Moscow.
(*Isadore Bleckman.*)

The engine compartment could use a little insulation, too. Something is always freezing up down there. We left Moab, Utah, on a wintry Friday afternoon, bound for the airport at Grand Junction, Colorado, so that I could catch the last plane to Denver and go on to New York for the *Sunday Morning* program. The distance from Moab to Grand Junction is not great, but the road is an exceedingly lonely one, through the region of stone windows and arches and canyon lands along the Colorado River. The wind rose, the snow began falling and the bus began slowing down.

"What's the matter?" I asked Izzy, who was driving.

"Won't go," he said.

He pressed the accelerator to the floor. The bus gave one last lurch forward into the blinding snow and stopped, right there in the middle of the road in the middle of nowhere in the middle of a blizzard.

"What's the next town?" Izzy asked.

"Cisco, Utah," I said, looking at the map.

"How far?"

"Too far to walk," I said.

We put on our parkas, went out into the storm and pried open the hatch to the engine compartment. Everything in there was coated thick with ice.

"Must be water in the gas line," Izzy said. "The carburetor's frozen up. Where's the ether spray?"

"We used up the ether spray back there in Green River," Larry said.

"Let's pour in some of that Drygas," I said.

"We used that up, too," Larry said.

"We need some alcohol," Izzy said.

"Well, we don't have any," Larry said. "Except the vodka."

We looked at one another.

I went into the bus and came back with a quart bottle of vodka, unopened. Larry opened it and solemnly poured the whole quart into the gas tank. Izzy climbed in and cranked the accelerator a few times. The engine started with a roar. We closed the door and were off.

A mile or two later, on a slight hill, the bus slowed to a stop again.

"There's always the scotch," Larry said.

The scotch got us to the top of the hill, but not much farther. We stopped again in the snow.

"Not the brandy!" I exclaimed. It was a fifth of VSOP, the good Hennessey.

"It's no use," Izzy said. "We have to dry out the carburetor somehow."

I remembered that Larry carries a small hair dryer in his sound case. He uses it to remove humidity from the tape recorder and the delicate circuit boards of the camera. I suggested using it on the carburetor.

Usually, at about this point in our breakdowns, an old rancher comes along in a pickup truck, stops and offers to help. All the old ranchers must have been home by the fire. Not a single soul passed that way in either direction that afternoon. If one had, he would have been treated to the sight of a motor home stranded in the storm with only its auxiliary generator running, and three snow-covered figures struggling to tape a hair dryer inside the engine compartment.

It took our entire supply of electrical tape, but we finally got the nozzle of the dryer aimed delicately at the carburetor. We closed the door to the engine compartment. We could hear the generator roaring and the hair dryer humming away in there. We felt foolish. Izzy waited a few minutes, then twisted the ignition key. The engine started right up.

We made it through the snow to Cisco, Utah, and up to Interstate 70. We made it across the state line into Colorado, running on Texaco regular, Smirnoff 90-proof, Dewar's White Label, and Clairol hair dryer power. We made it to the Grand Junction airport, just in time to see, above the low terminal roof, the tail of my airplane as it turned and taxied out to the runway.

We stopped at the curb outside the United counter, so that I could go in and ask about the first flight to Denver the next morning. I tried to think of something to be glad about.

I was glad we hadn't poured the Hennessey into the gas tank.

12

ON THE ROAD

I had the conceit that once under way, I would find stories at every country crossroads. We set out from New York in October in the rain and wandered aimlessly through small-town New England for a few rainy days without an idea in our heads. I began to get nervous, wondering whether an idea would ever come.

Then the sun came out and the wind came up and the bright foliage of the New Hampshire autumn shivered and began to fall. A shower of lemon and scarlet and gold washed across our windshield. In every town, people were out raking leaves and children were playing in piles of leaves. We got the camera out and did our first "On The Road" story just about how pretty it all was. An old friend, Sandy Socolow, maintains that the best story we've ever done was that first one, that they've all gone downhill from there.

"On The Road" required a change of gears for the *Evening News*, which in those days of racial violence and the Vietnam War certainly was not accustomed to spending time on autumn leaves; and for viewers, who had never seen peaceful glimpses of rural places on the Cronkite program; and for me, too. I was used to going fast and working hard. "On The Road" seemed to work best when I went slow and took it easy. I found that while it helped to have a story in mind up the road somewhere, the world would not come to an end if I never got there; I might find something more interesting along the way. It was best to take a deep breath, mosey along and soak up the moods of the country and the changes of weather and terrain. When I finally shook off the tempo of daily journalism and fell into the rhythms of the countryside, I didn't have to worry about finding stories any longer. They found me.

I had to revise my conception of the people who lived in the country, too. To judge from the news of the day, they were bitterly divided along racial or political lines, contentious and angry. But the people I actually met seemed neighborly and humane.

In Westerville, Ohio, Professor John Franklin Smith taught speech and dramatics at Otterbein College until he reached the mandatory retirement age of seventy.

"I loved my students," he said, "and I think they loved me."

He couldn't imagine leaving the students behind. So when he was forced to retire, he just kept working at the college. He had worked on for fifteen years—as janitor in the gym.

"During my years as a professor," he said, "I'd walk through here and see the man cleaning the floor. I knew what a mop was and what a bucket was. It was hard work at first, but I got on to it. It is necessary work, and I try to do it well."

I asked him which was more rewarding, being a professor or being a janitor.

This eighty-five-year-old man smiled and said, "Now, don't put me on the spot like that. I think I'd have to say every age in life has its own compensation."

We walked out across the campus together.

"I'm still looking ahead," he said. "I don't want to die. There's too much fun in this world, and a lot of good folks, a lot of them. And good books to read and fish to catch and pretty women to admire and good men to know. Why, life is a joy!"

At Pilottown, Louisiana, a community built on stilts near the mouth of the Mississippi River and reachable only by seaplane or boat, we met Andy Spirer, hunter and fisherman, reader of Greek in the original, and the only teacher, for ten years, in the one-room Pilottown schoolhouse. Why did he stay on in such a lonely place? "Well," he said, "they have trouble getting teachers to live out here, and somebody has to teach the kids."

On a little stream called Hunting Creek in Caroline County, Maryland, we came upon a 300-year-old gristmill still being operated by its eighty-one-year-old miller, Captain Frank Langrell. The Linchester mill ground corn for settlers in 1681, ground cornmeal for Washington's army nearly 100 years later and was grinding cornmeal yet. It must have been the oldest continually operated business in the country. But the mill didn't interest me as much as the miller. After sixty-five years beside his millstone, wasn't Frank Langrell tired of it all? "Yes," he said, "yes, I can't really say there's profit in it anymore, but these farmers count on me, you see. There's no other place to grind their corn, you see. . . ."

In Professor Smith and Andy Spirer and Frank Langrell, I saw Americans of a sort I had not known before, wedded to the places they lived and toiling not so much for themselves as for others. "It is necessary work . . ." "Somebody has to teach the kids . . ." "These farmers count on me, you see . . ." Their purposes and undertakings seemed entirely admirable to me. They had about them no delusions of superiority or motives of greed. I read the papers every day. The front pages were full of selfishness, arrogance and hostility toward others. The back roads were another country.

We wandered west. At Eagle Pass, Texas, on the Mexican border, we ran into Jo and Rumel Fuentes. They lived on a dirt street in a poor neighborhood. Every morning before dawn, Rumel Fuentes caught a bus to the nearest college, Southwest Texas Junior College in Uvalde. Uvalde is seventy miles away. It made for a long day, but three nights a week after coming home on the bus, Rumel taught American history classes for citizenship applicants. Two nights a week, he taught classes for high school dropouts. Washington had cut off funds for these courses several weeks before and most of the other teachers had left, but as long as the students kept studying, Rumel kept teaching.

Jo Fuentes had come to Eagle Pass from Ohio two years before as a Vista volunteer. During the mornings when Rumel was away in Uvalde, she, a Catholic, worked as a Planned Parenthood counselor. In the afternoons, she was the secretary at the Methodist church. Weekends, they both worked on the neighborhood center which they had persuaded the people to start building, and which was being paid for by the sale of tamales and old clothes.

They didn't see anything remarkable about their lives. Jo Fuentes said, "I think anybody who has the capability to do something about another person's sad situation should do it. It's not a matter of altruism or anything else. If you can do it, that's what you should do."

In Montana, we found a tough old rancher determined to save the wild horses of the Pryor Mountains if he had to do it all by himself. In California, we found a woman giving her life to the hummingbirds of Mojesca Canyon; she had a hundred hummingbird feeders hanging from the eaves of her porch. She said, "I know I can't save the world, but I can help out the hummingbirds."

That April, Martin Luther King, Jr., was murdered, and several American cities erupted in flames. In June, Robert Kennedy was murdered. I had known them both. I grieved for them, and for the country they had done so much to change for the better. I might have thought the country was now going mad if I hadn't been on the road. I had eyes and ears. I kept running into people who made me feel confident and reassured. In July, I ran into Pat Shannon Baker.

She was a young, white woman, the mother of three children, who lived in Reno, Nevada. The night Martin Luther King was killed, Pat Baker sat up late thinking, I have to do something about this. On her way to work, she often had passed a weedy vacant lot in a black neighborhood and wondered why the city hadn't turned it into a park. Now, she went to see her city councilman, who spoke of the strained budget and the difficulty of passing a bond issue. Pat Baker decided she couldn't wait for all that. She went to see people in the black neighborhood. She went to see garden supply houses and cement companies and surveyors and the heads of the construction unions and tough-minded contractors she had never met before. Pretty soon, her idea became everybody's idea.

At seven-thirty on a Friday morning, in a town not famous for early risers, a crowd began gathering at the vacant lot. By eight-thirty, 2,000 tons of donated topsoil was being spread by front-end loaders operated by heavy-equipment operators not used to working for free. They were working for free. I stood there and watched all this.

I watched a school custodian, an unemployed teenager, a roofer and a garage mechanic digging a ditch together. A junior high school kid assigned to saw two-by-fours to serve as cement forms sawed all day in the hot sun as if his life depended on it. A little girl carried water to the workers. Coastguardsmen, Marines and Seabees came by and pitched in. Cement was laid for a double tennis court and smoothed out by noon. A basketball court was in before the sun went down. Dozens of people worked all night.

Saturday morning, a crowd of several hundred showed up for work, black and white, old and young. An eighty-four-year-old man who came by to watch stayed all afternoon helping to plant trees; he said he needed the exercise. They sodded the lawn Saturday night and turned on the sprinkler system Sunday morning. By Sunday afternoon, the park was finished, with walks and grass and basketball courts and trees and benches.

They named it Pat Baker Park and asked her if she would like to say something. She said, "This was a great, big, black and white thing, that's what it was."

I went back there more than twenty years later. The grass was neatly mowed. The trees were tall and leafy. In the shade of the trees, people were sitting on the benches talking. Some kids who hadn't been born in 1968 were practicing gaudy hook shots on the basketball court.

I thought back to the weekend the park was built. A black man, leaning on his shovel, looked around and said, "This is the best damn thing that has happened since I came to Reno."

He didn't mean the park. He meant building the park.

In that first year on the road, I fell in love with my native land. I rode the Wabash Cannonball through Indiana and the *Delta Queen* down the Ohio River and the cable cars up and down the San Francisco hills. (The cable car story ran seven minutes and twelve seconds on the *Evening News*, a third of the broadcast, prompting Les Midgley, by then the *Evening News* producer, to remark, "Well, there's one we don't have to do again.") I spent time among Pennsylvania Dutchmen in Kutztown, and Greek sponge fishermen in Tarpon Springs, Florida.

I came upon M. C. Pinkstaff, the roadside poet of Gordon Junction, Illinois, proprietor of Pinkstaff's Two-Pump Gas Station and Poem Factory. He sold his gasoline for thirty-nine cents a gallon and his poems on local topics for ten cents apiece. His best-selling poem was "Morose Maud, the Mule That Kicked Down the Barn Door." He said he had noted differences among Americans in their appreciation of verse: "You take folks that are from south of the Ohio, they'll buy poems a little more readily than those from north of the river. And Hoosiers will buy it before a 'Llini will. Folks from the Hawkeye State, Iowa, they love poetry and will buy it far more readily than people from Minnesota will. You pry a dime out of somebody from Minnesota and you've done something, brother! When a Minnesotan goes somewhere for a week, he puts on a clean pair of overalls and puts a ten-dollar bill in his pocket, and never changes either one!"

I heard jazz music in the streets of New Orleans and brass bands in the streets of Bristol, Rhode Island. I listened to echoes in the ghost town of Bodie, California. I saw corncob pipes being made in Washington, Missouri, and windmills being built in Broken Arrow, Oklahoma. I walked half a day down into the Red River Gorge of Kentucky to find a cave Daniel Boone once camped in.

That first year, I sent back to New York forty-seven stories from twenty-three states, all of them my own discoveries. The biggest discovery of all was about myself: On the back roads of America, I felt at home at last. I knew I wanted to spend the rest of my life out there.

13

IZZY AND LARRY
AND CHARLIE AND ME

Working with a cameraman over a period of weeks or months is like having a love affair. You have to like him, to begin with. Then you have to woo him to keep him from running off with some other reporter. Slowly, you come to trust him, admire him and learn from him. You help him out whenever you can, try to cheer him up when he's down. After a while, you notice he's doing the same for you. The two of you find you both want to keep this good thing going.

After Jim Wilson left, I worked with a number of good cameramen, but none who were crazy about the idea of spending months at a time covering blacksmiths, loggers, Mail Pouch tobacco sign painters, sand castle builders, tombstone carvers, barbed wire collectors, backwoods hermits and muleback mailmen.

Until Izzy came along.

Isadore Bleckman came out from Chicago to meet me in Colorado. He was a nervous, intense little guy with a big moustache and darting eyes. His manner said, okay, where's the story, I don't have all day, let's get on with it. When it was his turn to drive the bus, he drove it faster than anybody ever had before, putting the swaying Travco through its paces on the mountain roads as if it were a sports car.

"Hey, man, slow down a little!" I said.

Izzy grumbled, "It's not the *Queen Mary*, you know."

This guy was talking back to me, even telling me how to drive the bus. I figured this was going to be a one-story relationship.

The story was deep in the woods up the north fork of the Gunnison River. Somebody had written to me about a man who lived up there in the West Elk Mountains tending a remote power station. The wild birds knew him so well that they'd perch on his shoulder and the skittish white-tailed deer would come out of the forest to take food from his hand.

It was all true. George Norris and his wife, Ann, had been feeding the deer for many winters. "C'mon, Cutter," he'd say, "C'mon, old Cakeeater. You better come runnin', Soap, or all the food will be gone!" And the wild deer would leap the picket fence into his yard, as docile as house pets in the presence of this one man they trusted. A great antlered buck stood nose to nose with Mr. Norris and took an oatcake from his mouth.

"I was deprived of the city life and schools," Mr. Norris said. "I just got what you might call an Indian's education. But even when I was a boy, I never liked hunting deer. Now, I wouldn't think of it. I wouldn't know where to hunt, because for thirty-five miles around here, all the deer are my friends. I'll never fire a rifle again."

I saw Izzy's eyes growing wider. The big-city boy had never had a day like this before. I figured these were probably the first deer he had ever seen close up. He shot the story from every angle, even climbing a tree to look down on the scene from above. Afterward, he couldn't resist trying to feed the deer himself, to see if they'd take morsels from a stranger. They would, as long as the stranger was in this particular backyard. Izzy was enchanted, by the remote place, by the deer, by George Norris's reverence for life.

The Norrises gave us dinner that night. Izzy enthused over the pictures he had made. I got the impression he had just shot the first story he had ever really enjoyed.

"By the way," he said, "this steak is terrific! Where do you get it?"

There was an awkward pause.

"It's venison," Mr. Norris said.

Izzy stopped chewing.

"Oh, not what you're thinking!" Mrs. Norris said. "Our son brought it to us from Wyoming."

Izzy had a little trouble finishing his meal, but afterward, on the long drive through the mountains back to our motel, all he could talk about was his first experience with deer, on the hoof and on the plate. "Where do we go next?" he asked.

We didn't know it that night, but where we were going next was to every part of every state, over and over again, for twenty years.

Izzy relaxed into the rhythms of the road, stopped looking at his watch and started driving a little slower. But he never lost his enthusiasm for new places and new experiences. He saw the road—he still does—through fresh eyes. He saw children swinging on a rope tied to a tree limb and said to me, "Boy, that's nice, isn't it? If you could think of something to say about it, I could sure make some pretty pictures." And the next thing the Cronkite news got from us was a pretty story just about children swinging on a rope.

We went to the fiddlers convention in Galax, Virginia, and Izzy, whose tastes ran more to Yehudi Menuhin, was charmed by a great country fiddler named Clark Kessinger. We still play Clark Kessinger fiddle tunes on the bus as we roll along, ballads and breakdowns we recorded in Galax on a hot day in August 1970. Izzy tasted his first oyster aboard the oyster-dredging skipjacks of Chesapeake Bay, and traveled with his first carnival out of Cape Girardeau, Missouri, (with Sunflower the Naked Lady, and Johnny the Geek, "60 Attractions 60," "Ladies In a Family Way Are Not Invited!") and rode his first steam train, the Sidewinder, hauling lumber and mixed cargo up into the hills out of Robbinsville, North Carolina. The last thing you need on a voyage of discovery is a jaded, worldly-wise traveling companion. Izzy was the opposite, a dazzled Odysseus, giddy with the wonders of the world and equal to all its perils.

I was very impressed when he climbed that tree at the Norrises'. That was nothing. Pictures other cameramen give up on, Izzy finds a way to make. In the course of our time together, I have watched him make pictures while hanging from a crane, riding a Ferris wheel, standing on the back of a circus elephant, floating on an inner tube, drifting in a hot-air balloon.

Off Maine, under way in a stiff breeze aboard *Victory Chimes*, last of the three-masted schooners, Izzy had himself hoisted to the top of the mast in a bos'n's chair; the crew on the heeling deck looked like scrambling termites from up there.

Izzy has put on roller skates to get just the dollying shot he wanted. He has shot from trains, planes, combines, tractors, racing cars, dune buggies, motorcycles, snowmobiles and countless helicopters. He has dived under the sea with an Aqua-Lung and climbed to the tip-top of the Golden Gate Bridge without a safety harness. He has shot from a one-horse open sleigh, a sailboard, a glider, a dugout canoe.

When we went out with a Coast Guard patrol boat into a wild sea off the Oregon coast, a crew member said, "The boat's designed to roll 360 degrees. Keep your lifeline hooked and watch the Chief. If the Chief keeps his cigar in his mouth, don't worry. If he spits out his cigar, take a deep breath, because we're about to roll."

Izzy said to me, "God, I hope we roll! What a picture!"

To ease his disappointment when we didn't, I said, "Do you realize if we'd gone under out there, we would have ruined a $50,000 camera?"

Izzy said, "Yeah, there is that."

On a story about a family of steeplejacks (a son swings into the picture at the top of the steeple and says, "Got a hammer, Ma?") naturally Izzy had to dangle out there with them. I stayed on the ground, afraid to look up.

When we did a story about a beer wagon drawn by forty horses, nothing would do but that Izzy ride backward on one of the lead horses so as to aim back at the driver; if he had fallen off, thirty-nine Belgian horses would have run over him.

When we did a story about an elderly farmer who flew kites for the amusement of children, Izzy wanted a shot from the *kite's* point of view; we hired a fifty-foot cherry picker to put him up in the sky with the kite in the foreground, the camera looking down the kite string to the farmer and the children far below. It was one of the loveliest pictures I've ever seen.

While working, Izzy is an acrobat. While waiting to work, he's a worried optimist. When rain interrupts a story, Izzy frets about the lost time, but always looks up into the downpour and says, "The sun's gonna come out. Just give it a minute or two." When we drove the bus off a desert road in Utah and got stuck in the sand, Izzy said, "The next guy to come along is going to be a Mormon farmer in a pickup truck. He's going to hook a chain to us and pull us out." That's just the way it happened. Izzy has kept my spirits up for twenty years.

We took on Charlie Quinlan, a former Chicago stagehand, as our electrician and traveling companion. Charlie didn't know a lot about motion picture lighting, but he was willing to work hard at stringing cables and hanging the lights where Izzy wanted them. Charlie diverted us with tales of the South Pacific, where he had spent World War II on a coal-fired destroyer, USS *Phelps*. The *Phelps* took part in all the great naval battles against the Japanese. Charlie didn't set foot on land for three years, until a kamikaze plane crashed into the bridge and killed all but one of the ship's officers. (That one was an ensign named Elmo Zumwalt, later Chief of Naval Operations.) The *Phelps* limped home to Pearl Harbor. As the small, crippled ship was passing Battleship Row, all hands were piped on deck. Charlie, head of the "black gang" in the engine room, came blinking up into the sunlight to hear a band playing on shore. The crews of all the battleships, in dress whites, stood at present arms along the rails.

"What's this for?" Charlie asked a buddy.

The buddy was weeping.

"It's for us," he said.

Charlie told us a hundred stories about his beloved ship and took time off every summer to attend a reunion of the crew. I asked what happened to the *Phelps* after the war.

Charlie said, "They sold it to Gillette and turned it into razor blades."

But most of Charlie's yarns were not poignant; most of them were funny. And he kept us amused with puns and spoonerisms (a crushing blow became a "blushing crow" in Quinlan-speak) and misunderstandings based on his slight hardness of hearing.

"Why are they always having steak dinners at the White House?"

"They're *state* dinners, Charlie."

He was a shade disorganized. Driving the bus in Amarillo one morning, Charlie cut across four lanes of traffic to make a left turn from the right lane—with a police car right behind him. The police car stopped us, of course. Two hefty cops wearing neat uniforms and dark glasses came aboard and asked the first thing cops always ask in such circumstances: "May I see your driver's license, sir?"

"Sure," Charlie said. "It's in my billfold."

The policemen waited.

"And my billfold is in the back there, in my suitcase."

Charlie climbed out of the driver's seat, went back and started moving boxes of lights and camera gear. Finally, he came to his suitcase, a huge leather number with straps, almost big enough to qualify as a trunk. He opened it on the floor and delved through piles of dirty clothes with the two Amarillo policemen as bemused spectators. Charlie saved the cost of doing laundry on the road by taking all his laundry home with him.

"Gotta be here," Charlie muttered.

"Charlie," I said, "if you don't mind telling me, what is your billfold doing in your suitcase?"

"Always hide it there," Charlie said. "Don't want to get it stolen."

Long minutes passed, with Charlie still unpacking his bag furiously right there in downtown Amarillo, flinging dirty socks and underwear everywhere. Even the cops could barely suppress their laughter.

After a while, one of them said, "Tell you what, sir. We'll just take your word there's a billfold in there somewhere. Next time, will you just get into the left lane to make a left turn?"

"Sure thing," Charlie said. He started piling his laundry back into the suitcase. While he did, I thanked the cops. They got into their car and drove away.

"Okay, Charlie," I said, "where's your driver's license?"

"It's in my billfold," Charlie said, climbing back into the driver's seat.

Charlie probably saved our lives with an alert job of high-speed driving one midnight on a lonely stretch of road in Nevada. The rest of us were napping when the bus suddenly lurched left, veered right, bumped along the shoulder and careered back onto the highway.

I woke up and hollered, "What the hell was *that?*"

Charlie said, "I don't know. A lot of critters on the road."

We backed up to find that Charlie had somehow steered right

through a big herd of wild burros clustered on the highway for warmth—without grazing even one of them.

Charlie was a quick thinker in times of trouble. In southern Illinois, we came upon a car that had just turned over in a ditch. Its wheels were still turning in the air and a little fire had started under the crushed hood. Other cars had stopped. Their drivers were standing around trying to figure out what to do. Charlie dashed out of the bus without a word, ran down the embankment and pulled two people out of the wreck before the fire could spread. Then he grabbed our fire extinguisher and put out the blaze.

"Fire control," he said later. "First thing you learn."

In the Navy, he meant.

Charlie helped perform another rescue on Interstate 80 in a Wyoming snowstorm. We had stopped on the shoulder to film the blowing snow and record the sound of the wind. A battered car with a broken windshield came out of the storm, slowed and stopped beside us. The face of the young woman behind the wheel was covered with blood. She said her car had been hit from behind by a speeding truck, then spun around and hit by another truck. When we opened the door to try to help her, her terrified pet Airedale leapt out and ran away into a snowy field.

"My dog, my dog!" she cried, and started after him.

Charlie took over. He grabbed her. "We'll take care of you," he said. "He"—pointing to me—"will take care of your dog."

She stood there bleeding and crying in the snow. Charlie picked her up and laid her on the floor of the bus. He cleaned her face with moist towels and held her hand while Izzy took the wheel and sped down the mountain toward the Laramie hospital. I walked around in the snow chasing the dog until I was able to calm him a little and coax him back into the wrecked car. On the way down the mountain, I met a lot of ambulances coming up with their lights flashing and their sirens wailing. The accident, we read in the papers the next day, was a seventeen-car pileup.

I made it into Laramie and found a boarding kennel for the dog. By the time I got to the hospital, they were just wheeling the young woman into an operating room. Months later, she sent a smiling picture of herself after reconstructive surgery on her face. "Just wanted you to know what I really look like," she said. She looked very pretty. In her note, she thanked us all.

But it was Charlie she addressed it to.

Soundmen came and went. We had a nervous husband who had to call home a couple times a day and soon left us because our long trips were breaking up his marriage. We had an affable Black Muslim who was lured away by one of the CBS bureaus. A moody young man with a guitar didn't pan out because he gave more attention to his music than to his work.

Izzy said, "We need a permanent soundman. Who's the best soundman in the business?"

I said, "Larry Gianneschi."

"Right," Izzy said. "Let's call Larry Gianneschi."

"Be serious," I said. For a lark, Larry Gianneschi had dropped in on "On The Road" in the early Jim Wilson days, but he was a soundman of great reputation who had worked with Murrow, was now working all over the world on important documentaries for *CBS Reports*, and was in the kind of demand that almost permitted him to choose his own assignments. It would take a lot of nerve to ask him to bring his big talent to a little project like ours.

"All it can cost us is the price of the phone call," Izzy said.

Larry Gianneschi said, "You guys are the only ones in television having any fun. When do I start?"

That was sometime in 1972. Larry has recorded the sound for nearly every "On The Road" story since.

You have to distinguish among Larry Gianneschis. Our Larry was born to the business. His father, Larry, was an old newsreel man. Our Larry's son Larry was getting started in television, as were his other sons, who must have grown up disappointed that they had to be named something else.

Larry is a man of sociable inclination, sensitive, polite and compatible. He did much more for us than aim a microphone. He thought up story ideas, helped out with the lighting, worked with Izzy on camera repairs and bus repairs and immediately stepped in to do a service for me.

The toughest moment of every story comes right at the beginning. You drive up into the yard of an old Iowa farmer who, sick and tired of farming, is building a yacht in his barnyard so he and his wife can see the world. Naturally, knowing what you're there for, the farmer takes you out back to see the yacht and starts telling you all about it. That's just what you *don't* want. Izzy is still fiddling with the camera and looking for angles. We're not quite ready yet. I have learned that we have to have the camera rolling the *first* time the farmer tells me about his unlikely project; the second time, he won't tell it as well. This is where Larry comes in. He engages the farmer in unrelated small talk. Have you had any rain this summer? How's the corn crop looking? This permits me to busy myself in the bus for the few minutes it takes Izzy to get all set up, then emerge for a spontaneous talk with our farmer. Larry and I never discussed this. It was just a job that he saw needed doing. He was a lot more than a soundman, right from the start.

Larry follows his own routine on the road. He rises earlier than everybody else, has himself a proper breakfast in the motel coffee shop while he peruses the morning paper (the rest of us usually settle for toast and coffee aboard the bus once we're under way) and prepares calmly for the day. Since Izzy is always the first each morning to take his turn at driving, and I'm up front with a map, navigating, Larry usually brews the coffee—he keeps the coffeepot going all day—and then wanders to his worktable at the back of the bus to work the crossword puzzle in peace and do a little maintenance on his sound equipment. We're so used to this that once we left a gas station in Carlsbad, New Mexico, and drove thirty miles before anybody noticed that Larry wasn't aboard. He said, "I figured you'd come back for me when you needed another pot of coffee."

Through most of the seventies, before I had to start finding an airport every weekend to fly back to New York for the *Sunday Morning* program, and before we switched over from film to videotape and lost Charlie Quinlan to new union rules that said we no longer needed a lighting man, "On The Road" was Izzy and Larry and Charlie and me. We covered hundreds of thousands of miles through all the states before 1976, and in that one year we revisited every state to report a moment of history from each one, our "On The Road" contribution to the Bicentennial.

We did stories about wrestlers and jugglers and mountain climbers, traffic cops, tattoo artists, gandy dancers, sheep shearers, bagel bakers, horseshoe players, rodeo riders, sorghum makers and seashell collectors. We ran to keep up with a 104-year-old jogger in California. We spent a day with a weight guesser at the Arizona State Fair. We met a man in Death Valley who lived in a house built out of beer bottles. We cruised Denver with a trumpet-playing taxi driver; I mean he drove with one hand and played the horn with the other. We passed the time of day in a one-parking-meter town, Lookingglass, Oregon; they were thinking about getting a streetlight next.

We did stories about ferryboats and fire trucks and pawnshops and driftwood and lightning and fog. We met a Texas horse trader, a Kansas mule dealer, a Florida pig auctioneer and an old wildcatter trying to coax oil out of a dry hole in Oklahoma. In Darwin, Minnesota, we spent a day with the owner of the world's largest ball of string. He kept adding to it while we talked. That's the trouble with owning the world's largest ball of string; you live in constant fear that somebody, somewhere, is making a larger ball of string.

At the end of 1977, I got sick and had to spend a couple of weeks in the hospital. Roger Mudd came to see me. He kidded me about "On The Road." "Give it up while there's still time!" he said. "You're a reporter and there are important things going on in the world! It's time you came in from the cornfields!"

I just laughed. Roger covered Congress, the Watergate hearings, all sorts of history-making events. I covered musical saw players, church suppers and greased pig contests. I wouldn't have traded jobs with him for anything. Nobody in journalism had better jobs than Izzy and Larry and Charlie and me.

14

CELEBRITY

*I*n the early days, before "On The Road" became a familiar part of the *Evening News*, nobody knew who we were. People would see us shooting film by the roadside and ask what was going on. Once, thinking we might somehow make a story of some farm kids flying kites in a field, we stopped and went to work, chasing those little boys and girls all over the place, Izzy lying on his back for a low angle, then jumping up and running after a kid and a kite; Larry running after him with his sound amplifier bouncing on his chest, the two of them connected by wires; Charlie Quinlan trotting along with a big silver reflector; I scribbling in a notebook. What rural parent, glancing through the kitchen window, could be prepared for such a sight? A mother finally came out of the house across the road to inquire just exactly what we thought we were doing.

"Madam," I said, "you're not going to believe this, but we are preparing a story for the *CBS Evening News* with Walter Cronkite."

Of course, she *didn't* believe it at first and tried to run us off. Izzy says in those days I started every new conversation, "Madam, you're not going to believe this . . ."

Gradually, we became better known. People commenced smiling and waving at the "On The Road" bus. This had a heady effect on us. In the first place, as veterans of stories like civil rights demonstrations, we were accustomed to being unwelcome wherever we went. I had covered the Freedom Rides in Mississippi and Alabama and found that every-body, the Freedom Riders, the Klansmen, the cops and the local popula-tion, suspected or despised the press; Izzy, Larry and Charlie had lately been dodging brickbats during protest marches in Chicago. "On The Road" was different. Patrons of small-town taverns would hail us as celebrities come to town and buy us rounds of beers. The editors of country weeklies would feature the news of our passing on page one, with photographs of us posed beside the bus. People would ask for autographs, "for the kids," they'd say. I signed bits of paper and restaurant menus and dollar bills. Once, a man asked me to sign the back of his T-shirt. Once, a man asked me to sign the blade of his chain saw. The peaceful stories of "On The Road" were making us popular; even, we fancied, making us loved!

Local boosters made us welcome everywhere. "Gee," I said to Izzy one day in Oklahoma, "a couple of months ago they made me a Kentucky Colonel, last month they made me an Arkansas Traveler, and this month I was inducted into the Kiowa tribe."

Izzy assumed the solemn expression of the rabbi at his Chicago synagogue. "My good man," he said to me sardonically, "you are slowly working your way up to Jew."

Occasionally, it got ridiculous. A producer and camera crew from the Public Broadcasting network traveled with us for a few days to make a documentary about "On The Road." As we shot a story in Leland, Michigan, about the morning coffee klatch in the firehouse, the PBS crew tagged along. The Traverse City television station heard we were nearby, and a cameraman-reporter showed up to shoot a story about us. "Hey," said the PBS producer, "a local station shooting a story! That's part of our story!" So, while we shot our story, the Traverse City newsman shot us shooting our story, and the PBS crew shot a story about him shooting us shooting our story. I felt I was a character in some sort of Kafka night-mare. The morning coffee drinkers probably were glad to see us all leave town.

In time, people stopped being surprised when we showed up in their small towns. It came to seem almost as if they were expecting us.

We went to Sopchoppy, in the Florida panhandle, to look into a story about worm grunting. Worm grunting is not practiced just everywhere. Maybe I'd better explain it:

You go out into the woods and pound a hardwood stake into the ground, preferably using a heavy truck spring to do the pounding. Then, you rub the truck spring sensually, but with a certain pressure, across the top of the stake. This sets up a vibration in the ground which you can feel in the soles of your feet. Earthworms must find the vibration disagreeable, for to escape it, they wriggle to the surface; whereupon, you pick up the worms and go fishing.

I didn't believe this when I first heard about it, but it turns out that some people around Sopchoppy make a living at it, selling their worms by the canful to Mr. M. B. Hodges's bait store. It will not surprise you to learn that if you go worm grunting in the National Forest, you have to have a federal Worm Gathering Permit displayed in the window of your pickup truck.

We parked the bus outside Mr. Hodges's store to inquire where we could find some worm grunting going on. An old man was sitting on a bench outside the store whittling—not carving anything, just making a pile of shavings the way old men do outside stores in the south. As I walked by, he looked up at me and said, in a soft, confidential drawl:

"I knew you guys would show up here sooner or later."

It was as if he had been sitting there waiting for us.

We were careful not to display our wondrous new importance to those we met, but the truth is we were beginning to feel like big shots. Therefore, it was good for us that a few days later, down the road in Fort Myers, we stopped the bus on a residential street to consult the map, and a woman came out of her house smiling.

I smiled, and she smiled, and I opened the door to accept the usual congratulations for our stories about America, or perhaps to sign another autograph.

She said, "I think I'd like a couple of loaves of rye today, please."

She thought we were the bread truck.

In the course of the years, we have also been mistaken for the library book van, and several times for the Red Cross Bloodmobile. (Izzy says the next time we are mistaken for the Bloodmobile, he is going to say,

"Just step to the rear of the bus and remove your garments, ma'am. The doctor will be with you in a moment.")

Such incidents have made us wear our fame a little more lightly. In one of the after-work seminars Ed Murrow used to conduct in Colbee's bar on 52nd Street back in New York, he said, "Just remember that even though you have a loud voice, even though your voice may reach 16 million people every time you speak, that doesn't make you any *smarter* than you were when your voice only reached the end of this bar." Those who work in the celebrity-making craft of television news ought to remember Murrow's dictum. Overweening pride is an occupational hazard.

Of course, sometimes there is an advantage to being recognized. The Police Chief of Nebraska City, Nebraska, paid us a visit as we were parking the bus on the main street to film the Arbor Day parade.

The Chief: "You shouldn't park here, you'll get in the way of the parade."

I: "Well, we sure do need to, Chief."

The Chief: "Say, you're that 'On The Road' feller, aren't you? Well, hell, all right then, go ahead."

But in general, we try to slip into town quietly, do our work unobtrusively and make our getaway before the Rotary Club invites us to lunch or the mayor shows up with the key to the city. And we try to make sure the story we are working on ends up being about the subject of the story and never about ourselves.

With respect to my own appearances on camera, we have adopted the Tricycle Principle. We were somewhere in the midwest, watching the local news on the television set in the bus before going out to supper. There was a feature about a children's tricycle race, cute little toddlers pedaling away and bumping into one another, an appealing story pretty well filmed and edited.

Izzy said, "You know what? Before this is over, the reporter is going to ride a tricycle."

"Oh, no!" I said. "That would ruin the whole thing."

Sure enough, the reporter signed off in close-up with a silly grin, the camera pulled back to show that he was perched on a tricycle, and he turned and pedaled clumsily away, making inane what had, until then, been charming. The anchor couple came on laughing to sign off the show.

The Tricycle Principle is simple: "When doing a tricycle story, don't ride a tricycle." The story is about children, dummy, not about you. Keep yourself out of it. Try to control your immodesty.

Even when some guy in a bar is buying you a beer.

Even when a smiling stranger comes up to you with a grease pen wanting you to autograph his chain saw.

15

LUCK

You'll think this is a whopper, and I wouldn't believe it either if I
hadn't been there. Tom Cosgrove will tell you it's the honest truth.

We were deep in the Okefenokee Swamp in an outboard motorboat
run by an old man who was born and brought up on the fringes of the
swamp and knew everything about it. We had left early in the morning,
thinking we'd make pictures in the swamp for an hour or two, but we kept
seeing more alligators, more herons and egrets and ibises, more flowering
water plants and thickets of cedar each more beautiful and mysterious
than the one before. In midafternoon, we were still out there filming.
Every time I figured we had enough for one day, Izzy noticed some new
wonder. On and on into the swamp we went.

It was hot, boiling hot, and muggy in the way that only certain places
on the continent ever become, the south Georgia swamp being one of
them. We were all sweaty and tired, and above all, we were thirsty. The
black swamp water looked too murky to drink. Anyway, it wasn't water
Cosgrove was thinking of that afternoon.

Tom Cosgrove, who was our soundman on this swing through the
south, was devoted to the healing qualities of beer. Any beer would do on
a hot day, but his beverage of choice was Budweiser. Long summer rides
in the bus when Cosgrove was along were punctuated by the staccato
sound of pop-tops popping back where he sat, and usually there were a

few empty Budweiser cans in the bus's trash bin at night when we got where we were going.

That steamy day in the Okefenokee, the rest of us could have used a beer, too, or anything at all to quench our terrible thirst, but it was Cosgrove who said finally, to nobody in particular, to all of us, to the great sweltering swamp itself:

"What I would give for a Budweiser right now!"

Not one minute later, in the middle of that watery wilderness, we noticed sunlight glinting from something bobbing in the water directly ahead of the boat. We slowed down beside whatever it was. Cosgrove leaned over the side, reached into the water and lifted out a six-pack of Budweiser beer.

The rest of us just looked at one another. Cosgrove set the dripping six-pack on the seat beside him and extracted a can from one of the plastic rings. He popped the top. He took several long, slow swallows and regarded the can thoughtfully.

He said, "Could be a little colder."

The old man who was running the boat thought the beer must have fallen out of somebody else's boat days or weeks before. Cosgrove gave as his own opinion that, considering the brand and all, it was a gift from the great spirit of the swamp to him alone, though he did bestow one can upon each of the rest of us. All I know is that every traveler needs a carefree and optimistic spirit, curiosity about his surroundings, powers of keen observation—and a little bit of dumb luck.

There was the time we were shooting a story commemorating General Washington's arduous crossing of the Delaware in the winter of '76. We went down to the riverbank at the place where he had started the crossing and found some old boats tied up, boats not much different from the ones the General had used to get his ragtag army over to Trenton— just the picture we were hoping to find. But the day was bright, not wintry-looking enough. Izzy said, "I wish to hell it would start to snow." We looked up at the sky. A cloud passed over the sun. It started to snow. The snow covered the boats; Izzy made his pictures, evocative of the Continental army's hardships in the snow; I made my little speech to the camera with big snowflakes falling all around me. Just as we finished shooting, the cloud passed by, the sun came out, it stopped snowing and didn't snow again for a week.

We have found, in the words of the golfer's epigram, that it's better to be lucky than good.

Once, looking for stories on the back roads of Ohio, we were suffering a week-long dry spell. A colorful beekeeper we'd been told about was away from home when we called on him, visiting a niece in Colorado or someplace. A promising old-time candy store had been sold and turned into a pizza joint. A venerable amusement park where we thought we might find a story had shut down for the season. We began to get a little discouraged.

We passed a farmhouse with a homemade banner stretched between two oak trees in the front yard. The banner said in huge letters: "WEL-COME HOME, ROGER!" We drove on for a mile or two. Somebody said, "Wonder who Roger is?"

We turned around, went back there and knocked on the door.

Roger was a soldier on his way home from the Vietnam War. His family knew he was coming, but wasn't sure what day he was going to arrive. Roger's mother was in the kitchen baking his favorite chocolate cake. Really—she was. His wife was there with a baby son Roger hadn't seen. We asked if they'd mind if we brought the camera into the house. Roger's mother said it would be all right if we'd give her a minute to fix her hair. I am sure we weren't there more than an hour, talking to those people who were all excited about Roger coming home. We never did see Roger, of course.

At my desk in the bus as we rolled on that afternoon, I wrote a simple story letting Roger represent all the GIs coming home to their families from Vietnam. We found an airport and shipped the film to New York, and Walter Cronkite put the story on the *Evening News* the next night.

Rarely has any of our stories caused such a reaction from viewers. It was just an account of waiting for Roger, that's all, but it resonated in the country. The CBS switchboard lighted up that night with dozens of calls from people moved by it in some way, and hundreds of letters came in, some of them asking that the story be repeated. There was so much interest nationwide that Cronkite felt compelled to report on the air a few nights later, "Oh, and by the way—Roger got home!"

That hour with Roger's family made it a good trip to Ohio, after all. I had done a fair amount of careful planning in preparation for the week's work, but careful planning got us nowhere. Then along came a banner stretched across a farmhouse yard.

Back at the office, people asked, "How do you *find* these stories?"

"Well," I said, "you do have to work at it."

All you really have to do is look out the window.

We stopped off in Douglas, Wyoming, to inquire into the jackalope phenomenon. I guess you know about the jackalope, the rare creature of the western plains. It seems to be a cross between the jackrabbit and the antelope. From its rabbit head sprout antelope horns. Jackalopes breed, it is said, only during flashes of lightning, so there aren't many of them. Cowboys singing songs around campfires at night report hearing jackalopes joining in from the surrounding darkness, in high tenor voices that are described as "unusual, but not unpleasing." They are timid animals unless cornered, when they have been known to attack. A jackalope in full charge, old-timers attest, can only be stopped with a buffalo gun.

Some people think jackalopes are creations of taxidermists with time on their hands. They say the same thing about the famous fur-bearing winter trout of Montana. All I know is that there are plenty of Wyoming bars with mounted jackalopes looking down inscrutably from the walls, and that in Douglas, where history records the first sighting, they have a jackalope statue right there on Center Street.

We hung around Douglas for the first couple of days of July 1978, and then, having absorbed as much jackalope lore as we could stand, decided to go on to Cheyenne to see what was doing there on Independence Day. The way to go from Douglas to Cheyenne is straight south on Interstate 25. It's a two-hour drive at the speed limit. But we remembered that stretch of interstate as a shade tedious, so we took off instead on a dirt road that goes about eighty miles over the hills to Medicine Bow. It was a road we'd never been on before. We planned to pick up old U.S. 30 at Medicine Bow and still make it to Cheyenne in plenty of time for supper.

But we never made it to Cheyenne at all. Not that trip. A few miles out of Douglas, we started noticing the wildflowers. There were patches of daisies and wild geraniums, stands of mountain columbine at the bottoms of the hills and vast fields of Indian paintbrush on the slopes. The farther we went along that road, the more spectacular the wildflower show became. There were thousands of flowers, millions of them. They grew to the horizon in every direction, a patchwork of brilliant white and blue and purple, yellow, orange and flaming red. We kept stopping the bus to get out and look at them.

After a while, Izzy said, "Do you suppose we ought to make some pictures?"

I said, "Sure. Do you have any film in your Leica?"

He said, "I mean television pictures."

Sometimes I am a little slow.

We went to work. Every time we saw a different variety, we stopped for Izzy to make wide shots and close-ups. There wasn't much sound for Larry to record except the whisper of the wind and the buzz of an occasional bee, so he scouted ahead for species of flowers we hadn't seen before. The trouble was he kept finding them far from the road. "Oh, man," he'd holler from some hilltop, "come look at this one!" and Izzy and I would trudge up there with the gear. Charlie Quinlan, following us with the bus, would shout from the road, "There's a whole bunch of iris-looking things down here by the creek!" and down the hill we'd plod. I suppose we walked fifteen or twenty miles of the eighty miles to Medicine Bow that day in quest of little bits of beauty.

When the sun went down, we had two or three hours of vivid wildflower pictures on tape, dozens of memories in our heads of the wild splendor we had seen—and one big problem: how to describe it in words. I didn't even know the names of most of the flowers. I was painfully aware that the big-city cynics on the *Evening News* would be skeptical right away when a shipment came in labeled "Wyoming Wildflowers." I couldn't accompany it with a script that said only, "My, look at all the flowers! Aren't they pretty?" We had lovely pictures, but we didn't have a story yet. I needed a little knowledge.

Knowledge, a wise old city editor once advised me, consists of knowing where to look it up. We had a wildflower book in the limited library aboard the bus, but not many of the flowers in there looked like the flowers we had on tape. Anyway, I couldn't take chances. I knew from experience that if I made a mistake and called a primrose a phlox, thousands of viewers, horticultural experts in numbers never before suspected, would materialize in the hinterlands and write identical letters calling me a blockhead. Where could I find, anywhere in the wilds of Wyoming, a dependable authority to save me from indignity?

I looked at the map. Nothing up ahead but Medicine Bow, Rock River, Laramie . . .

Laramie! Laramie was the capital of the state. More important, Laramie was the seat of the University of Wyoming, and universities have departments, don't they? And one of the departments would be, would it not, the Department of Botany? It was already after dark, and the next day was the Fourth of July, when the university would be shut down, but we drove on to Laramie and I went to bed that night happy in the certain knowledge that somewhere in the same city a Wyoming wildflower expert had to be sleeping.

His name turned out to be Dennis Knight. He was in his side yard cooking Fourth of July hamburgers for the neighbors by the time I tracked him down. Up his driveway into this tranquil holiday tableau rolled the "On The Road" bus full of demanding strangers interrupting everything.

"See, we have pictures of all these flowers," I said, "and we don't know what they are. Could you look at the tape and identify them for us?"

"When?" he said.

"Well—now," I said.

Dr. Dennis Knight, chairman of the Department of Botany at the University of Wyoming, who thought he was having a day off with his family, sighed a professorial sigh.

"Sure," he said. "Have a beer."

He spent most of the rest of that afternoon aboard the bus with us while his cookout went on without him.

I froze a frame on the monitor. "Daisy?" I guessed.

"Balsamroot," he said. "The bighorn sheep eat them in the spring."

"This one looks a little like a violet," I said.

"Blue flax," he said. "*Linum lewisii*. Named for Captain Meriwether Lewis. He found it out here and carried a specimen back to President Jefferson. The Indians used the stems to make fishing lines."

Dennis Knight's knowledge of those flowers was exhaustive, encyclopedic. If I had searched the world over, I could not have found anyone half so edifying on the subject. I couldn't type fast enough to record all the interesting things he knew.

"Sulphur flower," he said. "It's in the buckwheat family. Here, what do you think this one is?"

"Looks like a buttercup," I said.

"Bingo!" he said. "You got one!"

From time to time, Dr. Knight's kids, Charley and Christy, appeared at the door of the bus wondering when they could have their daddy back. But he was just warming up.

"Stonecrop. It's a *sedum*. Tough little thing. You think it's dead and gone, then it rains and there it is again."

I went back to the motel that night and wrote a beautiful, informed script about the wildflowers, full of nuance and understanding. There weren't any mistakes in it. The *Evening News* loved it. People who saw the story probably still think of me as some kind of naturalist. I am not, but I met a man who certainly is. He let me steal his Fourth of July and pick his brain of half a lifetime's knowledge all in one afternoon and never even murmured a complaint. I think he sort of enjoyed it.

What on earth led us to take the back road out of Douglas? What delivered Dennis Knight into our hands just when we had to find him?

I'd say the Almighty, if I didn't believe He has better things to do with His time than provide a wandering camera crew with fields of wildflowers and scholars on demand.

What it was was dumb luck.

16

DOWN BY THE RIVERSIDE

I started out thinking of America as highways and state lines. As I got to know it better, I began to think of it as rivers. Most of what I love about the country is a gift of the rivers: birchbark canoes and cottonwood pirogues, steamboats and trading scows; Huckleberry Finn, Mike Fink and Evangeline; blue herons and bald eagles and snowy egrets; the Grand Canyon and the Hudson palisades; Warren LeRuth's fancy restaurant in Gretna, Louisiana, where people come to dine wearing their cuff links and pearls, and the Silver Dollar Cafe in Ennis, Montana, where the customers eat without taking off their cowboy hats; the walnut-brown brick houses of the rich old merchants up on the bluffs, the tar paper shacks of the fishermen down on the flats; the sound of whistles, bells and foghorns in the night; jazz and crawfish and ferryboats and covered bridges. None of them would be there, in the country or in our memories, without the rivers.

I was born not far from the New River and brought up not far from the Catawba ("And we have heard the sorrowful silence of the river in October," Thomas Wolfe wrote. "Flow on, Catawba, to the sea."). I learned early that the towns with character there in North Carolina were the river towns—Elizabeth City on the Pasquotank, Edenton on the Chowan, New Bern on the Neuse.

The next river towns I came to know were also in my native region.

Proud old Charleston, South Carolina, (so they say in Charleston) is "where the Ashley and the Cooper rivers join to form the Atlantic Ocean." And if there is a finer place than Charleston in the spring, when azaleas bloom in every garden behind every wrought-iron gate on every winding street, I don't know it.

Unless, of course, it is Savannah (on the Savannah) in the spring, when the yellow forsythia gives way to the blue wisteria, which gives way to the dogwood, dazzling white. Then the citizens feel the urge to inhale April while strolling the cobblestones of the riverfront, which is crowded with shops and ships, now as ever; or to drive out to Desposito's across the Thunderbolt Bridge for a helping of hot, sweet, pink, miraculous shrimp, ordered by the pound, boiled in their shells, and served in a steaming pile.

Much of the fun and discovery of the country has occurred for me alongside one river or another. One day, the crew and I stopped to have our lunch on the banks of the Buffalo in the Ozarks, the first stream chosen by the country to be a national river. A man in overalls came along and said, "There's a woman up the road here you boys ought to meet." That's how we became acquainted with Violet Hensley, the whittling fiddler of Yellville, Arkansas. She sat on her front porch playing "Old Dan Tucker" and "Wildwood Flower" for us on different fiddles she'd carved herself out of native maple, patting a bare foot in time with the music until the moon started to come up from down in the valley of the Buffalo.

It was the Colorado River that led us to Robert P. McCulloch. He was a millionaire with big ideas. No other river on earth has cut such a labyrinth of deep gorges as the Colorado and no river has inspired more big ideas—most of them bad ones, like damming up the Grand Canyon. The dam builders have already flooded so many of the Colorado's canyons that the mighty river is now safe for water-skiers but not much to marvel at anymore. Robert P. McCulloch's big idea was completely outrageous but comparatively benign. He started by building his own dream town beside one of the lakes that the lower Colorado has become. But after he had done it, and named the town Lake Havasu City, and filled it with streets and houses and golf courses and all, he still wasn't satisfied. The city still needed something, a kind of centerpiece. Robert P. McCulloch thought the London Bridge would be nice. So he went to London and bought it. He shipped it over from the River Thames, every stone of it, and put it up in the Arizona desert, and only then detoured the Colorado so the London Bridge would have a river to cross. More than a million people make a special trip every year to see if it's true that the London Bridge is now in Arizona. It's true. People drive across the London Bridge and look out at the desert and grin.

I owe the Apple River in Wisconsin for leading me to Jack and Alice Raleigh. At the river's edge, they ran a place called River's Edge. Their sons still run it, dealing in inner tubes and frog's legs. What you do is rent an inner tube and put it in the Apple River and lie down on it. Then you float contentedly for an hour or two through the woods and pastures, meditating on the scenery, until you reach the town of Somerset. There, the Raleighs pick you up and dry you off and drive you back to their restaurant and serve you frog's legs. They have the toughest inner tubes and the tenderest frog's legs in Wisconsin.

It wouldn't be much of a country without the rivers, and the people who have figured out a way to make a living beside them. Not that all the river towns are charming. Most of them, to tell the truth, are tumbledown and sad. At Arkansas City on the Mississippi, Mark Twain asked a steamboat passenger who belonged there what sort of place it was. " 'Well,' said he, after considering, and with the air of one who wishes to take time and be accurate, 'it's a hell of a place.' A description," Mark Twain wrote, "which was photographic for exactness."

But something draws us to the riverside and keeps us there through winter freezes and spring floods. It was so from the beginning. There would be no Bunker Hill, no Beacon Hill, no Back Bay, no Boston Red Sox, no Boston, if there were no Charles River. John Winthrop and the first Bostonians chose the Charles because it offered easy access and the possibility of a quick getaway. Virginians chose the James River for the same reasons.

Later on, when Lewis and Clark set out to find what, if anything, might lie between the Mississippi and the Pacific, they traveled by river, and the river they traveled by, the Missouri, took them a long way west, upstream all the way. When the river forked, they named all the forks and followed what looked like the main one. In this way, those great trout streams, the Jefferson, Madison and Gallatin, got their names in honor of the President, Secretary of State and Secretary of the Treasury. (President Jefferson remarked dryly, "You went fairly far west before you found one to name for me.") Then when the Jefferson River forked, they named the branches for the shining attributes of the President—Philosophy, Philanthropy and Wisdom. (But these names were too much for the rough trappers and prospectors who followed. Those three rivers now are called Beaverhead, Ruby and Big Hole, though the intention of Lewis and Clark to honor their fellow Virginian's sagacity is preserved in the names of two cowtowns on the Big Hole River—Wise River and Wisdom. I wonder how many people who pass through Wisdom, Montana, are aware that it is *Thomas Jefferson's* wisdom that is commemorated there.)

Finally, Lewis and Clark and their tired men trudged up a mountain to what they took to be the headwaters of the Missouri, a spot where a little spring bubbled out of the ground. This was the place, Captain Lewis wrote in his diary, "in surch of which we have spent so many toilsome days and wristless nights." One of their privates, a man named Hugh McNeal, "exultingly stood with a foot on each side of this little rivulet and thanked his God that he had lived to bestride the mighty and heretofore deemed endless Missouri."

(If you don't mind sharp climbs on winding dirt roads, you can drive right to the same spot and step across the "Missouri" yourself. Izzy and Larry and Charlie and I did it, with Izzy driving and the rest of us pushing the bus around the steepest switchbacks. The little spring still bubbles there on the east side of the Lemhi Pass, just before you reach the Continental Divide and go plunging dangerously down into Idaho.)

Lewis and Clark thought the Salmon River might take them on to the Pacific, but they found that one too wild to ride. "The passage by canoe," Clark wrote, "is entirely impossible." It still is. The two captains had to look for a more placid passage, and found it in the Snake, which leads to the Columbia, which leads to the western sea. President Jefferson had told them he had a hunch the continent could be crossed by water, and they were able to come back and tell him he was pretty nearly right.

After Lewis and Clark returned to spread the word, Americans who were already moving west along the Ohio, the Cumberland and the

Tennessee were emboldened to make the great leap "across the wide Missouri," following the North Platte, that shallow, muddy river "too thick to drink and too thin to plow." You can still see the wagon ruts of those who went west in countless places in Nebraska and Wyoming. When the North Platte gave out, they followed a little river called the Sweetwater. Climb to the top of Independence Rock in Wyoming and you'll find the names of the pioneers up there: "Milo J. Ayer, age 29." "Fox, Cincinnati." "Ryan, Indianapolis." From the rocky height where they carved their names, all you can see is parched desert to the west, with the blue Sweetwater winding through it and the tracks of the Oregon Trail along the riverside. That sight tells you all you need to know about the importance of rivers to the people who rolled west in covered wagons.

The destiny of America—that it would become one country from sea to shining sea—was finally settled one fine day in 1848, the day James W. Marshall discovered gold at John Sutter's sawmill, which stood on the American River, which flows into the Sacramento, which flows into San Francisco Bay.

And that is the complete history of the United States of America from Boston Harbor to the Golden Gate—all rivers, twenty of them.

And I've hardly mentioned the greatest of them all, the one which figures largest in the country's history, the one that has such a hold on our imagination and our topsoil. The Mississippi River carries the mud of thirty states and two provinces 2,000 miles south to the delta and deposits 500 million tons of it there every year. The business of the Mississippi, which it will accomplish in time, is methodically to transport all of Illinois to the Gulf of Mexico. I've paddled my own canoe on Minnesota's placid Pigeon River, ridden a jet boat up the Rogue in Oregon and an oil-drum raft down the Tanana in Alaska, but when I traveled on Old Man River, I went in style—on the stern-wheeler *Delta Queen*, with the big river gliding by and the sun bouncing back into my eyes from the brass trim on the pilothouse and the steam calliope hooting and wheezing a tune from the stern. Oh, that was fine! I understood how Mark Twain felt the day of *his* first steamboat ride:

"I packed my valise and took passage. . . . When we presently got underway and went poking down the broad river, I became a new being and the subject of my own admiration. I was a traveler! A word had never tasted so good in my mouth before."

Just to recite the names of the Mississippi River ports of call is to compose a poem of mid-America: St. Paul, Red Wing, Winona, Prairie du Chien, Dubuque, Clinton, Rock Island, Keokuk, Hannibal, St. Louis, Cairo, Memphis, Vicksburg, Natchez, Baton Rouge, New Orleans!

New Orleans received more from the river than any other city, and gives back more to the visitor than any other. I lie awake in my bed in Room 9 of the Maison de Ville on Toulouse Street in the French Quarter, the room where Audubon once labored at his canvases and Tennessee Williams once struggled with the words of a play. The door to the courtyard is ajar. I can hear the soft splash of the fountain outside the door, and beyond that the brassy staccato of a trumpet from a jazz joint on Bourbon Street, and beyond that the moan of a tugboat horn from away the other side of Jackson Square on the river. This is the town of the tragic Manon Lescaut and the noble Le Moyne and the pirate Lafitte and Kate Townsend, the madam whose establishment had bed hangings of lace and chamber pots of gold; the town of Buddy Bolden, the horn player who drove himself mad with his own demoniacal cornet solos in the cribs of Storyville. (But his genius survived among certain admiring young members of his audience, young Bunk Johnson and Joe Oliver, young Louis Armstrong.) This is the town of L'Alouette, the suave fencing master, and Marie Laveau, the Voodoo Queen, and of numberless outrageous demagogues: Andy Jackson the populist-general-savior of the city, Ben Butler the carpetbagger, and the Kingfish, Huey Long. It is the town of Rex, Lord of Misrule, and the Carnival Krewe of Comus. And it is the town of a certain Mr. Moriarty, who had his deceased wife buried in Metairie Cemetery in a monumental tomb with four great grieving sculpted statues at the corners, representing, so it is said in New Orleans, "Faith, Hope, Charity and Mrs. Moriarty."

Once upon a time, as a young reporter from New York, I sat at a back table of the Acme Oyster Bar on Iberville Street through a long afternoon of oysters and bourbon whisky in the company of Earl Long, a roughhewn, slightly demented man who happened, at the time, to be Governor of the state, and Blaze Starr, a kindly stripper who was his mistress.

Governor Long patiently explained to me the folkways, mores, history, culture and politics of New Orleans. When I got up to leave, Miss Starr summarized for me: "There ain't any place like it, honey." And I have found that truly, there ain't. Every other large American city reminds the visitor faintly of someplace else—Seattle of San Francisco, Atlanta of Kansas City, Chicago of New York. New Orleans refers only to itself.

If there were no Mississippi River, there would be no Galena, Illinois, with its steamboat Gothic mansions and its memories of Ulysses S. Grant, who went off to war from Galena as drillmaster of the local volunteers. There would be no Ste. Genevieve, Missouri, a French village lost in time beside the timeless river. There would be no Greenville, Mississippi, and therefore no Doe's Eat Place serving hot tamales and iced tea at tables in the kitchen, and this would be a loss to the world. The Mississippi River gives many satisfactions.

Oh, so do they all. As I sort through remembered pleasures, Madison, Indiana, comes to mind, old Madison on the Ohio, largest city of the state for a little while there, now content to be merely the most evocative, its Greek Revival houses aging gently in the sun; and Sistersville, West Virginia, where a sumptuous Victorian suite in the Wells Inn still sets you back about $35 and a rocking chair is waiting for you on the porch; and a few miles down the Ohio and across the river, Marietta, Ohio, named for Marie Antoinette in her lifetime, where you can take an eccentric corner room in the Lafayette Hotel and watch the river life go by.

Some of our greatest river cities turned away from their rivers for a while there, but now they're turning back. Pittsburgh has done so, with its inviting Point State Park right downtown on the rivers. St. Louis's Gateway Arch soars over a riverfront rebirth. Detroit has reclaimed a part of its riverside from the ramshackle warehouses and vacant lots and transformed it into a stretch of graceful glass towers and plazas and fountains fronting on the river. Even New York—the greatest river city of them all, which has come to ignore its greatest river—is talking about replacing the broken-down piers along the majestic Hudson with green parks and public walkways.

Every city lucky enough to be on a river ought to take as its model San Antonio. Izzy and Larry and I drove into San Antonio one time to have a bent axle straightened, found that our rooms in a former convent school now known as La Mansion Hotel came with balconies overlooking the San Antonio River—and stayed for a week. I have been back there often to walk on the Paseo del Rio, the winding walk along the river, past shops and sidewalk cafes, under the shade trees and the arched foot-bridges. The San Antonio River was a forgotten storm drain until the thirties when the WPA went to work landscaping it and building paths beside it. Now it is the most inviting feature of the city. You can catch a water taxi to the public library in San Antonio! Visitors take a table beside the river, order a pitcher of sangría, and forget that this was the afternoon they were going to visit the Alamo.

Highways are handy, ribbons of concrete, man-made. But if you are in search of the authentic America, seek out the little river that runs under the bridge at Concord. Pay your respects to the Suwannee, the Shenandoah, the Appomattox. Walk in the grass beside the Little Bighorn and think about what happened there. Spend an afternoon waist-deep in the Henrys Fork with a fly rod in your hand, in the fall when the trumpeter swans fly low over the river. Walk down to the banks of the Missouri, which used to change its course so often that farmers along it complained they never knew whether their crop was going to be corn or catfish.

America is a great story, and there is a river on every page of it.

17

MR. BLACK

*G*eorge Black was a brickmaker. He turned out to be a pretty good diplomat for the State Department, too, but that part of the story comes later. George Black was a brickmaker, the craft he and his brother chose when their father died in 1889.

"We aren't going to get to go to school," his brother, fourteen, said to George, eleven. "We're going to have to work for a living. If we haul ourselves up and make men out of ourselves, even if we don't know A from B, we'll make somebody call us 'Mr. Black' someday."

Mr. Black quoted his brother with pride more than eighty years later. He was a tall, dignified old man. Everybody called him Mr. Black.

The little boys, George and his brother, setting out on their own in 1889, walked the forty miles from Randleman, North Carolina, to Winston-Salem. They apprenticed themselves to a brickmaker for a while, and after they learned the trade, they started their own business while they were still in their teens. Since well before the turn of the century, George Black had been making bricks the way I watched him do it one afternoon in his backyard.

He had a mule hitched to what he called a "mud mill." With his giant, practiced hands, Mr. Black scooped up the mud mixed by the paddles of the mill as the mule plodded in a circle, and packed the mud expertly into six-brick forms ready for the kiln.

"How many bricks do you figure you've made in your life?" I asked him.

"Oh, Lord," he said. "I don't know. I'd be most afraid to know." He handed a finished form to one of the neighborhood youngsters who were serving as stackers that day, and impatiently awaited another stack of empties.

"I made a million bricks in one year," he said. "Mr. R. J. Reynolds rode out here on a white horse. He always rode a white horse, you know. He asked me if I thought I could make a thousand thousand bricks. He said he had in mind to build a tobacco factory. I studied and said yes, I could. I did, too, and you can go downtown and see them if you want to. That building's still there. They're all my bricks. Yes sir."

I found myself filled with admiration for this man standing in a pit before me in mud up to his elbows. He had made a life of the basic elements, water and earth and fire. And he had made the building blocks of a city.

Mr. Black dressed up in his Sunday suit the next day and took me on a stroll about Winston-Salem.

"These bricks we're walking on," he said, as we passed through the restored village of Old Salem, "I made these only about forty years ago. They're holding up nice. Yeah."

He pointed with his cane. "I made the bricks for that building over there." It was a schoolhouse. "I made the bricks for the Old Home Church over there," he said. "I made the bricks for that brick wall yonder." Wherever we walked, he pointed out the work of his own hands.

When we reached the block-long R. J. Reynolds factory, he said, "I believe I told you wrong about this job. It wasn't a million bricks. It ended up being a million and a half." He leaned on his walking stick and looked up at the massive structure. "Made these bricks six at a time," he said. "Put 'em out on the board and put 'em in a kiln and burned 'em for a dollar and a half a day. You don't know it but that was good pay in those days. Yes sir."

We walked on. "Made all these bricks six at a time," Mr. Black said, "and I'm going to make some more yet!"

The morning after our story about Mr. Black went on the air, I was sitting on the edge of my bed in a motel room, rubbing my eyes and trying to figure out where to go next, when the phone rang. It was the CBS News State Department Correspondent of the time, Marvin Kalb.

Of course, that made it a red-letter day for me right there. I wasn't used to getting phone calls from Marvin Kalb.

He said, "There's a guy at the Agency for International Development who wants to talk to you. His name is Harvey J. Witherell. He's on the Guyana desk over there. I think he probably *is* the Guyana desk. I don't know what he wants with you, but he's been calling me all morning. I wish you'd give him a ring and get him off my neck."

"Sure, Marvin," I said.

"If it turns out to be anything I can help you with, let me know," Marvin said generously, and a little wearily. The life of a State Department Correspondent must be hard. He has the whole world to worry about all the time.

When I reached Harvey J. Witherell, his voice was trembling with excitement.

"I hear you had a story about a brickmaker on television last night," he said.

"Yep," I said.

"Oh, gosh, I've been looking all over this country for a brickmaker who still does the job by hand," Harvey J. Witherell said. "I didn't think there were any left. What's he like?"

"He's a nice man," I said.

"You see," Harvey J. Witherell said, "the government of Guyana wants us to send a brickmaker down there. They have a Five Year Plan or something like that to rebuild the whole country in brick. There's no shortage of raw materials, I mean there's plenty of mud in Guyana, but they don't want to build a big brick factory. They want somebody to go village-to-village for a couple of weeks to teach people how to make bricks for themselves."

"Well," I said, "I've got just the man for you, Harvey, but he *is* ninety-two years old. . . ."

"I don't care how old he is," Harvey said. "I think he's the last brickmaker." I gave him Mr. Black's address and telephone number. "You have made my day!" said Harvey J. Witherell.

When I called Mr. Black to warn him what was coming, he said he had already had a call from Washington.

"Where is Guyana?" Mr. Black asked.

"It's a little country in South America," I said.

Mr. Black said, "My, my."

The very next day, on official government business and carrying his government briefcase, Harvey J. Witherell caught a plane from Washington to Winston-Salem. He and Mr. Black hit it off. They came to an agreement that amounted to one of the best deals in the history of American foreign aid: Mr. Black would go to Guyana for ten days. He would take his granddaughter, Evelyn Abrams, who also knew how to make bricks, and a kid from the neighborhood, Thomas Brabham, and they would go down there and teach those people how to make bricks. Mr. Black would be paid $100 per day. Not much, I thought when I heard about it, but better than the dollar and a half he got from R. J. Reynolds.

Harvey J. Witherell was awash with a feeling of accomplishment.

He said, "This is a wonderful thing you're going to do, Mr. Black. We in Washington very much appreciate it."

There was no false modesty in Mr. Black. He said, "I believe you have picked the best man to do the job for the U.S.A."

Planning commenced.

No government planning is ever done simply, of course. Harvey J. Witherell had to formulate a detailed proposal for his own superiors and for higher-ups in the Department of State. He filled out reports in triplicate. He mapped the projected journey hour-by-hour and village-by-village. He developed plans and exigency plans. He put in travel orders and meal requisitions. There are forms for these things, and Harvey J. Witherell followed the forms.

All this planning had to be coordinated with the U.S. Embassy in Guyana, of course, and with the office of the Guyanese Prime Minister, Forbes Burnham, and the whole thing had to have a name. It was given the name "Operation Black Jack." It became a pretty big deal.

Cables began flying back and forth between Washington and Georgetown, the capital of Guyana, all of them bearing the capitalized admonition: "EXPEDITE." Later, somebody sneaked copies of those cables out of the State Department for me to read. (This did not constitute another Pentagon Papers case; they were not classified documents.) I was astonished by their number and by the baroque majesty of their prose. All this urgent intercontinental communication just to arrange for an elderly maker of bricks to show a few foreigners how it is done! A new appreciation of my government arose in my breast as I perused that tall stack of Operation Black Jack cables.

Harvey J. Witherell was thrilled; his big project was proceeding apace. George Black was thrilled; he had rarely been out of the county, and now he was about to be transported to a foreign land as an official representative of the United States of America. I was pretty excited myself; as Latin American Correspondent ten years before, I had been to Guyana a number of times on assignment. I figured I still had credit in some of the bars of Georgetown, and this would be a chance to get back there and look up some old friends.

As I awaited final word of the departure date, however, calamity struck.

Some high official of the Agency for International Development, some administrator whose job it was to review agency proposals and give them final approval, some insensible overseer, reading one of the forms Harvey J. Witherell had prepared in triplicate describing Mr. Black and the perfect match of the man to the mission, said to himself, wait a minute, this man is *ninety-two years old!* He reached for a stamp, one that said "CANCELLED," or perhaps "DENIED," stamped this stamp all over the proposal, and sent it tumbling back down through the bureaucracy, where it landed with a thud on the desk of Harvey J. Witherell.

He called me again, this time almost in tears.

"It's all off," he said. "They say he's too old."

"Well, Harvey," I said. "Way it goes. You sure tried hard."

By now, I liked Harvey J. Witherell. He was one of those bureaucrats we're always hearing about. He had spent twenty years or more in government service. Now, he was hovering on the brink of actually *doing* something. It didn't seem fair for Harvey's big idea to die this way, officially branded a bad idea. I felt the pain of his disappointment over the phone, and did my best to cheer him up.

"Too bad," I said.

"Yeah, too bad," he said. "Well, so long." And he hung up. It was over.

That is, it *would* have been over, except that right then we all got a lesson in how one branch of government doesn't always know what the other branch is doing.

Mr. Black, naturally, had been going around telling people about how he was going to Guyana. There was a good newspaper in Winston-Salem, the *Sentinel*. Somebody on the newspaper heard about Mr. Black's forthcoming trip and said, "That's a pretty good story." The *Sentinel* ran the story on page one: "Mr. Black Is Going to Guyana."

The people at the United Press wire service read the *Winston-Salem Sentinel*. Somebody there said, "That's a pretty good story." The UPI picked up the story and transmitted it nationwide: "Mr. Black Is Going to Guyana."

The Washington Post subscribes to the United Press wire service. Some editor there said, "That's a pretty good story." *The Washington Post* printed it with a wirephoto of Mr. Black and his mud mill: "Mr. Black Is Going to Guyana."

The White House reads *The Washington Post*. Somebody at the White House said, "That's a pretty good story," and showed it to somebody else who said, "Wouldn't it be wonderful if the President would see this man off?"

The timing could not have been more perfect. On precisely the same day Mr. Black's trip to Guyana was being cancelled by the State Department, the White House was inviting Mr. Black to stop off in Washington on his way to Guyana for the State Department, to meet President Nixon in the Oval Office!

Harvey J. Witherell, sitting there amid the wreckage of his dream, let his eye fall on the President's appointment schedule for the next week as published in the Official Register.

"10 A.M. Wednesday:" one item read. "George Black, brickmaker of Winston-Salem, N.C., who is going to Guyana to teach brickmaking at the invitation of U.S. AID."

This made Harvey J. Witherell feel much better. Whistling a little tune, he tore out this item, highlighted it with a yellow marker, and confidently sent it back up through the bureaucracy to the official who had stamped his idea "CANCELLED."

Of course, all the wheels that hours before had rolled backward to a halt now started running fast forward again. The project just stamped "CANCELLED" was restamped "HIGH PRIORITY." Harvey called me to say I'd better make airplane reservations for Guyana after all. He said he didn't have time to talk. He said Mr. Black was coming to Washington to meet the President.

Naturally, nobody at the White House thought to ask Mr. Black how he was going to *get* to Washington. He got there by making the first airplane flight of his life. His granddaughter, Evelyn Abrams, sitting beside him on the plane, said it might as well have been his hundredth flight, that's how composed he was. The White House told Mr. Black, "Bring your family with you." He did. He brought about thirty-two of them, uncles, aunts, nephews, nieces and cousins from all up and down the eastern seaboard.

The guard at the White House gate said, "Oh, no, this is way too many people." They discussed it. The guard said, "I'll tell you what. I'll let half of you in."

At a White House "photo opportunity" they open the door to the President's office for three minutes, and a herd of animals comes in, pushing and shoving. These are reporters and photographers, competing for the most appealing photograph of the President and his visitor, and straining for the quotable remark. I was one of the animals that day.

"This is a very nice family you have here, Mr. Black," said President Nixon.

"This is only half of them!" Mr. Black exclaimed. "The other half are waiting out there on the street. The man wouldn't let them in!"

The reporters scribbled notes.

"Why, that won't do," President Nixon said, and soon the other half of Mr. Black's family crowded into the Oval Office, filling it nearly to overflowing.

So George Black got to meet the President, and so did his close and distant relatives. He did go to Guyana. I went along. There, Mr. Black taught brickmaking with such energy that he exhausted his official hosts, his village pupils, and a retinue of U.S. government hirelings, one of whom was probably the very official who had told Harvey J. Witherell that Mr. Black was too old for this trip.

The problem was that in their attempts at brickmaking, the villagers kept getting it wrong, and Mr. Black wanted to stay in every village until they got it right. One day, Mrs. Forbes Burnham, wife of the Prime Minister, fashionably dressed in a riding outfit, came out to one of the villages in a limousine to be photographed for the local press with the visiting American brickmaker. Mr. Black nodded to her, extended a muddy hand, and went back to teaching brickmaking.

"He is quite a man," Mrs. Burnham said, as someone came up with a towel to wipe the mud from her hand.

He was, too.

I don't have many souvenirs from my adventures on the road, but from the story of George Black, I have two. The first is one of his bricks, solid and strong, like the man who made it. The second is a photograph of President Richard Nixon, standing awkwardly erect in the Oval Office flanked by Mr. Black and his granddaughter and some of the other family members. The head of the Agency for International Development is in the picture, too.

As for Harvey J. Witherell, the brave bureaucrat who had made this moment possible, he was in the room that day, only to find himself shoved rudely aside by a wire service photographer who said, "Excuse me, buddy, let me get through here." He stepped in front of Harvey, and so did all the other photographers. Flashbulbs were popping. Immortality in the government archives was being bestowed. In the moment of his greatest achievement, Harvey had been pushed into the shadows.

But bureaucrats are nothing if not nimble. For in a corner of this photograph, one other white face appears at the extreme left, wearing the insouciant expression of a man who has just elbowed his way back into the picture.

It is the face of Harvey J. Witherell.

18

FLIGHT

Every December, on the anniversary of the Wright brothers' first
flight, a motley fraternity of pilots, aerospace engineers and writers
about aviation gathers at Kitty Hawk, North Carolina. After an all-night
party, these celebrants assemble bleary-eyed on the sand dunes where
Wilbur and Orville's craft of hickory sticks stuck together with Arnstein's
Bicycle Cement first started forward into the wind. At the precise moment of the Wrights' lift-off in 1903, two Navy jets representing the two
brothers come roaring in low from the sea, rise to clear the sand dunes,
kick in their afterburners over the Wright monument, and then, in a
thundering instant that rattles the earth, turn straight up into the sky and
climb until they are out of sight. The day is often raw and windy, but the
faithful club members are always out there for this small, moving ceremony. They style themselves the "Man Will Never Fly Society." Their
motto is, "Birds fly. Men drink."

I am not a member, but when I am bouncing around up there among
thunderstorms, I always recall the society's name and credo with profound appreciation.

To beat a deadline, I once flew from Montevideo to Buenos Aires in
an open-cockpit biplane piloted by a Uruguayan teenager decked out,
reassuringly he thought, in helmet, goggles, white scarf and gloves. I
have flown up the Amazon in an ancient commercial seaplane, landing in

the river at each village along the way for passengers and mail to be rowed out from shore. I have skimmed under the fog a few feet above the waves on my way to an Eskimo settlement on an island in the Bering Sea. ("Don't fly with that guy," I was told back in Nome. "He always comes back with seaweed on his struts." But there wasn't any choice.) Three times in two days, I was forced by the pressure of a story to fly with a San Francisco daredevil who was willing to land, and a little later take off again, at the North Lake Tahoe airport, which was closed to landings and takeoffs at the time by snow and ice.

I have flown in airplanes that lost engine power aloft, once in a four-engine plane that lost three of its engines, once in a twin-engine plane that lost first one and then the other, and ended up nose-down in a field of sagebrush in eastern Oregon. I have flown in a glider, which had no engines to begin with, of course, with a pilot who aimed the craft straight at the sea cliffs of La Jolla, California, counting on the updrafts to lift us to safety. They did, but I have not wished to fly in a glider since.

Like every other reporter who covered the Vietnam War, I have a number of times flown in helicopters that were being shot at. U.S. chopper pilots had conflicting theories about gunfire avoidance: fly high, out of the range of enemy bullets, or fly fast and low over the treetops to give the enemy no time to aim. Both schools of thought had fervent adherents. Advocates of both, I noticed, often came home with bullet holes in their helicopters.

I have three times been in airplanes that were struck by lightning, an Army Beaver and two commercial jets. (American Airlines captain to his stunned and silent passengers after the deafening crack and blast of white light inside the cabin: "Folks, we seem to have experienced a negative electrical discharge . . .")

"There are old pilots and there are bold pilots," goes the familiar saying around the hangars. "There are no old, bold pilots."

Oh, I don't know:

There was Weldy Phipps, who flew his Twin Otter out of Resolute in the Northwest Territories well into his seventies, using a sextant for celestial navigation and doing the calculations in his head. They say he landed once in a clearing to pick up a Tlingit Indian woman who needed a fast trip to a hospital, and found that he didn't have enough room to take off again. After he made the woman comfortable in the back of the plane, he tied the tail of the Otter to a tree with a rope, revved the engines to full power, gave the signal for somebody to cut the rope with a chain saw, and bounced the plane out of there. It was Weldy who flew the supply plane for the Plaisted Expedition. I was aboard several times when he landed on pans of ice floating far offshore in the Arctic Ocean. His method was to taxi around on skis after landing while his passenger tumbled out of the plane with an ice ax to see whether the pan was thick enough to land on.

There was Edna Gardner Whyte, who was eighty when we met her. She was giving flying lessons in Roanoke, Texas, which she felt well enough qualified to do after 30,000 hours in the air. She had 123 aviation trophies on the shelves in her living room, and to show us that she could still handle an airplane, she took Izzy up for some aerial acrobatics. After a snap roll or two, Izzy lost interest in his work. He can be heard moaning softly on the sound track of the tape he was shooting.

"That's good for your veins," said eighty-year-old Edna Gardner Whyte. "Only two and a half gs! Want another one?"

"No, ma'am," said Izzy, politely.

Then there was the old man in Kansas, an old, bold pilot if ever we met one. We never caught his name. We were doing a story about Stan Herd, an artist whose canvases are eighty-acre fields. Stan Herd plants crops—soybeans, milo, alfalfa, sunflowers—in patterns which when viewed from the air become lovely pictures, vases of flowers on checkered tablecloths, or western landscapes, or portraits of Indian chiefs. Seen from the ground, they're just a jumble of crops; you have to be in an airplane to appreciate them. A few miles from where Stan was working in a field with his tractor, we spotted an old J-2 Piper Cub parked in a barnyard. Izzy knocked on the door of the owner, an elderly farmer with a competent air about him, and explained our need.

"Sure, I'll take you up," the farmer said.

"We need to take the door off so I can make pictures," Izzy said.

"Fine!" the old man said.

Up there at 2,000 feet over Stan's field, making pictures from the Cub with the door off, Izzy remarked, "How long ago did you get your ticket?"

"Ticket?" the man asked.

"You know," Izzy said, "your pilot's license."

"Hell, I don't have any pilot's license," the old farmer said. "I just found this thing wrecked out here and patched it up and taught myself to fly it."

Of all the flyers into whose hands we have placed our lives, Don Sheldon is the one I'll always be most thankful for. We had heard of him before we met him. Everybody in south central Alaska had heard of him.

Wandering around Alaska one spring, we thought we'd make some pictures of Mount McKinley—Denali, the great mountain of the continent. On clear days, the old giant can be seen from a hundred miles or more away, but, as usual, we wanted close-ups. We drove to Talkeetna, the village that has always served as headquarters for expeditions to McKinley, and was best known as the home of Don Sheldon, the fabled mountain pilot. He turned out to be a slender, unassuming man with thinning hair. He wore a plaid shirt, army pants and work boots. Very modest-looking, I thought, for a legend. He said he was free for a couple of days and we engaged him to fly us up to the mountain. As we helped him roll his ski-equipped, single-engine Cessna out of the hangar, he made gentle jokes about the dangers of mountain flying.

"Never know what we'll run into up there," he said, shaking his head and smiling. "You sure you boys want to do this? Well, let's fuel 'er up then."

I noticed he pumped his gas through a chamois strainer.

Light, fluffy cumulus clouds floated above the Alaska Range when we approached, Izzy riding beside Sheldon up front and a soundman named Stan Roginski strapped in behind with me. Izzy thought it would make a wonderful shot to fly through a cloud straight at the mountain with the camera rolling, so that when we came out of the cloud, the sunlit peak of McKinley would appear suddenly and dramatically.

"Let's try that cloud over there," Izzy said, and the mountain scenery tilted dizzily as Don Sheldon banked one way, then the other, to oblige. We flew toward the mountain through one cloud after another. Izzy was never satisfied that we had captured quite the desired spectacular effect. There were a lot of clouds to try, and we tried most of them. I found myself gripping the armrests and trying to keep my breakfast down each time we broke through into the sunlight, steered straight for Mount McKinley and veered sharply away at the last minute.

"Let's try that one over there," Izzy said, pointing to yet another cloud close to the peak.

"If we try that one," Don Sheldon said, "it will ruin my reputation."

"What do you mean?" Izzy asked.

Sheldon said calmly, "That one's got rocks in it."

"Look," I said, "is there someplace we can set this thing down for a while? Maybe we need a rest."

"I know just the place," the pilot said, putting the plane over on one wing again and tilting the nose sickeningly downward. "I think I even brought along a Thermos of coffee for you boys. We'll take a little coffee break." He set the plane's skis for landing, dropped the flaps and, a few minutes later, brought us to a bumpy stop in the snow in a big curved bowl, an ice field of the Ruth Glacier.

When Sheldon shut down the engine and we stepped out into the sunlight, I was nearly blinded by the brilliance of the white world around us. The glacier formed a vast, silent basin surrounded by massive slopes, a universe of ice and rock. Range upon range of mountains stretched before us into the measureless distance, and behind us, towering almost straight up from the ice field, rose Denali itself, with snow blowing from its summit thousands of feet overhead.

After a long silence, one of us said, "Good God!"

"Yep," Don Sheldon said, "I've always sort of liked this place myself."

We spent a long time just standing there before we remembered we were supposed to be making pictures. Don Sheldon tramped about thoughtfully in the snow while we worked.

When it was time to go, he had a little news for us.

"Good news and bad news," he said. "The good news is that the sun hasn't gone down yet and I can still get this plane out of here and back home before dark.

"The bad news is that the sun has made the snow so mushy that I can't take off with all of you on board."

I gulped, "You *can't?*"

"Nope," he said. "Too much weight. Best I can do now is take one of you back to Talkeetna, and maybe some of your gear. Two of you are going to have to spend the night up here, I'm afraid. I'll come back for you in the morning."

I looked around, imagining the nighttime temperature on the glacier. Also imagining wolves and polar bears.

"Nothing up here to hurt you," Don Sheldon said. "I'll dig a couple of sleeping bags out of the plane for you."

While he was doing so, he added, "Oh, and you won't have to be alone, either." He nodded toward a rocky outcrop about a mile away at the edge of the ice field. "You can't see it from here, but there's a cozy one-room cabin on the other side of that rock. Some of the climbers use it for a base camp. There's a Catholic priest in there now on some kind of a retreat. He's a nice guy. Father Ron is what I call him. He's been up here awhile. He won't mind a little company."

Sheldon held up the bedrolls. "Who wants these?" he asked.

I was still letting all this news sink in, about the necessity for two of us to spend the night in this wilderness, and then about there being a *cabin* in this unlikely place, and not only a cabin but also a *priest.* . . .

I heard Izzy say, "I'll stay." He shouldered his camera and the tape recorder and took one of the bedrolls. Then I heard myself say, "Sure, I'll stay, too." Don Sheldon handed me the other roll of bedding and a long length of rope.

"Better rope yourselves together when you walk over there," he said. "You know. Crevasses. See you tomorrow."

He climbed into the pilot's seat with Stan beside him, started the engine, and began his takeoff run down the glacier. The plane lifted off and turned toward home. We watched until it vanished among the mountains.

Izzy tied one end of the rope around his waist and handed me the other end, regarding my 220-pound bulk doubtfully. "If one of us falls into a hole in the ice," he said, "it better be me, I guess." We started across the glacier with the setting sun casting our shadows a hundred yards ahead of us and creating imaginary hidden crevasses every few steps.

It must have taken us nearly an hour to make it off the ice and into the rocks of the mountain. When we started up, we could see a big, red-bearded man wearing a bright parka coming down toward us, carrying a coiled rope of his own over one shoulder, and in his hand, a staff. He looked like a Biblical prophet of the mountains.

"Good afternoon, Father," I said.

"Never mind the Father blather!" he boomed cheerily. "Sorry to be late in greeting you! The truth is I wasn't expecting company! Haven't seen another soul since sometime last month! Here, let me carry some of that load for you."

He talked loudly all the way up the hill, not stopping even to ask where we had come from and what we were doing there. It had been weeks, I guess, since he had heard the sound of his own voice.

"I suppose Don Sheldon dropped you off," he said, "unless you took a wrong turn on a stroll in Anchorage and hoofed it up here. Don likes to show off his shelter. He built it himself, you know. He got tired of climbers freezing in the storms. Tough work, you know, having to fly their bodies back down and all, so he flew a few loads of lumber and nails up here—and here we are. Welcome to our humble abode!"

The cabin was small, six-sided and half buried in snow. Inside, sleeping shelves were built up off the floor under a ring of windows. A wood stove squatted in the center of the room with a fire crackling inside. That's all there was to the place. It looked very good to me.

"I am pleased to offer you northern exposures with a view of the mountains," Father Ron said, dumping our bedrolls on the shelf. "All the exposures have a view of the mountains. The menu tonight is stew. That is the menu every night." He walked outside, dug around in the snow for a black iron pot full of beef and beans, came back in and set it on the stove. "Dinner will be served shortly," he said, "but first the cocktail hour." From his duffel bag on the floor under the shelf, he produced a bottle of Christian Brothers brandy. "We like to support the brothers in their good work," he said. He unscrewed the cap and passed the bottle ceremoniously to Izzy to drink first.

Over tin bowls of stew, Father Ron told us that he had come to Alaska seeking solitude in the loneliest place he could find. Somebody in Talkeetna had told him about the Mount McKinley shelter and he had talked Don Sheldon into flying him up here. He was escaping a critical bishop in Boston or someplace. He said this sojourn in the mountains was partly for religious reflection and partly for figuring out what to do with his life.

"Well," I said, "I guess it doesn't help your solitude much for a couple of strangers to show up at dinnertime and stay all night."

"I am very glad to have your company," Father Ron said solemnly. "I've never been alone for so long before. Let me tell you what I have discovered about being alone: it is a great gift, but it is damned lonely."

I laughed.

"Solitude is hard to come by in this world," he went on. "It is a priceless luxury. Only the very rich can afford it—and paupers like me. Everybody else in the world dreams of splendid isolation, workers from their bosses, husbands from their wives, but they can only dream, you see. They are in the grip of daily life, and daily life must be lived with others."

I said I envied him his escape from daily life.

"Yes," he said, "it offers communion with God. But about this time of day, you find yourself in need of some kind of human communion, somebody to have a drink with, or a debate. God listens well, but doesn't talk much. Moses went to the mountaintop to talk with God, but you'll remember that he came right back down again. And I have found out why. The pressure is too great up here. It is not natural to human beings to talk only with God. The tension accumulates. . . ."

We all fell silent, thinking about this.

"But now," Father Ron said, "the after-dinner show! Look over your shoulder."

In the sky behind us, a faint white light was shimmering. It grew brighter, changed to a shade of purple, then pink and suddenly shot in a streak to the dome of the sky. Izzy and I stood up and stared through the window.

"*Aurora borealis*," Father Ron said. "It is Latin, meaning 'the northern dawn.' "

I had seen the northern lights before, glowing dimly on some northern horizon. This was different, a display of brilliant pastels that trembled over the silhouettes of the mountains, a big Wurlitzer jukebox in the sky. Ripples of color rose in layers from bottom to top and unexpectedly sent bright streamers flying so high that we had to draw close to the windows to see where they ended above our heads.

"Charged particles from the sun entering the atmosphere of the earth," Father Ron intoned. He was used to the show.

"If you gentlemen will excuse me, I am going to retire," he said, and soon he was snoring lightly in his sleeping bag. But Izzy and I sat there on the shelf through the short subarctic night watching those bright rivers of light transform the dark world. For one night only, we had the best seats on the planet for nature's most spectacular show. It faded away only with the rising of the sun. Both of us were left awed and exhausted. Neither of us has ever been able to describe that night adequately to others, though we did our best to tell Father Ron what he had missed as soon as he wakened.

"Very good, very good," he said, with a sort of pride of ownership. "We do our best to satisfy our guests in this inn. How do you take your coffee? Black, I hope."

We were just roping ourselves together at the edge of the ice field when Don Sheldon's silver Cessna appeared overhead, turned upwind and landed. Father Ron helped carry our gear out to the plane. He took off his mittens to shake hands. Izzy and I climbed aboard, waved once, and left the big, bearded prophet standing there on the glacier, alone again with only God to talk to. I have not seen or heard of him since. I hope he worked it all out up there in the mountains, but have no way of knowing.

"Pretty nice night?" Don Sheldon asked over the engine noise.

"It was okay," I said. "Not a very good place to sleep though, what with the lights coming in the window."

He chuckled. "I thought you might not mind it up there," he said. "I haven't seen every place, but it's the prettiest place I've ever seen."

"Well," I said, "me too. How can I ever thank you, Don?"

He said, "Don't thank me. I wanted to take you home with me last night. Thank the soft snow on that glacier."

That's what he said, but I wonder. I wonder whether Don Sheldon sized us up as a couple of guys who thought we were in a bigger hurry than we really were and would benefit from a night to slow down and look around and think about this place where we were.

I can't ask him. Don Sheldon had cancer then, knew he had it, and died less than a year later. You can find his name on the new Geological Survey map of Mount McKinley, printed in small letters on a white patch that represents the ice field where he landed us for coffee and wouldn't take us home from until we'd spent the night, the place he said was the prettiest he'd ever seen. The beautiful big white bowl of the Ruth Glacier where the northern lights put on their show every night is forever named the Don Sheldon Amphitheater.

19

ALUMINUM TUBES
WITH WINGS

*T*hese days, I am on the road during the week, but I always have to get back to New York on the weekend to work on the *Sunday Morning* program. So I spend a lot of time in the lines at the airline counters. Most people who have to go somewhere in America nowadays wait in those same lines. I can remember when people in those lines laughed and chatted, anticipating the exciting trips they were about to make up above the clouds. Now, they wait glumly and check their watches. This is because airline travel has changed, and they know they're not going to have any fun up there.

Once, you could fly from Denver, Colorado, to Elko, Nevada, on the same airliner. You could have a drink and a smoke and a hot meal served on a real plate and watch the mountains go by. It was always a little bumpy over the mountains, but the stewardesses never looked worried. They made the trip so nice that when it was over, you sort of hated to get off the plane.

Today, you can't go from Denver to Elko. You go to Salt Lake City instead. Your plane leaves Denver at the same time about sixty other planes are trying to leave, for Denver has become a hub for United and Continental, and you arrive in Salt Lake City at the same time about thirty other planes are trying to land, for Salt Lake City is a hub for Delta. When the plane finally makes it to an open gate, you step off into a swarming hell of connecting passengers, all of whom started their trips in Denver or Boise or Los Angeles in an attempt to get to Elko or Billings or Idaho Falls. All of them are in Salt Lake City, where none of them wishes to be. They crisscross in the maze, their suit bags flying behind them, running and cursing from Terminal C to Terminal A (for a master airline computer hums all day to assure that no passenger may ever depart from the same concourse at which he landed). For a distraught and agitated hour, they jam the bars, toilets and telephone booths and sprint down the endless corridors until the last gate is shut, the last jetway retracted and the last winged aluminum tube has departed with its cargo of sweaty passengers and misdirected luggage to wait in line out on the taxiway. Then an otherworldly peace descends upon Salt Lake City International Airport. A few lost souls wander dazed in the strange silence, having been left behind. And you—you who remember the old, easy days when airplanes flew from Denver to Elko—you are one of these. For the plane you were looking for in Salt Lake City, designated by Delta as Delta Flight 5857, is known to the people who actually fly it as Sky West 5857. This is a little trick played on you by the big airlines. Nobody back in Denver ever mentioned anything called Sky West, or that the airplane in question is the sort you must bend deeply to enter and double your legs under your chin to sit down in after divining its distant parking place. So you—you who still think of passenger airplanes as DC-9s or -10s, or at least -6s or -7s—watch from a window as something known as a Fairchild Swearingen Metro leaves without you. There will be another flight to Elko in two hours and thirty-two minutes. An Embraer EMB-110 Bandeirante, which is made in Brazil. I used to live in Brazil and watch them make things there. This Brazilian plane, they say, will go to Elko after a while. In the meantime, you have a big, quiet airport pretty much all to yourself in which to reflect on the improvement in North American air travel over the years.

Or you can rent a car and drive to Elko. At seventy miles per hour, which is as slow as anybody drives out here, and with a two-and-a-half-hour head start, you'll beat the Embraer to Nevada, and the road takes you over the Donner Trail through the Great Salt Flats, and through Wendover astride the Utah–Nevada line, my favorite state-line town, even more wonderful than Texarkana (Texas–Arkansas) where the courthouse was built on the state line and fugitives have to be extradited from one end of the hall to the other. For peculiarity, Wendover also beats Virgilina (Virginia–North Carolina) or Monida (Montana–Idaho) or Florala (Florida–Alabama), all places I have visited more than once, as it happens. Wendover is my state-line darling, for here in a single step you leave modest Mormon Utah Wendover, a town of tidy houses with prim lace curtains at the windows, and enter gaudy Nevada Wendover with neon signs that flash the words "Liquor" and "Keno" and "Casino" back into sleeping Wendover, Utah, through the desert night. One step in the same town takes you from Mountain time at midnight an hour back into Pacific time where the evening is young yet. It is the step Adam made, one step from the garden to the fast lane. Most wanderers through Wendover, children of Adam, prefer the Nevada side of town.

So you may not make it to Elko tonight after all. But at least you've made it out of the Salt Lake City hub.

Cities *want* to be airline hubs. The theory, I guess, is that a certain number of passengers will miss their planes and spend nights in town, dining and dancing and spending money freely, shopping the next morning for washer-dryers, and, who knows, station wagons, before winging on to their destinations. But regular travelers hate these wretched sprawling terminals, and eventually, by extension, the cities whose names they bear: Chicago, Atlanta, Pittsburgh, St. Louis, Dallas, Denver, Minneapolis–St. Paul. (Old question in the south: "If you die and go to hell, do you have to change in Atlanta?" Answer: "If you die in Georgia, Alabama or Mississippi, yes, you do.")

"For Your Convenience" are the words I dread. Whenever they make an airport ghastlier, they put up a sign that says they are doing it for my convenience. At friendly little old Raleigh–Durham, for example, an airport where I land often for down-home reasons collegial and familial, I used to get off the plane, walk across the street to the rental car lot, adjust the rearview mirror on the Cutlass, and be off to Chapel Hill. One day I saw a sign in the airport lobby: "For Your Convenience . . ." Now I wait for the Hertz bus in a throng at the curb. When the bus finally arrives, after the buses of Avis, National, Budget, Alamo, Sheraton, Ramada,

Holiday Inn and Airport Employees have passed, I wait for it to drive me a mile out into the piney woods and then wind through the parking lot dropping off other customers. Eventually, the driver hollers my name, points to a car, hands me my rental contract, opens the door and says, "Have a nice day." But the nice days are over. American Airlines, which never even bothered to fly to Raleigh–Durham in the nice days, now deposits thousands of passengers there whether they want to be there or not, and after an hour or two, at its convenience, picks most of these same people up and flies them somewhere else. Raleigh and Durham are very proud that their airport is now a hub. So far, it's not a big enough hub to be notorious, but it's growing and may yet become nationally despised.

Most steady customers of the airlines mention Atlanta Hartsfield and Chicago O'Hare as the abattoirs of the continent, but I have more often been hacked and bloodied at Minneapolis–St. Paul. Victims attempting connections at Minneapolis must run a fiendish gauntlet, a corridor constructed in a former cornfield on the bluffs above the Minnesota River. There is plenty of room in the cornfield to add hundreds of yards to this corridor, and every couple of years, they do. When the pathetic connecting passenger finally drags his suitcase to its end with the seconds ticking away before the departure of his outgoing flight, the smile of triumph on his face suddenly vanishes. He discovers he has not reached his goal at all. What he saw in the glimmering distance was only a mirage, the main terminal, where he now must pass out of the security zone, struggle the length of the building, line up to pass through *another* security gate and then pant down *another* interminable hallway in order to miss a connection on the same airline he came in on! I have missed so many flights on this airline and dawdled away so much time in the Minneapolis airport that employees of the gift shops and newsstands there nod to me as I pass. They think I work there too. I will not mention the name of the airline. It knows which one it is.

I miss the vanished airlines whose names described the wonderful destinations to which their planes flew directly: Western, Piedmont, Allegheny, Southern, Ozark, North Central. I miss the orderly, regulated days when I knew the airline to call if I wanted to fly from, say, Los Angeles to San Francisco. In that case, the airline was United. Everybody knew this. Flights every hour on the hour. Do you know who flies from Los Angeles to San Francisco today? Delta. (Delta used to mean the *Mississippi* Delta, for heaven's sake! Delta was how you got to New Orleans.) United still flies to San Francisco, as it happens. Also Continental, USAir, American, America West, Southwest, Northwest, Westair, Pan Am and Alaska Airlines, just to list the planes that depart before ten o'clock in the morning.

This is called competition by theorists in faraway Washington, D.C., who brought it about, free market in action, good for the public. At least one miserable member of the public, trapped aboard a cramped airplane on a Los Angeles airport taxiway, calls it chaos. The country cheered when Ronald Reagan fired all those uppity air traffic controllers, and now—how many years later?—the captain is still saying on the intercom, "Well, we're thirteenth in line to take off, folks, and we've been informed of an air traffic delay for spacing on the way up to the Bay Area, so if you'll just sit back and make yourselves comfortable for a while . . ."

You could drive to San Francisco, if they'd only let you off the plane. It is one of the great trips on the continent, up the trail of Spanish missions, San Buenaventura, Santa Barbara, Santa Maria, San Luis Obispo . . . (Then comes San Simeon, which is the most splendid of all, but should not be confused with the missions built by the Spanish padres. It was built by William Randolph Hearst, a sugar-padre, off on a mission of his own.) . . . San Carlos de Borromeo, Santa Cruz, San Jose. You could stop at Point Lobos, the country's most breathtaking meeting place of land and sea, and watch the sea otters floating around out there on their backs opening clams on their tummies. You could go shopping in Carmel, and walk around Monterey in the footsteps of the great Steinbeck, and play a quick nine holes at Pebble Beach, and buy a sack of artichokes in Castroville, Artichoke Capital of the World. California Route 1, *that's* the way to get to San Francisco.

But I know, I know. You have to meet a hot business prospect at Tadich's Grill at noon. Well, as the captain just said, sit back and make yourself comfortable. Tadich's stays open all afternoon, and this unsympathetic, unregulated corporation into whose hands you have put yourself will drop you off by the bay by and by.

I miss the fine old hand of government interference. I miss the comfortable seats and the considerate captains with gray at their temples who conducted historical tours of the landscape passing below.

"General Custer marched down from Bismarck into these Black Hills and camped at a little spot you can see down there on the right. They call it Custer now." On his flights from Denver up into the Dakotas, Captain Larry Beardsley of Frontier Airlines used to keep his passengers straining for a look at historic rivers and crumbled forts. "On up to our left about fifteen miles is the famous old western town, Deadwood City, home of Wild Bill Hickok and Calamity Jane. Wild Bill was killed in a poker game, as you no doubt recall, holding aces and eights at the time, the 'dead man's hand' . . ."

Often, when he had a few minutes to spare, Larry Beardsley would bank his Boeing 737 in a tight 360-degree turn around Mount Rushmore so that people seated on *both* sides of the plane could see the sculpted presidents; when Frontier was gobbled up by a bigger company and the new owners told him to knock it off, Captain Beardsley got so bored that he retired. Something went out of aviation that day.

They are all retired, it seems to me, the airline people who loved flying, except from the television commercials where the flight attendants still smile and bring an extra pillow. On the planes, they do not smile. They serve bad food wordlessly, pick up the empty trays mechanically and spend the rest of the flight in the galley talking about their dates and their days off. Their union representative explains that this is because they are not there to serve passengers, they are there to assure safety.

Please do not speak to me of safety. Please smile and make this trip pass as quickly and pleasantly as you can. I will do my part by smiling back, though I do not much want to be up here in the first place. Birds fly, men drink. Safety is the job of whoever's up there in the cockpit flying this thing.

I have accumulated many free miles in the airlines' frequent flyer programs. But there is a catch. To use those miles, I have to take another trip on an airline.

20

PERILS

"Thrice I have suffered shipwreck," wrote Saint Paul one day when his nerves were jangled by travel, "A night and a day I have been in the deep, in journeyings often, in perils of waters, in perils of robbers, in perils by mine own countrymen and by the heathen, in the city and the wilderness and the sea . . . in weariness and painfulness and cold."

I know. It's not all fun out there.

It helps if you make it a rule never to eat in any restaurant with kings, foxes, coaches or horses in the name. Beware of the word "gourmet." If a restaurant says it serves gourmet food, you are going to get a frozen dinner that has been warmed up in the microwave.

Do not eat in a restaurant on the top of a building. If you *must* eat in a restaurant on the top of a building, never eat in one that revolves.

Do not try to find a good restaurant in Kansas. There is much good home cooking in Kansas, but there are no good restaurants. There used to be one: the dining room of the hotel in the cowtown of Alma, but the proprietor got disgusted and moved to California, where his cooking would be appreciated. When you cross the Missouri River headed west, pack a peanut butter sandwich, for there is nothing to eat until you get to Denver.

When you go out to dinner, leave the television set on and a "Do Not

Disturb" sign on the doorknob. This may keep the maid's boyfriend from entering and stealing your suit.

Never sleep on the side of the bed next to the telephone. That is where everybody else sleeps, for the convenience of answering the morning wake-up call, and that is where beefy traveling salesmen sit during the day to call their clients. The mattress on that side of the bed is always broken down, and you will find your slumber interrupted by the need to keep grasping the uphill sheet to keep from rolling off toward the telephone.

The interstate highway system is a wonderful thing. It makes it possible to go from coast to coast without seeing anything or meeting anybody. If the United States interests you, stay off the interstates.

Carry a rubber sink stopper in your pocket. The mechanical arrangements for keeping water in motel room sinks never work.

If you rub a thin film of soap on the bathroom mirror, it will keep it from steaming up while you take your shower.

When making motel reservations, say, "Down and out, up front." They will know what you mean. A room that is downstairs with an outside entrance is easy to reach, preventing the tendonitis that afflicts the suitcase-carrying arms of travelers who convey bags down halls and up stairs. A room that is also near the front of the building will be farthest from the diesel refrigerator trucks that are invariably parked all night with their engines running. They park in back.

Always ask for dry toast at breakfast, with butter on the side, so they do not slather that greasy stuff on your toast back in the kitchen. I don't know what it is, but it isn't butter.

Pay for your breakfast with paper money only. Save all the quarters you get in change. You are going to need plenty of quarters as the day goes along, at newspaper boxes, toll booths and Coke machines. The traveler setting out without a pocketful of quarters in America today is a soldier going into battle without ammo.

If you are going from New York to Washington, avoid both the Pan Am Shuttle and the Trump Shuttle. Save time and aggravation by going on the train. Take the club car on the way down, for on the southbound Metroliner, they hook the club car right behind the engine, making for a trip smooth enough for you to read the papers and do the crossword puzzle at 100 miles per hour. Ride in an ordinary coach on the way back, however. Northbound, the club car is always the last car on the train, not the first, and it snaps around on the curves like the business end of a whip, requiring you to hold on with both hands while your complimentary seafood tidbits slide off the tray into your lap.

West of the Mississippi, travel, if possible, with your own coffeepot. The coffee gets progressively weaker from Illinois westward. My theory for this is that the pioneers ran out of coffee as they traveled west and had to re-use the grounds. Their descendants grew up liking it that way. The weakest coffee in America is served in Brookings, South Dakota. Some say Salt Lake City, but they are people who have not yet been to Brookings.

Never be without a pint of vodka. There are still dry counties in this country.

Never be without a big safety pin. The curtains of motel room windows never quite meet in the middle. They must be pinned unless you want a direct shaft of bright sunlight to fall across your eyes in the morning an hour and a half before it's time to get up.

The best suitcase—I have tried them all—is the small Lark, which expands to give you a way to bring home all the stuff you didn't have with you when you left.

You could carry a knife, scissors, tweezers, magnifying glass, can opener, corkscrew, toothpick, awl and Phillips screwdriver—or you could carry a Swiss Army knife. I find an essential use for mine nearly every day on the road.

Hotel room radios never work. If you want a little news in the morning and a little Haydn at night, as I do, you should have a fifteen-band FM/long-wave/medium-wave/shortwave/alarm clock Sony ICF-7700 in your bag. It's the size of a paperback book, weighs less than a pound, and is always there to keep you company.

If you must work at night, carry a 100-watt light bulb. Forty-watt bulbs are manufactured exclusively for the motel trade, which puts them in the lamps in the rooms. They provide enough light to find your way to the bathroom, but not enough to read by.

If you don't like loud rock music, change the settings on the rental car radio as soon as you rent the car. The guys who wash rental cars all like rock music, and the push buttons of all rental cars are set for rock stations. Sometimes *all* the buttons are set for the *same* rock station.

Whatever you order in a cafe, do not order chili. Cafe chili is invariably disappointing and potentially lethal. Red Fenwick of Denver, a western historian, told me chili was invented by a Wyoming sheepherder to keep the feet of his sheepdogs warm on cold nights. He sent some to a Texas friend, who ate it by mistake, which Texans have been doing ever since.

Gift shops are well named. There's never anything in them that you would want to keep for yourself.

Gas station attendants become more polite the farther the gas station is located from the main highway.

If you have to travel by air and connect at a hub, carry a bandage with you and wrap it around your ankle. They will call you an electric cart.

21

ANIMAL TALES

We have spent a lot of time close to the creatures of wilderness, ranch and barnyard. At the Turkey Festival in Cuero, Texas, where they herd thousands of turkeys through the streets each year, we learned they always pray for sunshine on Festival Day. If it rains, turkeys look up with their mouths open to see what's hitting them on the head. They are so dumb that they forget to look back down, and if the rain continues, the turkeys are in danger of drowning right there on Main Street.

This is what we were told. You do not pick up this sort of fact in the reading rooms of libraries, you know. You have to be out there in the field, in intimate contact with birds and animals.

We did a story about Ralphy, the remarkable swimming pig of San Marcos, Texas, for example. To tell you the truth, we got kind of sweet on the pig's trainer, a pretty young woman in a bathing suit, and probably spent a day or two longer than we should have making pictures of Ralphy in his pool. We even hired an underwater housing for the camera so we could get shots from below of that little porker paddling along. In my script, I made a big deal of the pig's accomplishment.

After the story went on the air, I got a lot of letters from farmers saying, "You idiot, *any* pig can swim!"

So now I know about turkeys and pigs. I am still finding out about horses.

I was a hell-for-leather rider back when I was Hopalong Cassidy and my horse was a broomstick, but now I dread it when we have to ride real horses to get where we are going. We put as much of our gear as we can into saddlebags and carry the rest slung about our necks. Loaded down that way, we are even gawkier on horseback than we would be riding free, which would be plenty gawky. But every ride teaches us new lessons.

After a day on horseback in the Superstition Mountains of Arizona, where we were trying to put together a story about the Lost Dutchman gold mine, I found that the insides of my legs were chafed raw and bloody from shifting in the saddle.

"Too bad," the wrangler said. "You should have wore pantyhose."

So *that's* the cowboy's secret! Under the chaps and jeans and boots—pantyhose! That's something I know about horseback riding now, but I never worked up the nerve to go into a store and ask for a pair of pantyhose in my size. Horses remain a trial.

We went on a bison roundup outside Medora, North Dakota. For television purposes, I wanted to ride my horse up to the camera, manned by Izzy on the ground, and make a short, poignant speech about the noble buffalo. I rode up to the camera all right, but the horse wouldn't stop.

"You got to pull back on the reins!" the wrangler shouted.

We tried it again. The horse and I got to the camera and I pulled back on the reins. The horse kept going.

"You got to pull back *hard* on the reins," the wrangler said.

I got the horse turned around and headed back toward Izzy. This time I practically yanked the bit down the poor animal's throat. He galloped a few yards past the camera, into just the wrong position, and stopped.

I climbed down and gave my poignant speech dismounted.

"Too bad," the wrangler said. "You got to pull back on the reins."

A while later, we were covering a mule train carrying construction material to a dam site in the California Sierra. We had to ride horses to get up there. Larry's horse kept wanting to trot on the narrow trail. Larry tried to slow him down. The horse reared, kicking at the air with his front feet. Larry fell off backward and slid down the mountainside. He got his hands and face all scratched up and bruised his ribs something terrible.

"Too bad," the wrangler said. "You shouldn't have pulled back on the reins like that."

Even when we come out of our animal episodes uninjured, we usually look back on them with a certain wry regret.

A woman wrote me a letter from Ohio. She said her parakeet could say, "And that's the way it is," like Walter Cronkite. We went there right away, of course. As soon as she opened the door, the parakeet said, "And that's the way it is!" While we set up the lights and camera there in the living room, the parakeet watched us from inside his cage and said, "And that's the way it is!" We pointed the lens at the cage and started rolling. The parakeet looked at the camera and said:

"AAAAWK!"

The parakeet's owner said, "And that's the way it is!" to give him a cue.

The parakeet said, "AAAAWK!"

"And that's the way it is!" she said patiently.

He said, "AAAAWK!"

We turned off the lights to let the parakeet calm down. We went into the kitchen and had a cup of coffee and talked about the weather and other things. Then we sauntered back into the living room, pretending to pay no attention to the parakeet in his cage. The bird's owner thought this might work. We said nothing. The parakeet said nothing. We turned on the camera again.

The parakeet said, "AAAAWK!"

After an hour or two of this, we packed up, promising to return some other time. We said good-bye to the disappointed woman who wanted to see her parakeet on Walter Cronkite's news program. We closed the front door and started down the walk to the driveway, carrying our camera and lights. Behind us in the living room, we heard the parakeet say:

"And that's the way it is!"

Then there was the lovable little shopping center dog in Florida who carried people's packages for them in his teeth. He seemed to be owned by nobody, we were told. He was petted and fed by everybody. He was especially fond of small children.

We went to the shopping center on a day when it was raining lightly.

We saw the dog. A woman had given him a small plastic bag of groceries and he was walking along beside her toward her car, carrying the bag in his teeth. His tail was wagging. It was an adorable picture. We quickly set up the camera a long distance away so as not to disturb the scene, but the darling animal spotted us. He dropped the groceries in a puddle, growled, wheeled and raced toward us, baring his fangs and snarling. We retreated. He followed us back to the bus, snapping at our heels and barking.

"For heaven's sake," said somebody passing by, "leave the poor little dog alone!"

It appears there's just something about a television camera that four-legged creatures, wild and domestic, find disconcerting. If, in Nebraska, we see a panorama of the plains with three palominos in the foreground, the sort of picture any photographer aches to capture on film, our inclination these days is to drive on by, for we know from hard experience that those ponies will probably mosey away behind a hill before Izzy can focus on the scene. For a while there, Izzy used to whistle to them to show his friendly intentions. This just made them walk away faster. He tried offering them apples and sugar cubes, which they always rejected, for the very good reason that farmers and ranchers do not give their livestock apples and sugar cubes and the animals were unfamiliar with such delicacies. In our archives are many, many pictures of the rear ends of horses. Also of moose, antelope, deer, donkeys, pigs, sheep, polar bears, squirrels, mules and chickens, some walking away disdainfully, some galloping away in fright, but all departing.

Frequently, on the road, we stop to make pictures for the nature vignettes that always close the *Sunday Morning* program. Careful viewers of these short pieces will remember that the ducks are ordinarily flying—or swimming or waddling—*away* from the camera. We have seen much of nature, but usually of nature retreating.

The shyness of animals never has been more than a time-consuming inconvenience to us—except once in west Texas, when it became a mortification. I wanted to crawl under the bed in embarrassment. As it happened, there was no bed to crawl under for many miles.

We were covering the spring cattle roundup on a big ranch in west Texas, the Kokernot spread in the rough mountain rangeland around

Marfa and Alpine. The western landscape here is so rugged that the roundup can only be accomplished the old-fashioned way, by riders on horseback. The cowboys begin with a chuck wagon breakfast before dawn and then spend a hard day in the saddle, coaxing cows and calves out of the rocky ravines and down from the precipices where they have hidden themselves during the winter. Among those crags, there are wild cows that have gone unfound year after year. It is harsh, unfenced country, and it is cowboying at its hardest—sleeping on the ground at night, riding, roping and branding under the hot sun all day. A passing thunderstorm and a downpour of rain made things worse the day we were there.

As the sun finally went down, twenty or so riders, wet, miserable and exhausted, came toward camp, herding several hundred wet, miserable, loudly objecting cattle to the corral. As they neared the corral gate, at the end of their ride at last, we walked out beside the trail to make pictures of the scene. As the lead cows passed us, Izzy pressed the button and the Arriflex film camera started with a soft whir. Only long afterward did we speculate that the sound of an Arriflex camera in operation must be, to a cow, exactly the sound of a rattlesnake coiled and preparing to strike.

The first cows in the herd bolted away from the camera, nearly running down a couple of tired riders whose horses reared to escape the charge. This sudden wild commotion ran through the whole herd in an instant horrible to see. The next thing we knew, hundreds of cattle were stampeding back along the trail, headed for the hills again, with twenty cursing cowboys spurring their horses in mad pursuit.

We stood there, suddenly utterly alone. We watched the cattle thunder into the distance, the riders galloping at full speed to try to head them, until the whole chaotic horde of cattle, men and horses disappeared from our sight.

Izzy looked at me and said, "Did *I* do that?"

A couple of hours later, in the dark of night, having finally slowed, and stopped, and turned the cattle, the cowboys had them heading back our way again. As they neared the corral for the second time, we were watching from a hundred yards away. A single rider turned and rode over to us. He stopped his horse, touched the brim of his hat politely and looked down at us from the saddle. There was mud all over his face. He said, "The foreman told me to ask you if you'd mind not taking pictures this time."

When the gate to the corral was finally shut with the cattle inside and the horses put away for the night, the cowboys came struggling over to the campfire in the dark, carrying their saddles. They threw themselves down on the ground in silence to wait for their supper.

I said, "I sure am sorry. We never imagined anything like that would happen."

They just sat there, looking into the fire. Finally, one of them said, "Oh, hell, it don't matter. Some days, that's just the way it is."

I thought of that parakeet in Ohio.

22

WHAT THEY SAY

I met a man who told me that he and his wife were too hungry to wait until they got to Waco to have their lunch, so they stopped in Mexia, Texas, for a couple of hamburgers. They knew what town they were in, but they got to speculating about how to pronounce it—me-*hee*-a, or mex-*ee*-a, or *mex*-ya. "Excuse me," the man said to the waitress, "would you tell us how you say the name of this place?"

"Sure," she said, and pronounced it for them slowly:

"*Day*-ree-*queen*."

•

I walked into the barbershop in Dillon, Montana, needing a haircut. The barber was alone in there, sweeping up the place.

"Are you free?" I asked him.

"Nope," he said, "I charge seven dollars."

•

Sign on the door of a cafe in Evansville, Indiana: "Open 24 Hours a Day, 7 Days a Week. Closed Thursdays."

•

West Virginia hills are so steep that people who live in the valleys say they have to look up their chimneys to see their cows come home.

•

Rhododendron is called "laurel" by old-timers in the Blue Ridge Mountains. Laurel is "ivy." Ivy is "vine."

•

Song at a girls' basketball game in Eagle, Nebraska, to the tune of "My Country 'Tis of Thee":

> *There ain't no flies on us,*
> *There ain't no flies on us,*
> *No flies on us.*
> *There may be one or two*
> *Great big green flies on you.*
> *There ain't no flies on us,*
> *No flies on us.*

•

Chicago cabdriver's advice to a tourist inquiring the way to Lake Michigan: "Walk east 'til your hat floats."

•

New York restaurateur on why he never considered leaving Manhattan: "Every place else is a piece of raisin cake."

•

Great Plainsman Roger Welsch on how hard the wind blows on the Plains: "People don't bother with weather vanes. They just look out the window to see which way the barn is leaning."

•

Stranger to west Texan: "Mr. Jordan?"
West Texan, sticking out his hand: "Mr. Jordan was my daddy. I'm Joe."

•

In Minnesota, the birds sing in Swedish.

•

A paper bag in Virginia is a paper sack in Vermont. A burlap bag in Illinois is a tow sack in North Carolina is a grass sack in Arkansas is a croaker sack in Georgia.

•

What is called everywhere else the beach is called in New Jersey "the Shore."

•

Things learned from Mrs. Ora Watson of Deep Gap, North Carolina:
Never kill hogs or dig potatoes in the dark of the moon.
Never make soap or cut shingles in the light of the moon.
You'll have good luck if you see a red-haired girl riding a white mule.
If a rooster crows at night, there will be snow before morning.
If your nose itches, company is coming.
If the wind is from the south on March 22nd, the summer will be dry.
If a honeybee buzzes around your head, you are about to find some money.
If you need to stop a cut from bleeding, say the sixth verse of the sixteenth chapter of Ezekiel while walking toward the sunrise.

•

Signs seen by the side of the road:
"Park Hear."
"No Trustpassing."
"No Boats Aloud."
"No Congretating On The Driveway. Vialtors Will Be Proscuated."

•

After a night of drinking, University of Nebraska students might wake up with the "brown bottle flu." If they are also throwing up, that's "calling dinosaurs."

•

North Dakota farmer on his marriage of forty years:
    "Kissing don't last, but good cooking does."

•

Breakfast in east Tennessee, described by a Jonesboro innkeeper: "Get yourself a jug of good corn liquor, a thick beefsteak and a hound dog. Then feed the beefsteak to the hound dog."

•

The earth is so rich in Missouri that if you plant a nail, it will grow into a spike by morning.

•

How to say "I don't believe it" politely:
    In Iowa: "Could be."
    In Maine: "I imagine."
    In Wyoming: "You reckon?"
    In Arkansas: "That's a new one on me!"

•

Graffito on toilet stall wall in a truck stop in northern Idaho:
    "I hate this part of Texas."

•

Scrawled on the toilet seat paper cover dispenser in the Albuquerque airport:
    "Free Cowboy Hats!"

•

Scratched on the prophylactic machine in a truck stop in Iowa:
    "This gum tastes like rubber."

•

Jim Griffith of Tucson on the size of western mosquitoes:
    "There was one, I remember it was in the papers at the time, there

was one that come into Nellis Air Force Base, and they were about to fill it up with high-octane fuel until they realized it had the wrong markings on it."

•

Heard in the hills:
"She's as ugly as homemade soap."
"He's too blind to see through a barbed-wire fence."
"He's such a liar he has to get somebody else to call his hogs."
"She was born tired and raised lazy."
"He ain't worth the salt that goes into his bread."
"She's on the down-go. She ain't got the strength to brush the hen off the roost."

•

Q: How many Californians does it take to change a light bulb?
A: Six. One to change the bulb and five to share the experience.

•

Sign behind the bar in Laramie, Wyoming: "Don't Buy A Drink Before Seeing That Your Baby Has Shoes."

•

In Natchitoches, Louisiana, they say they have more morality and more immorality than any other town. There's nearly as much immorality down the road in Alexandria, they say, and no morality at all.

•

Pennsylvania Dutch farm wife to her husband:
"Throw the mule over the fence some hay."

•

Key Largo fisherman to his wife:
"I'll be home at day-down, right about the pink of the evenin'."

23

BRUSHES WITH
THE FAMOUS

*F*enwick, Connecticut, is a collection of fine old houses on the Long Island Sound, the sort of big, rambling, shingled dwellings that were called "cottages" by the wealthy Connecticut Yankees who summered there at the turn of the century. My friend Oliver Jensen, author and historian, lives in one of those houses, does his writing there at a window overlooking the Saybrook breakwater, and regales his guests in the evenings with yarns about American railroading and seafaring and the settlement of old New England. Izzy and Larry and I used to drop by to see Oliver whenever we needed a well-told historical tale.

We were filming one summer afternoon on the Jensens' spacious porch facing the sound when a ruckus arose out on the water. A boy had fallen out of the speedboat he had been driving. He was in the water about fifty yards offshore and the empty boat was roaring around him in circles, threatening on each pass to run him down—a really frightening situation for him and for the handful of people who could see his predicament from shore. Nobody was doing anything, though; nobody could figure out what to do.

Izzy, who spent part of his youth as a lifeguard on the beach at Venice, California, took one look at this scary state of affairs and sprinted for the dock of a big neighboring house where a rowboat was tied up. We watched him free the boat, jump in and start rowing as fast as he could toward the kid in the water. A few people on shore shouted encouragement. The youngster was still managing to escape the runaway boat's repeated passes by dodging away each time it came knifing by, but we could tell he was getting tired out there.

Izzy, rowing hard, planned to wait for the empty speedboat to go by, then rush in, pick up the boy and try to make a safe getaway. Just as he approached the scene, however, a couple of fast powerboats came speeding in from the sound. The driver of one of them fell in beside the runaway craft. A young passenger grasped the gunwale of the empty boat, steadied himself, then tumbled into the cockpit and shut down the engine. The other newly arrived boat stopped beside the boy in the water and plucked him to safety. Big cheers for this performance arose from the little knot of people watching.

Izzy, no longer needed, turned the rowboat around and made the long trip back to the dock where he started. When he got there, all tired out, a woman was standing on the dock wearing dark glasses and a scarf. She said, "I saw it all. You were quite magnificent. Thank you for what you did." Izzy held an oar up to her and said gruffly, "Pull me in, will you?" She did, and helped him tie up the boat.

Izzy came walking back to us from the dock of the big house looking shaken. He sat down on the steps of Oliver's porch.

"That was great, Iz," I said.

Izzy didn't say anything.

I said, "I mean you looked like the old lifeguard out there."

He still didn't say anything. I figured he was exhausted from his effort.

After a while, Izzy said, "Do you know who I just stuck an oar at and ordered to pull me in to the dock?"

"Who?" I said.

He said, "Katharine Hepburn."

I said, "Are you sure?"

Oliver Jensen laughed. "Whose dock did you think that was?" he said. "Whose rowboat did you think you were using?"

Izzy sat in silence another minute or two. Then he said, "Do you know what Katharine Hepburn said to me? She said I was magnificent. And do you know what I said to her?"

"What?"

"I said, 'Pull me in, will you?' "

I could tell he was miserable.

"Hell, she didn't mind, Iz," I said. "She *did* it, didn't she?"

He just looked out at the water.

I remember the day as the one on which Izzy reacted to danger so quickly and behaved so heroically. He remembers it as the day he failed for one horrible moment to recognize his favorite actress of all time and treated her as if she were a dockhand.

Our brushes with the famous have almost always been by accident like that. Famous people get plenty of coverage; battalions of reporters seek them out. So we intentionally go looking for people you wouldn't expect to read about on the front pages or see on the evening news. But when we've stumbled upon a household name, we have almost always found the person behind the name to be friendly and agreeable—even willing to pull a stranger in a rowboat into a dock when ordered to. I know that some rich, famous and powerful people enjoy acting rich, famous and powerful, but the best of them don't. Maybe it's their memories of youthful struggle, or a certain discomfort with the perquisites and praise that are lavished on them all the time, but it turns out that many celebrated people are just folks when you get to know them.

We were in Haines, Alaska, one fall, making pictures of eagles. Haines is at the end of the dusty 650-mile road that comes down from Fairbanks through the Yukon. If you want to go on from Haines, you have to fly or hire a fishing boat, because Haines is where the road runs out. There's a sawmill there and the Captain's Choice Motel on the harbor and Bell's Store and a good cafe bearing the unlikely name of Bamboo Room. Most of the people in Haines are very friendly to strangers and do not ask too many questions, for the town attracts travelers who seem to be running away from something somewhere else. People reach the end of the road in Haines and collect there for a few days or weeks. Some of them just stay. Among the permanent residents are a former New York debutante, the worldly son of a Wehrmacht officer who plotted against Hitler and an Indian woman who always walks in the middle of the street.

The eagles come in November. Bald eagles are scarce and endangered in most of the country, of course, but when the salmon run up the

Chilkat River in November to spawn and die, the eagles fly in by the hundreds to feed on their carcasses. You can drive a few miles out of Haines on the road to Klukwan and see flocks of bald eagles soaring nobly in the air, posing in the trees and behaving just like vultures among the dead salmon on the riverbank.

One morning, I was in Haines with Shad Northshield, founding producer of *Sunday Morning*, naturalist and old friend, and a cameraman named Bob Dunn. We were surprised to see a man walking down the street who bore a great resemblance to Senator Howard Baker. He had a camera in his hand and a film bag over his shoulder. He was accompanied by a small retinue of aides and greeters, which, I realized, meant that undoubtedly he *was* Senator Howard Baker. He was one of the country's most important politicians at the time, Senate Minority Leader, and, it was rumored, a likely candidate for President. As we met on the sidewalk, I said, "If you don't mind my saying so, this is a hell of a place to start your Presidential campaign."

He laughed and said, "I know you from television, and I'd say I'm here for the same reason you are. Which way are the eagles?"

I pointed north up the Klukwan road. Senator Baker had been in Anchorage the night before to make a speech. He was an avid photographer of considerable ability, and it was well known that he never went anywhere without his cameras and lenses. Somebody had told him about the eagles of Haines and he had decided to detour for a couple of hours on the way back to Washington for the rare chance at some head-and-shoulder close-ups of the national bird. It was beginning to snow. Somebody handed Senator Baker a parka. He pulled it on over his coat and tie and piled into a van to be driven off in search of eagle pictures.

We had eagle pictures of our own to make that day. The snowfall grew heavier along the river, coated the blue-green limbs of the spruce trees, and made for splendid portraits of the big birds in windblown wintry settings. When we got back to town after dark and walked down the slippery street to the Bamboo Room for our nightly steak, we were surprised to find Senator Baker there having dinner with two of his young aides.

"I thought you were leaving this afternoon," I said.

"Too much snow," he said cheerfully. "Airplane can't take off. Pull up a couple of chairs and join us!"

One of his assistants said, "We have to get the Senator back to Washington tomorrow. Any ideas?"

"Can't get back to Washington if the airplane can't take off," Senator Baker said with a shrug and a smile. He spent the evening comparing notes with Shad, a splendid photographer of birds, on the fine points of shutter speeds and lens apertures when photographing eagles in a snowstorm.

He was still smiling at breakfast the next morning, at lunch the next afternoon, and at dinner the next night. Back in Washington, the Senate was preparing to go into session with its Minority Leader snowbound in a small town at the end of the road 3,500 miles away. The snowstorm turned into a full-blast southeastern Alaska blizzard. Drifts piled up outside the Captain's Choice, which had found rooms for the Senator and his retinue. His aides fretted on the phones. Senator Baker walked happily around town in the heavy snow, freed by an act of God from whatever crushing national responsibilities awaited him at his office back at the Capitol. I imagined these were the first days he had enjoyed for many years with absolutely nothing to do.

Still another day went by before the storm passed and they were able to clear the snow from the airstrip at Haines. So we had another breakfast, lunch and dinner with Senator Howard Baker (G.O.P.–Tenn.). While his aides looked glumly out the window at the snow piling up, he told us funny inside tales of life at the top in Washington. He told us stories on Lyndon Johnson, Richard Nixon and George Bush, with the unspoken understanding that these yarns would not be retold anywhere outside the Bamboo Room Cafe. I got the impression his assistants thought their boss was being a little reckless with his storytelling, and the equally strong impression that he was having the time of his life. He was the most agreeable big-time politician I had ever come across—certainly the funniest Republican—and he struck me as wise and humane besides. I decided that if he did run for President, I might have to vote for him.

The blizzard ended, the sun came out, and we all left Haines and the snow and the eagles behind us and went our separate ways. Howard Baker didn't run for President. He became President Ronald Reagan's chief of staff instead, at a time when the Reagan White House was beleaguered and much in need of help. I sent him a telegram: "MY GOD, LOOK WHERE YOU'RE SNOWED IN NOW!" but I never got a reply. By then, his joyful respite in a small town in Alaska, the gift of the snowflakes, was long past and Howard Baker was up to his ears in affairs of state again.

I've always been a little diffident when meeting people who are very well known, reluctant to take up too much of their time. This is not the approved attitude for reporters, I know; how far would Mike Wallace have come if he had been the least bit in awe of moguls, mobsters, presidents and kings? (To tell you the truth, after thirty years of acquaintance, I find I am still a little bit in awe of Mike Wallace!)

But the great Eudora Welty, who should have been writing that afternoon, insisted that I spend a couple of hours with her in her parlor in Jackson, Mississippi. She even opened a bottle of old bourbon so fine that it didn't have a label, only a number inscribed by pen in a fine hand, a gift, she said, from her friend Robert MacNeil of PBS. She talked about her Mississippi upbringing and her days in journalism, thoughtfully about the art of the short story, about good young writers she hoped to encourage, and when I left, walked me down her sidewalk to the curb and bestowed on me a parting smile that felt like a benediction. I knew about her genius from reading her books; that afternoon, I learned about Eudora Welty's generosity.

Andrew Wyeth and his son Jamie spent the better part of a day with Shad, Izzy, Larry and me, strolling about the splendid, small Wyeth museum in Pennsylvania. It was a day in March when the brown landscape around Chadds Ford looked like a melancholy Andrew Wyeth painting.

"Yes," he said, "I like Pennsylvania this time of year, this open country with patches of snow and the feeling of deep earth below. My father and I were great friends, but we had arguments. He said, 'Andy, you paint this country only in its severe feeling.' 'Well,' I said, 'that's what I like about it.' If you get to know these farmers here intimately, as I have, you know they have had a tough time, and you begin to realize the power of this country, and its somber mood."

He looked out across the land in silence for a while.

"I can look at that hill there. To me, it's not just a hill with snow on it. It's a hill that I know. In painting it, I can fly across the valley and land on the top of that hill and be a part of that hill. It's part of me. I've played there. I've walked over it. It's real.

"I just find the more I look, the more I see, the more I feel, and I want to go deeper. I have not exhausted the ground I stand on. . . ."

I have met a lot of men and women who seemed inseparable from their times and places, but none so much an element of the land as that one man in that one place, Andrew Wyeth in Pennsylvania in the spring.

The Wyeths take care for their privacy, as they must, but they can still make a new acquaintance feel like an old friend. Jamie and his graceful wife, Phyllis, invited Shad and me to dinner at their farmhouse that night. I was distracted from the Wyeth conversation by the Wyeths all over the walls. They were hanging there casually, wonderful pictures I had seen before only in books.

I had a note from Andrew Wyeth when I got home: "Come back and see us at the Mill again when you have more time." I know I'll never do that, not, heaven knows, because of any shortage of my time, but out of consideration for his. I'd hate to interrupt the old lion in his den on a day when he happened to have some surpassing new masterpiece half finished on his easel. There is plenty of artistic chitchat in this world, but there can never be enough Wyeths.

By another accident of timing, I spent a few days in the company of Marlon Brando. He wasn't very good company. For Brando, I guess I have to make an exception to my rule that the very famous, down deep, are just like you and me. Marlon Brando is not one bit like you and me.

I was covering a big public squabble between the state of Washington and the Puyallup Indians over fishing rights. The Indians claimed they had the right to fish for salmon out of season on their reservation; the state said that would ruin fishing everywhere in Puget Sound. The dispute dragged on for weeks, with the Puyallups catching fish and the state Fish and Game wardens issuing them citations and taking them into court.

A few days before a big Indian demonstration was planned for the state capitol steps in Olympia, Marlon Brando showed up from Hollywood and moved into a suite on the same floor of the same hotel where I was staying. I don't think anybody invited him, but Brando was eager to be known as a supporter of Indian causes, and he brought along a beautiful brunette secretary to handle his press releases. The reporters all crowded around the movie star, of course. I noticed this did not exactly thrill the Puyallup fishermen, who saw the attention the press had been giving to their struggle suddenly shift over to Brando. Hearing that he was in Olympia, Brando groupies came rushing to town from all over the northwest. One of them, a pretty, star-struck farm girl from Yakima, was more persistent than the rest. She climbed atop a soft-drink vending machine outside Brando's hotel room door, one of those low, old-fashioned boxes that gave you a Coke for a nickel, and sat there with her legs dangling down. Whatever the hour I walked down the hall, she was there. She said her name was Flo. Every time Brando entered or left the room, she was there, looking at him from atop the Coke machine. He never spoke to her. She never spoke to him. She was just there. After a couple of days, this began to irritate the gorgeous secretary who was occupying Brando's suite. I heard the two of them arguing about Flo in the coffee shop one morning.

Brando's trip was going sour in other ways, too. His aim was to catch an illegal salmon on reservation waters, get arrested and make headlines to publicize the Indian cause. Morning after morning, he went out and trolled a salmon lure from a boat with a flotilla of photographers following and the Fish and Game officers watching from a respectful distance. The problem was that Marlon Brando was a movie star, not a fisherman. He couldn't catch a fish. He worked at it, from midmorning until late afternoon, in bright sun and driving rain, but the salmon would not yield to his fame. This became a joke to everybody but Brando. The reporters and photographers started drifting away to other assignments, which made Brando moody and angry. One day, around a little bend close to shore, he found a dead salmon floating in the water. He plucked it out and went looking for the Fish and Game boat. He presented this deceased relic to the officers triumphantly, expecting to be arrested at last. The chief of the detail regarded the limp fish suspiciously, sniffed it, and handed it back.

"I'm sorry, Mr. Brando," he said. "This one won't do." Brando headed for shore in disgust.

He went out drinking with Hunter Thompson, who gained fame later as the gonzo journalist chronicler of the Hell's Angels and other misfits, like the Presidential Press Corps. At the time, Hunter was a relatively orthodox reporter for a Dow Jones weekly, *The National Observer.* I knew him from Rio, where I had once lent him bail money to get out of jail after he had slugged a guy who had kicked a dog in a bar. Hunter told Brando he suspected I was growing tired of the Indian fishing story and was about to pull out with the CBS crew. Brando went to a phone, called me at the hotel and spoke to me as seriously as a man with several double scotches under his belt can speak. He said, "If you leave this town before I catch a fish, you scum, I will find you wherever you are and kill you with my own hands."

That night, he had another quarrel with his beautiful dark-haired companion. She went storming out of the suite carrying her suitcase and took a limousine to the Seattle–Tacoma airport. I thought about Brando's threat. I decided there was no way *Marlon Brando* was going to stalk *me* around the country. So I decided to give up, too, on the long-running saga of the Puyallups and the movie star and made plane reservations for the next morning.

I don't think Marlon Brando helped the Indian cause much, or furthered his own reputation either as Indian rights crusader or salmon fisherman. The press and the public, and maybe the fish, too, were all pretty weary of him before he left town. There weren't any winners.

Except Flo.

As I was passing Brando's suite on my way to bed that night, the door opened, and Brando himself stood in the doorway. He ignored me. He looked straight at Flo, the adoring farm girl from Yakima, who was still sitting atop the Coke machine with her legs dangling off. She looked back at him. She hopped down and walked into his room, and Marlon Brando followed her and closed the door.

Other brushes with the famous, let's see:

We keep running into Pete Seeger, who could give Brando lessons in dedication to causes. Clean rivers, racial justice, homes for the homeless, gay rights, you give the demonstration and Pete will come sing at it. I admire him for his passion, and I like his singing. Pete Seeger is the legitimate heir to Woody Guthrie and all the wandering troubadours of history. Inscribed around the rim of his banjo are the words "This Machine Surrounds Hate and Forces It to Surrender."

I'll always be glad I met Archibald MacLeish. I was knocked out by his poems in college. Like a lot of other people, I thought he must have written them directly to me. Soon after the new satellite made it possible, I moderated a transatlantic television discussion in which MacLeish took part from New York, as did Prime Minister Harold Wilson from London. This was a brand-new thing. The picture was one-way only. Those of us in New York could see the participants in London; they could only hear us. Somebody said to me before the program started, "I don't think Wilson and MacLeish have ever met. Maybe you ought to introduce them." So I said, "Excuse me, Prime Minister . . ." On the screen, MacLeish and I could see him look up at the camera. "Before we begin," I said, "I would like to introduce Mr. Archibald MacLeish."

"Indeed, indeed," Wilson said, "I am very glad to meet you, Mr. MacLeish!" As he spoke, the Prime Minister of Great Britain stood up to acknowledge the blind introduction of a man who was thousands of miles away. Seeing this, MacLeish also stood. And I, feeling awkward but not knowing what else to do, stood up too.

"I very much admire your poems," Wilson said, and started saying one of them: " 'A poem should be palpable and mute . . . as a globed fruit . . .' " When he finished quoting "Ars Poetica" to its author, the Prime Minister sat down and presently the program began. When we were off the air, MacLeish said to me, "Wasn't that the damnedest thing, Wilson standing up that way? That's a lesson in the intimacy of television, the power of it. We were all on the same program, so to him it was as if we were all in the same room."

I saw Archibald MacLeish one or two times again before he died, was always impressed that erudition and humanity could come together so felicitously in one man, and was proud of our acquaintance. I always wanted to hear him talk about poetry. He always wanted to talk about television, about Prime Minister Wilson standing up that time in London to acknowledge the introduction of someone in New York. "Just the damnedest thing," he said. "It will become commonplace, I suppose."

Whenever I see Ted Koppel's nightly worldwide panel discussions which today's technology have made perfectly commonplace, I always think of the great old poet who saw the future coming.

Alf Landon was interested in communications, too. "As Maine goes, so goes the nation" was the truism in Presidential elections until Alf Landon came along. He was the progressive Republican Governor of Kansas who lost the Presidency to Franklin D. Roosevelt in the famous landslide of 1936. Even his home state, where Governor Landon was very popular, went for FDR that year. Landon carried only rock-ribbed Republican Maine and Vermont—"leading," he never tired of joking, "to the familiar political saying, 'As Maine goes, so goes Vermont.' "

Alf Landon was well up into his eighties when Izzy and Larry and I went to see him to ask him about the changes he had noticed in the lives of Kansas farmers over the years. He sat in a rocking chair on his big front porch in Topeka dressed in boots and jodhpurs, fresh from his daily horseback ride.

"Communications!" he said. "That's the ticket! That's the thing that's made all the difference in the farmer's life."

I told him I expected him to say improved feed and seed and fertilizer and farm machinery.

"Communications!" he repeated. "The seed question was all settled way back at the beginning when the Russian immigrants came out here on the Union Pacific Railroad with those hard, red winter wheat seeds in their pockets. That's the wheat that feeds the whole country now. Most years, it helps feed several other countries, including Russia, where it came from in the first place.

"No, the Kansas farmer always had good land and good seed. But the problem was he lived an isolated life, see? He and his family didn't know what was going on. He could be a good farmer, but he had no way to be a good citizen. And do you know what changed that? It wasn't FDR. It was . . ."

He leaned forward and confided the secret of Kansas progress:

"RFD!"

"Rural Free Delivery?"

"Correct!" Alf Landon said. "It was the idea of the Democrats. I remember when it came in," he said, his eyes twinkling as he leaned back in his rocking chair.

I checked later and found he would have remembered the start of rural mail delivery, all right. It was an innovation of the second Cleveland administration. That's how far back Alf Landon's political memory went.

"All the bankers and merchants were against it," he said. "They thought it was a terrible waste of money. But it made all the difference to the farmers, see? It meant they didn't have to wait 'til Saturday when they came to town to find out the news. They could get a newspaper in the mailbox every day and read the news after supper and discuss it around the table. That's when farmers became as smart as everybody else."

I agreed that it is pretty hard to find a hayseed in the country anymore. The old vaudeville figure of fun, the country bumpkin, seems to have vanished from the land.

"Yes," Alf Landon said, "if you think you've found one, and ask him how his sorghum crop is coming along, he's liable to reply with some smart remark he heard on the Johnny Carson show. Everybody knows all the same news and the same jokes now. There aren't any country hicks for the politicians and the traveling salesmen to trick. That's good for the country, see?"

We never passed through Topeka after that without paying our respects to Governor Landon. He rode his horse every day until he was ninety-three, saw his daughter, Nancy Kassebaum, elected to the U.S. Senate—probably not without some advice from her old man—and lived on to be 100, never losing interest in the welfare of Kansas farmers or the beneficial effects of spreading the news around so everybody can be in on it.

I have always had heroes. Some of them became friends, people I work with who do the same things I do and outdo me: Morley Safer, Harry Reasoner, Andy Rooney, Bruce Morton, Dick Threlkeld, Charles Osgood, Tom Fenton and John Leonard, whose television essays on *Sunday Morning*, full of metaphor and allusion, always leave me dazzled.

My line of work has given me the chance to meet others I long admired from afar; not once do I remember being disappointed.

I sat next to Mickey Mantle on an airplane flight from Dallas to New York, hesitantly introduced myself and was rewarded with a guileless Oklahoma grin and a string of great yarns about those other heroes, Casey and Billy and Whitey.

I went to a dinner honoring Norman Corwin, the princely user of words who, with *On a Note of Triumph* and other masterpieces, elevated the radio documentary beyond mere craft to art. I have held Corwin in reverent respect since I first came upon a book of his radio plays when I was in high school; I can hardly believe that now I carry on a regular correspondence with him, getting more than I give.

I saw Adlai Stevenson, Hubert Humphrey and John F. Kennedy close up. I spent a day talking with Eleanor Roosevelt, after she amiably permitted me to pin a microphone to the bra of her corset.

I met people who were better at what they did than anybody else: the sculptor, Henry Moore; the sportswriter, Red Smith; the singer, Mabel Mercer; the author, Teddy White. They were everything I'd imagined they'd be.

Plenty of reporters meet more celebrities in a month than I have met in a lifetime on the road, but I am contented with this register of congenial artists, writers and politicians—and one egomaniacal actor for spice. I have one more name to add.

Except on records, I had never heard Vladimir Horowitz play the piano until the day he played for me in his living room. He was eighty-two years old. He hadn't played much in public for many years, and when he did play a concert, tickets were notoriously hard to come by. Anyway, I thought this wasn't a bad way for me to begin my encounter with the fabled maestro—leaning on his Steinway while he sat at the keyboard pounding away mercilessly to make a musical point.

"This is what is wrong with pianists today!" he shouted over the sound of the music. "They treat the piano as if it were a percussive instrument! No, no! It is all wrong, you see." He stopped pounding and caressed the same notes of Chopin from the piano softly and slowly, with his palms below the keyboard, his long fingers arching upward to touch the keys. "More like this," he said. He played for a few more seconds. "Is better," he said, looking up for agreement.

Who was I to disagree? I was a former third-chair, third clarinet player in the high school band. He was Horowitz, the last of the Romantics, the transcendent pianist of the world. I wasn't exactly alone with him. To begin with, no stranger ever was alone with Horowitz; he was eternally guarded and attended by his formidable wife, Wanda, daughter of Toscanini. She defended him from fools, reporters and autograph-seekers—I was there that day in all three of these capacities—and she defended him from himself. The great man had human tendencies. While strolling down the street, he might have popped into a bar for a few beers with the boys had it not been for Wanda's stern hand on his elbow.

Besides, on this day, the Horowitz living room in New York was cluttered with lights, cables, cameras and TV technicians. Izzy and Larry were there, and Shad Northshield, among many others. A momentous announcement had recently rocked the world of classical music: Horowitz was going to play a concert in the land of his birth, the Soviet Union, to be telecast worldwide. By inflexible tradition, all Horowitz concerts began at four P.M. on Sunday afternoon. Four in the afternoon Moscow time is Sunday morning in New York. *Sunday Morning!* Shad quickly negotiated with Peter Gelb, Horowitz's manager, the right to broadcast the concert on CBS as an expanded version of our *Sunday Morning* program. We were all crowded into the Horowitz town house for a predeparture interview, with the great man at center stage and Wanda an unsmiling presence off camera.

"I think that is enough piano playing," she said to her husband. "And more than enough criticism of other pianists. Do come back and sit on the sofa." He obeyed, and the cameras dutifully refocused on him as he settled into the soft cushions and took an envelope from his inside jacket pocket.

"Look," he said, "I even have a letter from my niece in Kharkov!" I said, "Will you read it to us?"

"But it is in Russian," he said coyly. "You won't understand it."

"But you can translate," I said.

"Ahh!" he said with a playful smile. "You want it in English! It is written in Russian. But very well, I shall try:

" 'Dear Volodya, is it true you are coming? We will come to meet you at the airport. . . . We will be so happy to see you. I have always dreamed of hearing you in concert, and now my dream will come true. . . . We are waiting for you.' "

Horowitz looked up from his translation of the letter to say, "I last saw her when she was nine years old. Now she is seventy!"

Horowitz left Russia in 1925, a beautiful twenty-two-year-old boy from Kiev. He was already celebrated in his homeland for the pyrotechnics of his piano style. Even the Bolshevik border guards knew who he was. One of them, Horowitz remembered, put a hand on his shoulder and told him gravely, "While you are gone, do not forget your motherland." Horowitz was touched by this admonition, but also profoundly relieved that the guard didn't require him to remove his shoes, for in them were hidden thousands of American dollars to finance his concert tour of Germany.

His exit visa permitted him to be gone for six months. He overstayed it by sixty years. He received his United States citizenship in 1942, and often said he had no wish to return to the Soviet Union.

But with old age, he began to yield to a desire to see Russia once more before he died. When the cultural exchange agreement between the United States and the Soviet Union was reinstated in 1985, Horowitz wondered aloud to Peter Gelb if he might not return as "an ambassador of peace." Gelb knew right away, of course, that a Horowitz concert in Moscow would become, automatically, one of the musical events of the century. He dashed off to Washington to start making arrangements. When he was able to assure the finicky maestro and the doubtful Wanda that the trip could be carried off in the customary Horowitz style— comfortable apartment in Spaso House, residence of the American ambassador; the Steinway company's chief technician on hand to tend Horowitz's own piano; a supply of Dover sole flown in daily from Paris— Horowitz said yes, and the trip was announced.

Mikhail Gorbachev's policy of *glasnost*, openness, had not taken hold in Russia in the spring of 1986. Though they had agreed to it, the Soviets were not, in fact, particularly open to the return of a native who had skipped the country more than sixty years before, no matter how famous he had become in the meantime. The impending concert was big news among music lovers in the United States. In Moscow, there was nothing in the newspapers or on the radio or television. The great event was announced only on a single poster that appeared one morning on the pale yellow wall of the Moscow Conservatory of Music. The poster said a piano recital would be presented at four P.M. Sunday, April 20, by "Vladimir Horowitz (USA)." In a music-loving city like Moscow, however, one poster was all it took. The news was all over town within hours. As it turned out, 1,400 seats in the conservatory's beautiful Great Hall were reserved for government officials and members of the diplomatic corps, leaving only 400 tickets for sale to the general public. People stayed up all night in a long line to buy those precious few. Minutes after the box office opened in the morning, the concert was sold out.

Elena Dolberg, the niece who wrote to Horowitz from Kharkov, did come to the Moscow airport to meet her celebrated uncle as Horowitz and his entourage stepped off a flight from Paris. Volodya was back at last, and the two old relatives ignored our television lights and a small crowd of European reporters for a time as they sat in a corner of the airport lounge holding hands and exchanging reminiscences.

After that, we didn't see much of Horowitz. He secluded himself in Ambassador Arthur Hartman's capacious official residence under the watchful eye of Wanda, making a pilgrimage only to the house of the composer Aleksandr Scriabin, who had praised the playing of the young Horowitz once upon a time. There, on Scriabin's piano, he played Scriabin études to the delight of Scriabin's daughter Yelena and a small group of American onlookers. He seemed to want to stay and play longer, but—well, you know. Wanda. She guided him toward the door.

The Soviets weren't much help to our little band of visitors from CBS. I arrived on an Aeroflot flight from London with Al Balisky, the genial chief tape editor of *Sunday Morning*. He wasn't so genial when the immigration officials got through with him. First, a sharp-eyed officer discovered a spot of smudged ink on his visa and led Al away to a holding room for an hour and a half while this possible forgery was straightened out. Then, while minutely searching his luggage, they found a music cassette he had brought along for diversion featuring Sly and the Family Stone, and we had to wait another hour for the censor of rock music to be summoned. By the time this functionary showed up, declared Sly harmless to the Soviet state and waved us into the country, the night was getting late. We were tired and famished on the long taxi ride to the Intourist Hotel. All the hotel bars and restaurants had closed, except for a crowded roof cafe where a woman was frying beefsteaks on a grill. Around us, people were eating steaks. Al walked up to the counter and caught the cook's attention. "Two steaks," he said, holding up two fingers. "*Nyet* steaks!" she exclaimed. She scooped the steaks off the grill, put them all in a refrigerator and pointed to the only food that was left—a single bit of smoked fish on a tiny round of stale brown bread, the last of the early evening hors d'oeuvres. Al paid her for it, said, "Welcome to Moscow, Charles," and bit the morsel in half. He handed me the other half. I swallowed it, and we went to bed wondering what kind of country it is that cooks steaks and then puts them in the icebox for the night.

We had plenty to do to prepare for the concert. But if you were a foreign TV journalist in Moscow in those days, you didn't do anything without a "keeper," an official from Gostelradio who went everywhere with you, served as interpreter and censor, and undoubtedly turned in a report on your activities to the KGB each evening. Our keeper was an attractive young woman named Nona. Nona kept telling Izzy and Larry and me all the things we couldn't take pictures of and making a nuisance of herself, but we understood that was her job and kidded her along. Nona was working on improving her English. She carried a little notebook full of colloquialisms she had picked up from other camera crews, with English definitions.

"This town is giving me the heebie-jeebies," Larry said one day.

"Please, what is heebie-jeebies?" Nona said. We explained and she wrote it down.

We needed to build a small camera platform for the concert. "Maybe we can find a few two-by-fours somewhere," Izzy said.

"Please," Nona said, "what is two-by-four?"

One day when we were in a hurry, our taxi driver made a U-turn to get us into the conservatory driveway. A policeman wearing white gloves appeared from behind a post and motioned the taxi over to the curb.

"Tell him to fuck off," Izzy said.

Nona got out and talked to the cop and got the cabdriver off the hook. When she came back to the car, Izzy said, "I noticed you didn't put 'fuck off' in your notebook."

Nona said, "I've already got that one."

On the Friday afternoon before the concert, Horowitz came to the hall to rehearse. The hall was packed with music students and their professors. Horowitz paced about on the stage, meticulously checking the lighting and the placement of the piano. He sat down at the piano and played a few dissonant chords, clowning with Izzy, who was up there respectfully taping the whole thing. Then, sensing the expectations of the audience, he began to play seriously. A great silence settled on the hall. The rehearsal became a concert, prelude to the advertised one to follow. Peter Gelb stood beaming offstage. He said later that this "rehearsal" was one of the finest Horowitz performances he had ever heard.

The students cheered Horowitz for many minutes. They followed him into the conservatory courtyard and mobbed his car. In spite of the best efforts of a cordon of police, it took nearly half an hour for the limousine to make it fifty feet to the street. And after the car had escaped the crowd of young admirers and sped away, the students remained in the courtyard in small groups, discussing what they had heard.

It was raining two days later when the afternoon of the formal concert arrived. I got to the hall three hours early and had to work my way through a huge crowd standing under umbrellas in the street. These were people who knew they would not hear a note. They just wanted to be able to say they were there.

At the appointed hour, the applause began as a thunderclap from the seats at stage right as a slight old man in a dark blue suit and tidy gray bow tie appeared in the wings. The applause swept through the audience and was joined by cheers as he shambled to the center of the stage, gave the crowd a shrug and a nervous grin, patted his piano as if to reassure the instrument and himself, and sat down to wait for silence.

I was watching from a box at the back of the great hall. When that small man alone on that big stage put his fingers upon the keys to play the first notes of a Scarlatti sonata, a chill ran down my back. Vladimir Horowitz (USA), at the age of eighty-two, after an absence of more than sixty years, was playing again in the country of his birth.

He played with great subtlety and great power. He gave the crowd rainbows and thunderstorms, while looking down at his fingers with a bemused expression, as if he were as astonished as the rest of us by the remarkable, nimble things those fingers could do. It was a hell of a performance, which millions of people have heard by now. The Deutsche Grammophon recording of it became the worldwide classical best-seller for more than a year. By the time Horowitz reached the music of the Russian composers Rachmaninoff and Scriabin, many in the audience were weeping.

At intermission, a concertgoer said, "It is not human. It can only come from heaven." "He is the only pianist who can play colors," said another. A Soviet pianist in the audience told an interviewer, "His music is just bits of beauty flowing through the air." The headline on page one of *The New York Times* next day read "For Horowitz in Moscow, Bravos and Tears."

On the lofty State Department–Foreign Ministry level, relations between the United States and the Soviet Union were tense just then. The U.S. Air Force had bombed Libya, and the Soviet government had reacted angrily. The world's television screens had been full of warlike images for a week. Now, on those same screens, appeared the wistful image of a great Russian-born American pianist playing for a Russian audience Schumann's tender "Träumerei," one of the *Scenes from Childhood*. The emotional message implied by Horowitz's choice of encores was lost on nobody in the hall, and he played the piece gently, softly, as if lost in a private reverie.

Back home in New York, my friend Andy Rooney, who often plays curmudgeon on *60 Minutes*, let his private sensibilities show through in his syndicated newspaper column the next day. He wrote:

> During the latter part of the concert, watching this eighty-two-year-old genius play, I found mist forming in my eyes for some mysterious reason I could not explain. I was not sad. I was exultant. It had something to do with my pride, at that very moment, in being a part of the same civilization that this great and endearing man playing the piano was part of.
>
> Almost at the same instant I felt the suggestion of tears in my eyes, the television camera left Horowitz's fingers on the keyboard and

dissolved to the face of a Soviet citizen in the audience. He did not look like the enemy. His eyes were closed, his head tilted slightly backward so that his face was up . . . and one lone teardrop ran down his cheek.

It was the same teardrop running down mine.

24

THE DENTIST

I went back to the Soviet Union in May 1988. Sometimes—once in a great while—a story on television actually brings people together, and touches them, and helps make their lives whole. I watched this happen that spring. The man who made it happen was a retired Russian dentist.

I carry around in my head memories of hundreds of people I have met in these years of wandering. The memory of this one man haunts me. Hardly a day goes by that I don't think of Nikita Zakaravich Aseyev.

He was a stocky old bulldog of a man who barged into the hotel where I was staying in Moscow while I helped out with coverage of the Reagan–Gorbachev summit meeting. The hotel, the gigantic Rossiya which looms behind Red Square, was closed to Soviet citizens that week. All comings and goings were regulated by KGB men at the doors wearing red armbands inscribed "I am here to help you." "Pals," the wry Muscovites call these grim-faced guards. Those of us who had rooms and temporary offices in the hotel—mostly American and Western European reporters—wore credentials on chains around our necks to get us into the building past the Pals. Dr. Aseyev got in on his medals.

He wore his World War II medals on the lapels of his suit coat, as do many old soldiers in the Soviet Union. When the KGB men stopped him at the front door of the Rossiya, an acquaintance of mine happened to be there watching. He reported that the old man erupted in indignation.

He thundered, "What do you mean I cannot enter? You children, you pups! You have the gall to tell a veteran of the Great Patriotic War he cannot pass into a common hotel lobby?"

He slapped the place over his heart where his medals hung.

"Where were you?" he demanded of the young chief of the guard detail, who had come striding over to see what the shouting was about. "Where were *you* when I received these honors for helping repel the fascist hordes from our precious motherland?"

His voice rose even louder as he theatrically answered his own question. "Cowering in a safe corner, a child who never heard the guns!" he roared. "Or suckling at your mother's breast!"

The KGB men looked at one another with resignation. The chief of the detail started to speak, but the old man interrupted him.

"Where were *you* when the Gestapo gave me *this?*" he shouted, pointing dramatically to a deep scar in his skull over his right eye.

A little crowd of Western reporters was beginning to gather. The raving old man poked the KGB chief in the chest with a stubby finger.

"Where were *you?*" he roared at the top of his lungs. He jutted out his old square chin and paused for a reply.

The KGB man shrugged. Without a word, he unhooked the chain that barred the door and stood aside.

The old man marched into the lobby of the Rossiya Hotel looking satisfied, his medals swinging from his chest.

He approached the first person in his path and demanded to see a representative of American television. "CBS, third floor," he was told.

Minutes later, he showed up in the CBS News offices, a chunky, obviously unofficial character ranting in Russian, insisting that he be heard. As it happened, everybody in the place was busily preoccupied, preparing for coverage of what seemed more important at the time: the final meeting of the week between the President of the United States and the General Secretary of the Communist Party of the Soviet Union. A young assistant, a Russian-speaking foreign student at Moscow's Pushkin Institute who had been hired by CBS for the week of summit duty, took the old man into a vacant room in order to get him out of the hall, calm him down and get rid of him. The student listened to a few minutes of what seemed to be a carefully rehearsed speech, explained that everybody was too busy to hear his story at the moment, walked the old man back down to the hotel lobby and sent him home in a CBS-hired taxi—but only after making a solemn promise that a reporter from CBS News would see him next morning.

And that is how it happened that the next morning, I went for a walk in a park with Dr. Nikita Zakaravich Aseyev.

He wore his medals. He carried a walking stick in one hand and a worn shopping bag in the other. The tail of his sport shirt hung out over his trousers, which did not match his suit coat. We were accompanied by an interpreter, but Dr. Aseyev kept forgetting to wait for his words to be put into English. He was in a great rush to say what he had to say.

"You have to help me," he said. "You are my hope. Everybody lives in hope, you know, and I am no different. For more than forty years, I have waited for this chance, and now it has come."

He shifted his cane to the hand that held the shopping bag and grasped my arm.

"You can speak to America, is this not true?" he asked, and went on before I could answer. "You must help me find some Americans I knew during the war. I have to thank them for saving my life and the lives of many other Russian soldiers."

We sat down on a park bench. He pointed to the scar in his forehead.

"A memory of the Gestapo," he said. "Not a very happy memory. I have another in the side of my body."

He cleared his throat and began:

"We were all prisoners of the Germans at a big concentration camp at Fürstenberg on the Oder River. There were eight thousand American soldiers there, captured in North Africa. The camp was laid out this way."

With his cane, he drew a map on the ground in front of the bench.

"Here the town . . . here the river and the railroad tracks . . . here the camp, Stalag 3-B. The Gestapo barracks were here, near the gate," he said, "here the French prisoners, the Polish, the Yugoslav, the partisans." He indicated each compound by drawing large rectangles in the dirt. "Here," he said, drawing the largest enclosure of all, "the Russians. And next to us," he said, finishing his map, "just across the wire fence—the Americans.

"Nearly every Friday, the Americans each received a five-kilo food parcel from the Red Cross. But the Germans gave us only one liter of turnip soup per day, and one liter of water. It wasn't enough to keep us alive. We were dying by the tens, and then by the hundreds. The Americans could see this. Twenty-five thousand men died in that concentration camp. . . ."

His eyes looked past me for a moment, into the distance.

"I could tell you many stories about those who died," he said softly. He paused, still looking away. Then, abruptly, returning to me, "But that is not what I am here to do. It's the Americans I want to talk about, you see.

"In all the camp, I was the only dentist. Every living person, can, of course get sick, and the Germans permitted me to treat the Americans. There was no dental surgery. I just accepted patients in an ordinary chair, even when I had to perform complicated operations. I treated hundreds of American soldiers, and I believe there were never any complications afterwards, even in such conditions as perhaps you can imagine. I was the only Russian permitted any contact with the Americans, and the Americans respected me. All eight thousand of them knew me, or had heard about me, and understood that I was a very good specialist, and they held me in respect.

"One day, after I had been there about a year, two American brothers named Wowczuk, Michael and Peter, and a third American whose name I forget, spoke to me about conditions in the Russian compound. These brothers I knew by now. They were from Chicago, workers in the stockyards, and I understood already that they were very good people. We were alone in the room that was the dental clinic. This was the beginning of the thing I want to tell you. The brothers Wowczuk and this other, whose name I cannot remember, proposed a plot by which the Americans would smuggle food to the Russians. They told me that not only the three of them, but many others of the Americans were willing to participate. I instantly agreed. That is how it all started."

"Wasn't this dangerous?" I asked.

Dr. Aseyev threw up his hands. "Oh, of course!" he exclaimed. "We would have been shot if they had caught us. Merely to be found outside the barracks at night was a shooting offense, and many men were executed in that camp for much less!"

"How did the Americans get the food to you?"

The old man smiled to remember. "They waited until the sentry had passed at night and threw the parcels over the fence," he said. "The fence was only eight meters high. Those Americans were strong! They could have thrown those things a hundred meters!" He laughed.

"I organized a group on our side to rush out to the fence and retrieve the packages. In one night, we received 1,350 parcels in this way."

Dr. Aseyev took my arm again and gripped it tightly.

"Do you realize what I am saying?" he asked me. "This was nearly seven thousand kilos of food in one night! Do you understand what this food meant on our side of the wire, where men were dying every night of starvation?"

He released my arm. "This went on," he said, "at least one night a week for many months. At least one night a week, the Americans, many different ones, risked their lives to collect food parcels and dash out at night to throw them to us. Not one parcel ever failed to make it across the wire. Not one ever was wasted."

"Why do you think the Americans did this?" I asked.

"Because we were allies," Dr. Aseyev answered. "And because they were good men."

He reached for the old plastic shopping bag lying beside him on the bench and brought out a fuzzy photograph.

"This was a good man, too," he said. "This was a German corporal, one of the guard detail. He stumbled into knowledge of what we were doing almost from the first night. He turned his back and let us continue. He was a soldier of the Wehrmacht, but he did not like seeing enemy soldiers starve. After the war, I wrote to his family and they sent me this portrait of him." He handed the photograph to me. "I had a copy made yesterday," Dr. Aseyev said. "It is for you to take home to America. With perfect assurance, you may tell people that Corporal Alfred Jung was an exceptional member of the human race."

"What happened to him?" I asked, looking at the unfocused image of a young man in a German Army uniform.

"The day the plot was finally discovered," Dr. Aseyev said, "they took him out and guillotined him."

He set the shopping bag back on the bench.

"What else do you have there?" I asked.

"I will show you presently," Dr. Aseyev said. "But now I want to tell you about the behavior of the Americans when the plot was discovered.

"All eight thousand American prisoners were assembled on the parade ground in a great semicircle. This was late in May 1944. It was a hot day. Four SS officers went down the line of them saying to each one, 'Give us the name of the Russian who organized this plot.' For three hours in the sun, with nothing to drink, the Americans stood in absolute silence. They stood there with clenched lips. The German officers threatened them with severe reprisal. They stood in silence. Not one word was spoken. Not one American gave the name of the Russian Dr. Aseyev.

"Finally, to bring the thing to an end, the brothers Wowczuk, Peter and Michael, stepped forward. 'We did it,' they said. 'The whole thing was our idea.' A squad of German guards seized them, and the two brothers were driven out of the camp in a closed truck. Later, I learned that they were taken to another camp, a place for special punishment, where they were questioned every day for four months by the Gestapo—and the Gestapo was the Gestapo, you know! I was afraid for them, but I had no fear for myself. I knew that Michael and Peter would never reveal my name, and they did not."

Dr. Aseyev smiled and lowered his voice. "Later, we were all moved to a different camp," he said, "and do you know—I found Michael and Peter there. And within a few days, we had organized the plot all over again!"

He beamed triumphantly, and started rummaging around again in his shopping bag.

"After the war," he said, "I wrote down the names of those Americans so I could never forget them." He showed me a carbon copy of a document of several pages, typed in Cyrillic characters and dated September 1, 1949.

"This is for you," he said. "It is the only extra copy, so do not lose it. It tells the names of the Americans and what I remember about them. For now, I will tell you the names only."

Gravely, he began to read.

"Wowczuk, Michael.

"Wowczuk, Peter.

"Oh," he said, "Bennett! I just thought of Bennett. He isn't on the list. He was on his deathbed and I did an operation on him. I don't know his first name.

"Jarema, William. He was from New York.

"Harold Symmonds. He was from Mississippi. He lived on that famous river of yours.

"Walhaug, Lloyd. He was a farmer from Illinois.

"Emil Vierling, thirty years old, also a farmer.

"Gut. He was a medic.

"Gasprich. How I loved Gasprich!"

He looked up from the paper in his hand to say emotionally, "What good men they were! What good men they all were!"

He took out a handkerchief and wiped his eyes. "I loved these guys," he said. He continued reading:

"Brockman. Doctor. Captain. I will tell you more about Brockman. . . .

"Dr. Hughes. He was a good friend.

"Dr. Amrich."

I sat on a park bench in Moscow listening to these American names pronounced in a Russian accent. I knew I was hearing a roll call of heroes.

"There were others not written down here," Dr. Aseyev said. "They all took part in smuggling food. I remember Rossbridge, Tossi, Snow— from California, I think—Mangelomani, Audeni . . ."

He leaned forward and said to me, "There were four of us Russian doctors in the camp who took an oath one night that after the war we would find a way to thank these Americans. You see, I am getting old now. This is my chance.

"Now, now because of you," he said, "if these guys are still alive they will know I remember—this dentist who loved them, and whom they did not betray."

He stopped. He exhaled deeply, handed me the list of names and slumped back on the bench. After forty-three years, Nikita Zakaravich Aseyev had just fulfilled an oath.

I invited him to lunch at the Rossiya Hotel. The KGB men stood aside as we entered, not wishing to tangle with him again. At the lunch table, where we were joined by CBS News producer Peter Schweitzer and others, Dr. Aseyev produced more keepsakes from his shopping bag.

"Oh," he said, "oh . . . These are my darlings, my treasures!"

There were photographs of the abandoned camp, clipped from a Soviet newspaper after the war. There were snapshots of the Russian medical doctors who had survived the ordeal of Stalag 3-B with him. There were more medals, wrapped in tissue. Finally, there was a crude cigarette case made of hammered tin.

"Late in the war," said Dr. Aseyev, "Dr. Brockman, who was a gentleman, and with whom I had many long and searching conversations, left the camp. He and some others learned they had been exchanged for German prisoners. Before he left, he came to me and gave me this. It was the only thing he had to give me."

Into the top of the case was scratched the inscription "To N. Z. Aseyev from Sidney Brockman, Captain, U.S. Army."

After lunch, I walked Dr. Aseyev to the taxi that would take him home.

"I know you will not fail me," he said.

I extended my hand, but he didn't take it. Instead, he gave me a vigorous military salute, stepped into the taxi with his cane and shopping bag, and shut the door. As he was driven away, he looked back, and I said good-bye to him in the only way that was now possible. I stood at attention in my best imitation of the form I learned once in the Army Reserve, and returned his salute.

The next morning, June 4, I left Moscow for London by Aeroflot jet, carrying in my hand an orange CBS News shipping bag with the word "URGENT" printed on it in red capital letters. The bag contained the videotape cassettes of Dr. Aseyev's story. All our news shipments are labelled "URGENT." This one, I felt, really was. On arrival in London, I went straight to the CBS News offices in Knightsbridge, where Al Balisky was waiting for me in an editing room. As we sat with the door closed screening the cassettes, I noticed Al's eyes growing moist.

"Imagine," he said gruffly. "The old guy remembered all these years."

Then, without saying anything more, he began the hard job of editing Dr. Aseyev's story into a form that would fit the stringent time requirements of that night's *Evening News.* Once more, on tape, Dr. Aseyev recalled the names.

"Wowczuk . . . Symmonds . . . Jarema . . . Brockman . . ."

"Listen to these names back there in America," I said. "If your name is on this list, an old soldier is saying thank you."

Watching the news that night, William Jarema, retired New York City police detective, felt tears spring to his eyes. "It was a different kind of weeping," he explained a few days later, still unable to speak without choking up. "These are tears of joy. We were like brothers. I thought he was dead."

Dr. Sidney Brockman, retired from the San Antonio, Texas, Health Department, also wept that night. "We were all very close to Dr. Aseyev," he explained later. "We all had tremendous respect for the man, because we knew the Russian prisoners were having things mighty rough.

"In the wintertime, when the Russian prisoners died in their barracks, their comrades did not report their death to the Germans. They brought them out and stood them up for roll call so that their bodies would be counted for rations."

He took out a handkerchief, just as Dr. Aseyev had done on the park bench, and dabbed at his eyes.

"How could we not try to help them?" he asked.

But to risk his own life for them?

"It was part of the game," Dr. Brockman said. "We had all risked our lives to begin with or we wouldn't have been in that place. What was one more risk?"

He said, "Look, I have not believed in being a professional prisoner of war. What happened is done with. I want to forget it if I can." Against his will, he started to weep again.

"But I can't," he said. He paused for a while to collect himself.

"I appreciate Dr. Aseyev remembering me. I have never forgotten him. I will never forget him. What more can I say?"

He got up, went to a cedar chest in a hall closet, and after a time found what he was looking for. "I keep it in here where it's safe and where I don't have to look at it very often," he said. "I took it with me when I left the camp. It's about the only thing I've kept from the war."

It was a cigarette case fashioned of scrap wood, patiently handmade. He opened the case and shook a small metal plaque into his hand.

The plaque read: "To Sidney Brockman from N. Z. Aseyev."

The typewritten pages Dr. Aseyev entrusted to me on the park bench, when translated, give further details of the sacrifice and heroism that ennobled a miserable place once known as Stalag 3-B. When he wrote these notes in 1949, they were meant only as a memorandum to himself, insurance against forgetting some men he had vowed never to forget. But as I read his unadorned recital of bravery and brotherhood in a dark time, I could not help thinking of his notes as a message to the world.

AMERICAN ANTI-FASCIST PRISONERS OF WAR,
MEMBERS OF THE UNDERGROUND IN THE CONCENTRATION CAMP 3-B
IN THE TOWN OF FURSTENBERG-ON-ODER, 1942–1945. GERMANY.

1. Michael Wowczuk. Senior sergeant. 25–30 years old, blond, native of the town of Chicago, former worker at a slaughterhouse . . . active member of the underground . . . organizer of help to our prisoners of war and to our partisans. Continually informed me about the situation on the Soviet–German fronts . . . In the American blocks, there were two radios under the platforms in barracks 13 and 15. Michael Wowczuk continually organized collection of food parcels . . .

2. Peter Wowczuk. Brother of Michael. 35 years. Blond. Was always with Michael. He helped Michael in all undertakings to organize more food provisions for our prisoners. He also obtained English leaflets, translated them into Russian, and passed them to me in the American medical unit. He also actively helped Michael in collecting food

parcels for Soviet partisans in May, 1944. He also was imprisoned with Michael together with a third whose surname I have forgotten in a prison in Frankfurt-on-Oder. There they were convicted by a fascist tribunal. The Germans were seeking the name of the Russian Communist who helped organize food parcels for the Soviet partisans. Neither they nor the other 8,000 American POW's gave me up as the organizer, though the Gestapo sought me for four months. The brothers Wowczuk and the third person during four months in the prison were subjected to interrogations, but did not give my name and thus saved me from death at the hands of the Gestapo.

3. William Jarema. 25–30 years. Native of the town of New York. Formerly a New York courier. A remarkable and warmhearted person. Active member of the underground. Constant companion of the Wowczuk brothers. Constant organizer amongst the Americans of collection of food parcels for Soviet prisoners of war and also for our long-suffering tormented partisans.

4. Harold Symmonds. 20–25. Blond. Senior sergeant. Medic with the American infirmary with whom I had a close friendship, especially when I worked in their infirmary where there was not even a dentist's chair for the dentist. So Harold Symmonds always stood behind an ordinary chair and held the head of the patient as if he were a headrest, and also helped me in my specialist work where necessary. . . .

He always said that such a war as the fascists had conducted against all countries would not happen again, that Marshal Stalin would come to an agreement with our President Roosevelt and that then there would be no war.

Harold Symmonds was from the town of Mississippi. His house was on the banks of the river. He studied in a technical college for three years, but since he didn't have enough money to continue studying, he was forced to take out a contract with the Army for two years. Then the war started and he was sent to Africa, either to Tunis or Algiers. I don't remember very well, but as I understand they were captured in the fortress of Tobruk, taken captive by Rommel's army, and ended up with us. . . .

Symmonds was a good antifascist underground member for more than three years, and when we were liberated from captivity in the town of Luckenwald in April 1945 by the tanks, Symmonds came to our meeting and seeing me, ran to embrace me. He took me in both arms and wept for joy that both he and I were alive. In all my life, I can't remember such tears, especially from a young man, such as those wept by my dear friend, my American savior, and all of them, 8,000 men, were my saviors when they stood on the parade ground in May, 1944, in a semicircle before the head of the Gestapo, Krautzer, who expected that one of them would step forward and say who was the organizer of the collection of food parcels for the Russian partisans, but no one gave the name of the Russian Dr. Aseyev.

5. Lloyd Walhaug. American medic . . . Walhaug was 20–25 years old, a farmer from the state of Illinois . . . Loved to joke, very communicative, helped in every way the Soviet POW's, especially in throwing food parcels over the wire barricade . . . He continually told the Americans that the Russians were good people and that they were suffering from starvation, being driven to hard labor and being brought home dead from work. He would say, "Why, why, why? It is not their fault that the Germans don't feed them but force them to work, beat them and kill them." Lloyd Walhaug in Luckenwald in Camp 3-A obtained for our underground, I do not know how, much medication and many bandages, three liters of iodine, 500 bandages, 300 vials of 2% novocaine . . .

6. Emil Vierling. A farmer with a lettuce plantation from the state of Iowa. He was an active underground member, often threw materials from the infirmary courtyard over the wire barrier. Next door to the infirmary was the general camp bath area in which worked 17 of our Soviet doctors who were assigned to this wash area with great difficulty through the fascist Dr. Kruger who agreed to the doctors being taken from heavy work on the railway and uprooting tree stumps in the forest. It was necessary to save these doctors by feeding them and this was achieved. The bath area was common to all foreigners . . . The American medics collected food, packed it in bags and kept

it in the infirmary stores and upon my direction, the American medics threw the bags to our doctors in the wash area under cover of darkness. . . .

7. Gut. Medic of the American infirmary. An American of Spanish origin, 20–25 years, brunet, a quiet type, rarely entered into conversation . . . but helped to collect food parcels in the infirmary . . . and threw food sacks to our doctors. I remember [Gut's parcels being picked up by] the surgeon from the town of Voronezh, Nikolai Alekseevich Petrov. . . . But in general, I remember hazily.

8. Gasprich. A huge man, 35, blond, from New York, one of the organizers of the collection of food parcels. . . . After we were moved to Concentration Camp 3-A, he became representative of the American Red Cross. In Camp 3-A in February, 1945, he learned that I also had arrived and came to visit me. Michael and Peter Wowczuk, William Jarema, Gasprich and I organized amongst the Americans the collection of 800 5-kilogram parcels which were conveyed to our block in the first days of April. This helped to put a stop to the recruitment of our starving people into Vlasov's criminal plot. [A scheme by which Russian prisoners were offered normal food rations and release from the camp in return for joining the German Army and fighting on the German side.] The attempt collapsed and burst like a soap bubble. In this way, the Americans helped me fulfill the tasks set by the underground group opposing fascism in Camp 3-A. The head of the underground unit was Pilot Captain Victor Ivanovich Yuschenko.

9. Brockman. Doctor. Captain. Blond. . . . He was very communicative and related to me very well. He always greeted me in the infirmary with some chocolate and invariably opened a golden cigarette case and said, "Please, Doctor, have a smoke." He said that he was apolitical, although I didn't ask about that. He put questions to me such as, "Tell me, Doctor, is it true that in Russia when a child is born it is taken from its mother?" I asked him where he got that idea. He said that's what they write in American newspapers. I said to him that a newspaper is just a bit of paper and you can write any nonsense you like on it, but if you want the truth I'll tell you. This conversation took place

in the presence of my convoy, Alfred Jung, who brought me to visit Brockman at his invitation, illegally, under cover of darkness. I told Brockman that we have nurseries, thousands of them, and if any mother decides to work in industry or anywhere else, then she can leave her child in a nursery and after work collect her child and take it home. We have thousands of nurseries in the USSR!

Brockman looked hard at me and listened attentively. Then raising both hands, he said loudly, "Very good, Doctor. We don't have that in America!"

As far as politics was concerned, of course, he was a gentleman with a batman like a baron. He treated me to good food that night, even omelet with sausage. Before the convoy left, having turned out the light in the corridor, Brockman entrusted to me one food parcel and another one to his batman, and having said good-bye, we left with the two parcels by the camp road and the convoy took me to the Soviet block and returned with the batman.

10. Hughes. Doctor, captain, blond, perhaps 35 years old. A fine person. He sympathized with the Soviet POW's whom the Germans treated so cruelly. "Why?" he always asked me. What could I answer to his why? Especially since I knew where I was and amongst whom. So I always answered I don't know. Dr. Hughes gave the Soviet POW's much food from his personal supply. He would say to me, "I would like you to accept for the Russian prisoners . . ."

Dr. Hughes was killed when the town of Brandenburg was bombed by American aviation, along with the Yugoslav Doctor Rado Savlevich Manchino. He also was a fine person.

11. Amrich. Doctor, captain, brunet from New York. I did not know this person well. He always kept to himself, talked little. On rare occasions, he spoke to me in English. Once in the American infirmary, I stood by the window and looked at the forest, which was situated not far away to the east of the infirmary. Dr. Amrich came up to me and said, "Tell me, Doctor, is it true that in Kiev at Babi Yar the Germans shot 90,000 Jews?" I answered that this was a fact, that I personally in September, 1941, talked with people who were there. Amrich

burst into tears and I could not get him to calm down. Oh no, I thought, now I am in trouble. Amrich will tell the Germans and I'll get a bullet in the head. But everything turned out all right. Amrich calmed down. He was a Jew.

N. Aseyev
1 September, 1949.

I did my best to deliver Dr. Aseyev's message of gratitude and remembrance to all those on his list. I found that some have died, among them the brave brothers Wowczuk. One or two find the memory of Stalag 3-B so painful that they refuse to discuss it, even now, even on the telephone. In spite of a diligent search by the Military Field Branch of the Department of Defense and by the Center of Military History in Washington, several remain unaccounted for. By recent act of Congress, World War II prisoners of war have been awarded decorations, years after their imprisonment. So far as I know, none of the heroes of Stalag 3-B has ever been honored for what he did there, except in the memory of an aging Russian dentist.

"It was a terrific operation," William Jarema said. "Terrific. We were repaid many times by our feeling of satisfaction, knowing we helped people in need.

"See, when you're starving, it is an awful feeling, your stomach tightens up on you. People don't know how it feels. If you've ever been starving yourself, you can't just walk away from a person who's starving. We were all in trouble in that camp, and we did everything we could to help one another."

He thought about it for a minute and said, "There ought to be more of that in the world today."

25

REGRETS

I knew it was going to be a long, lonely drive, and that's what it turned out to be. I rented a Peugeot in Lima, stowed a sack of meat pies and some water bottles in the back seat and half a dozen five-gallon cans of gas in the trunk and set out north along the coast road one afternoon in February, midsummer in Peru. After three or four hours, I turned off to the right into a side road and started climbing up into the Andes. The road turned into a dirt track about the time night came on.

I was headed for a primitive village hundreds of miles up in the mountains. Willard Van Dyke, the famous pioneer filmmaker, was up there working on a documentary for CBS about the life of the Quechua Indians, descendants of the proud Incas who were turned into serfs by the Spanish and who still live in thrall to faraway landowners. I was to spend a week or two helping out on interviews and working on the script, and I had been delayed by having to attend an attempted *coup d'état* in Bolivia or somewhere. Van Dyke, I knew, was waiting for me, and there was no way to send a message to him, so I figured it was better to drive all night than to keep him wondering for another day whatever the hell had become of his reporter.

At first, I passed through occasional little settlements of six or eight huts with the light of kerosene lanterns showing at the windows, but then the lights went out and there were no more signs of civilization at all except the winding dirt trail that I followed up and up toward the top of the cordillera. I was utterly alone up there in the dark, and driving carefully. There were no guardrails and my headlights showed me what I would have been able to do if I took any sharp curve a little too fast. I would have been able to whistle sixteen bars of the Peruvian national anthem in thin air on the way down. The stars came out, looking like headlights in the black sky. I'd have welcomed a pair of real headlights coming down the hill as a sign that other human beings coexisted in that starry night, but none ever came. I had heard stories of bandits, and half expected to find armed men in the road around every bend, but no bandits appeared. No animals crossed the road. I was the last creature on earth, driving a French car up a Peruvian mountain in the desolate darkness.

I kept checking my watch, so I know it was just after two A.M. when I heard the loud ping under the hood. The accelerator started flopping under my foot and the car slowed down and stopped in the middle of the narrow trail. I cursed and kicked the accelerator. It lay dead on the floor.

I set the hand brake and got out. A vertical slope rose a few feet to the left of the car and a chasm fell off a few feet to the right. I reached inside and turned off the car's lights. Whatever my other problems were, I knew I didn't need a dead battery. After that, I didn't know what to do. I stood there for a while in the dark beside the dead car, cold and scared. I thought after a while, well, lift the hood. That's what people do, isn't it? I fumbled around until I figured out how to lift the hood of a Peugeot and got it open. It was too dark to see anything in there. I remembered a battery penlight that I once had carried in my shaving kit and wondered if it might still be there. After another few minutes of groping in the dark— ridiculous thing to be doing, I thought to myself, throwing things out of your suitcase onto a dirt road in the Andes in the middle of the night—I found the shaving kit, and inside it, under the soap and the razor and the laxative pills and the bottle of paregoric and the aspirin and deodorant and Swiss Army knife and house keys and collar stays, my hand fell around the little flashlight. The battery will be gone, I thought. But it wasn't. I remember that tiny light coming on in that great darkness as one of the glad moments of my life.

I shined it around under the hood of the car until I found a broken wire hanging loose. When I jiggled the wire, I discovered that it went inside the car and made the gas pedal move. I am not much of a mechanic, but it didn't take much of a mechanic to figure out that this was the accelerator cable, and that it was busted in the middle. I found the other end up by the carburetor. I held the little flashlight in my teeth, took the broken ends of the wire in my hands and brought them together. How could I make them *stay* together? I could think of only one way. I tied them together in a knot.

I closed the hood, got back into the car and turned the ignition key. In neutral, the engine raced with a roar I had not heard from a motionless car since the fifties, when the hot-rodders of my youth gunned their motors before "scratching off" from the Central High School parking lot. I shifted into low and the Peugeot scratched off. The rear wheels spun, dug in, and drove the car crazily toward the next steep curve. I jammed on the brakes. The car slid to the edge of the precipice, cornered like a Maserati at Le Mans and roared into the uphill straightaway. Another curve coming up. Another hard, fast slide and another rocket ride up the mountain. The accelerator, I calculate, was tied down to about fifty miles per hour; on that road, thirty was a suicidal speed. I drove with my foot on the brake and one hand on the gearshift lever, dropping her back into neutral as we approached the most perilous turns. Several times when I smelled the brake lining beginning to burn I coasted to an uphill stop to let the brakes cool off and my heartbeat slow down. Then back into gear and back into orbit, skidding up and around the mountain again.

I was so intent on the driving that I didn't notice at first that I was beginning to see farther up the road than the range of my headlights. Daylight was arriving. The curves became gentler and finally the road straightened out. I had reached the top, the great high plateau that divides the coastal range of the Andes from the snowcapped Cordillera Blanca away to the east. I could see in the early morning light the thin line of the road stretching miles ahead to the north over a treeless, rolling plain dotted with small lakes. The meaning sank in: I wasn't going to drive over a cliff. The cliffs were all behind me. I had made it.

I stopped the car and turned off the damned roaring motor. The silence was the most profound I had ever known. I stepped out, feeling weak and dizzy from the thin air and the lack of sleep and the relief at having come through the crisis. I unwrapped a meat pie and ate it slowly, leaning against the car in the morning cold, looking around at the mountains. I uncorked a bottle of water and drank most of it down. Just as I was preparing to climb back into the car, dreading the thought of having to listen to that insane racing motor again, I heard another sound, a human sound, a faint and muffled shout.

I knew the altitude had made me light-headed. I could see nothing but the two mountain ranges and the vast, vacant plateau. But I heard it again, the same sound, a shout. I scanned the landscape more carefully—and saw him, a man running uphill toward me from the direction of a lake which lay below the road a mile or so ahead.

Good God, where had he come from? What was he doing in this barren place? I thought of bandits and of ambush. I thought of turning the car around and escaping the way I had come, but that would take me back into the hairpin turns of the mountain, downhill this time, with the car really out of control. He shouted again. He was scrambling and stumbling toward me over the rocks as fast as he could, but he still had a few hundred yards of hill to climb before he reached the road. I leapt into the car, started it, slammed it into gear and bolted straight ahead. He altered his course to intercept me on the road. As I grew closer, I could tell he was wearing a black woolen coat and an Indian balaclava hood pulled down over his face. He was carrying something in one hand—a club, a gun? He ran toward a point in the road ahead, waving his free hand at me. I drove for my life, terrified.

He reached the road an instant ahead of the car, lifted the hood from his face, raised the thing he was carrying high in the air and shouted at me at the top of his voice. As I roared past, I caught a glimpse of what it was he was holding.

It was a fish.

He was trying to sell me a fish.

The poor man had been fishing all night on the shore of that godforsaken lake, trying to stay warm in his black coat and his face mask, in the hope of catching a fish he could sell for a few *soles* at the roadside. My car, appearing so early in the morning, must have seemed sent from heaven. We were the only two souls in the wilderness. We met as if by destiny. But one of us was from another world, and wildly misunderstanding. I sped past him like a maniac, leaving him standing there in the dust. In the rearview mirror, I could see him put his fish down in the grass and sit down beside it to catch his breath.

I could have gone back. I could have apologized, and bought the fish. But I knew I couldn't explain to him. He was probably a Quechua speaker who did not understand Spanish. Anyway, there is no language for putting into words the embarrassment of acting foolishly out of fear. I drove on, using the brake and the gearshift until I came to a small settlement beside a river where I found a man with a length of strong wire who could help me replace the accelerator cable.

Sometimes at night before sleeping, little regrets come back to me. The guy with the fish comes back. The reporter's existence is one of perpetual motion. He wraps up one story, gets started on the next one and thinks he must be accomplishing something. But the good memories are all of stopping and staying awhile. I realize I've always driven too fast through life, carrying in my baggage too much impatience and apprehension, missing too many chances, passing too many good people in the dust.

Nobody ever knew the Minnesota north woods better than Bill Magie. After he died, the other guides and outfitters put a plaque on a boulder in the middle of a lake in the Boundary Waters canoe country. It says on the plaque:

> *Think on this land of lakes and forests.*
> *It cannot survive man's greed*
> *without man's selfless dedication.*
> *William H. Magie,*
> *friend of the wilderness,*
> *devoted most of his life to this cause.*
> *Now, it is yours.*

I spent a day doing a story about Bill. He was already seventy-six. Every summer, he said good-bye to Lucille, his understanding wife, left her behind in Superior, Wisconsin, and went up into the Minnesota woods to camp alone beside a lake with his old dog, Murphy. He hired himself out guiding canoeists. Bill Magie remembered everything that had ever happened to him in a lifetime guiding in the Minnesota–Ontario wilderness. He told about the hunting trip he took Knute Rockne on back in the twenties and about the night he crawled inside a moose he had shot to keep from freezing and all about his mapping expeditions in winters past. "I'm the only man alive that's walked from Lake Superior to Lake of the Woods on the ice and carried a transit on his shoulder all the way," he said. Bill Magie was a wonderful man and such a good storyteller that we were able to finish up our story about him before the sun went down.

Over supper, he said to me earnestly, "You know, I want to take one more long canoe trip before I get too old to carry a canoe on the portages. I believe I like you well enough to invite you to come along with me."

I could tell he meant it. I felt honored and a little abashed.

"I don't know much about canoes," I said.

"I could teach you everything," he said. "You like fishing, hell, we'll catch our supper every night and listen to the loons and live off the land the way I used to. I'll promise you this: I can take you to some lakes that damn few people have ever seen. I'd like to see them one more time myself."

"How long a trip are you talking about?" I asked him.

"We could do the whole thing in six weeks, maybe eight," he said. "We'll leave the Fourth of July next summer and be back the end of August. How about it?"

I didn't know how to answer. I could never take that much time away from work, but his invitation was so eager and heartfelt that I hated to tell him so.

I said, "Six or eight weeks is kind of a long time for me, Bill."

"The hell it is," he said. "It's six or eight weeks is all it is. What are you going to do for six or eight weeks that would be better than this?"

I told him I'd think about it and let him know.

He wrote me letters over the winter to make sure I was thinking about it. In one of them, he said if it was money I was worrying about, why of course he wasn't planning to charge me for guide service, he thought I understood that. "Just your grub is all you'd have to pay for," he said. "Write me soon."

But I never did write him, and after a while he gave up on me. I found later that he never made the long canoe trip. He spent the next summer around Moose Lake, guiding a few tourists on overnight camping outings, telling them some of his stories around the campfire and paddling them back the next day. A year or two later, Lucille Magie wrote to me from Superior to tell me that Bill had died.

I wish with all my heart I had made the long canoe trip with Bill Magic. I can't remember what I was doing from the Fourth of July to the end of August the summer he wanted to go fish every night and listen to the loons and see those distant lakes one more time. What could I have been doing that would have been better than that?

There was a flood one spring in West Virginia and the assignment desk sent me to meet a camera crew in Charleston. I got there late at night and drove around looking for a place to stay. Even the ma-and-pa motels and the tourist courts were all filled with people who had been flooded out of their houses. I wound up at the desk of a seedy hotel on a side street run by a burly tattooed night manager in shirt-sleeves and a mentally retarded bellboy in a dirty uniform. The bellboy slumbered in a lobby chair with a pornographic magazine open on his lap until, in a parody of Grand Hotel style, the manager tapped the bell on the desk.

"What?" said the startled sleeper.

"Room four twenty-six, that's what," the manager said.

The bellboy picked up my bag with a yawn and opened the door to the elevator, the old lever-operated variety. On the way up, he looked me over.

"You need anything?" he asked.

"Nope," I said. "Just some sleep."

By now, he had overshot the fourth floor. As he coaxed the lift back down in fits and jolts, he said, "You know what I mean. You *need* anything?"

"Nope," I said.

He got the elevator door open at last. "Where's my room?" I asked.

"I got a lot better room," he said with an idiot leer. He dug a key out of his pocket, opened a door across from the elevator and switched on the ceiling light with a flourish. There on the bed, uncovered by so much as a sheet, a young woman lay naked. She turned her head to the door and smiled.

"Hello, honey," she said to me.

"It's my cousin," the bellboy said proudly.

I stood there gaping. She had dirty blonde hair that fell to her shoulders. Her sleepy eyes were blue. She was pretty.

"Well, come on in," she said. She sat up in bed and pulled the sheet up around herself. A gesture of modesty for my sake.

"I'm Sally," she said.

"I can't come in," I stammered. "I mean, nice to meet you, Sally, but it's a mistake. It's the wrong room."

She looked back at me. "Well," she said. "All right."

She lay back down and turned to the wall. She said, "Turn the light out, Luther."

Luther did, and shut the door, and walked ahead of me down the hall. At the door of 426, he handed me the key and walked away disgustedly. He said over his shoulder, "You're crazy, man."

One of us is crazy, I thought. My room was tiny and stuffy. The window, painted shut, overlooked an air shaft. A spindly floor lamp tilted from its base beside a horsehide chair. There was a cheap veneer desk with nothing but a Western Union blank in the dusty drawer. Luther was right. Sally's *was* a better room. I sat down on the edge of the lumpy bed, a little shaken, and started to take off my shoes. Outside in the hall, a bell started ringing.

"Forget it, it's nothing," the manager said on the phone. I could hear his switchboard buzzing like crazy.

"Yeah, but what is it?" I asked him.

"It's the fire alarm," he said. "It'll go off. It happens all the time. It's nothing."

I undressed, got into bed and waited for the bell to stop ringing. Pretty soon, there was a commotion in the hall, somebody banging on the doors and shouting, "Get up! Get up! Get out of here!" I got up and cracked the door. It was Sally. She was barefoot and wrapped in a chenille bedspread.

"The guy downstairs says it's nothing," I said.

"It's not nothing!" she hollered. "I smell smoke. Get out of here!" She went on down the hall pounding on doors and shouting.

I put on my shirt and pants, went out and found a stairway and made it down to the lobby. The lobby was full of smoke, so I went out onto the street. Luther and the tattooed desk clerk were already safely there, I noticed. Other people kept coming down the stairs and out of the smoky lobby until there were maybe fifty of us standing on the sidewalk. After a while, the fire trucks came and the first firemen jumped off and went running into the hotel while the others hooked up hoses. It turned out to be a fire in a storeroom in the back of the fleabag hotel, and the firemen had it out in a few minutes. But they wouldn't let us back into the building until the smoke was aired out, so we stood out there half dressed in the dark for another couple of hours with the red and white lights of the fire trucks flashing over our heads and the truck radios crackling. A little shower came past, and we all flattened ourselves against the buildings to try to stay dry. I found myself standing next to Sally. She was still wrapped in her bedspread. She was perfectly calm.

"Well, thanks for saving my life," I said.

"That's all right," she said.

"And I'm sorry for barging in on you like that before."

"That's all right," she said.

"Well," I said, "I guess now we're going to get rained on."

She looked up at the sky.

"Yeah," she said.

Her blonde hair was all wet and matted and shining in the lights of the fire trucks. She lifted a corner of the bedspread off her shoulder.

She smiled. She said, "Are you still sure you don't want to get under here with me?"

It was five o'clock in the morning. The first light was appearing in the gray sky. People were going back into the hotel and trudging up the stairs. I was weary and lonely. She was still smiling. She touched my hand. . . .

I kissed her chastely on the cheek, went up and got my bag and walked down the street in the drizzle, looking for breakfast.

This was about thirty years ago. Harry Golden, the old editor and author who lived in my hometown, told me when I was a young newspaper reporter, "When you get to be my age, sonny, all you ever think about are the women you could have gone to bed with and didn't."

I laughed then.

26

A PLACE TO COME
HOME TO

*T*here is a cabin in a grove of cottonwoods beside a western river. The cabin, and a timber bridge across a creek to give access to the cabin, are the only disturbances of nature along the river. The river runs, as it has for centuries, between deep-cut banks, leaving gravel bars on the insides of its frequent bends. When Lewis and Clark passed a few miles away in 1805, they sent one of their sergeants to explore westward up the river. He reported tough going through thickets of wild roses on the banks. The roses are still there, a few steps from where the cabin now stands. They still discourage travel along the river.

Ring-necked pheasants and sharp-tailed grouse, however, find cover in the briars the year round and nourishment in the rose hips of late summer. Hundreds of smaller birds chortle and tweet unseen in the heart of the thicket, protected there from the marsh hawk who appears in the afternoons to hang in the thermals overhead.

Upriver, the roses give way to young willows, which crowd the banks. Deer have made paths through the willows, and follow these paths to drink from the river in late afternoon before they retreat to the tall grass of the river bottom meadow to bed down for the night.

Every few hundred yards, a creek enters the main stream. These creeks are the homes of beavers, whose broad tooth marks girdle every cottonwood within falling distance of water. The beavers are notoriously busy, and also very patient. They may wait for many seasons for a huge and ancient tree to fall, wait until the bright, deep indentation of their gnawing and the yellow wood chips they have left at the base of the tree have been turned gray by weather. They know one winter a storm will come and seize the tree by its spreading upper branches and wrench it down across the creek, and the giant will be theirs. Beavers like their cottonwoods horizontal. Nobody traps beavers here any longer, so they proliferate. When it comes to dam-building, they could give lessons to the U.S. Army Corps of Engineers. Their dams are built to last, and if breached, are quickly repaired. In these creeks, the beavers reveal their instinctive intention: to turn all the flowing waters this side of the Continental Divide into a series of placid ponds stretching downstream to the Gulf of Mexico.

Late in spring, if there has been much snow in the mountains, the quiet river rises, becomes a torrent, forces the beavers into a flurry of dam-mending, and robs them of their patiently felled and stripped cottonwood trunks. These are hurtled down the river into great logjams in the bends, where they may remain through many drier springs when the river has not the force to propel them farther. Under these piles of wreckage, in the quiet currents and eddies, live the largest brown trout of the river. They venture out at dusk to sip mayflies, caddis flies, drowned ants or grasshoppers, according to the season, their rises from the depths creating awesome circles on the dark surface of the water. In the faster current below the logjams the rainbow trout feed on such insects as have floated past the marauding browns. The rainbows rise more exuberantly, sometimes arching unexpectedly out of the water and falling back with a splash, disturbing the grave peace of the river after sundown.

Elk, migrating moose and wandering brown bears are visitors to this place, but always move on after a few days. Sandhill cranes arrive in spring to spend the short summer in the meadows, and Canada geese claim the shallows of the river for a month or two. The year-round residents are the less spectacular common creatures of the west, the white-tailed and mule deer, the raccoon, muskrat, porcupine and skunk, gray turkey and blue heron. All, by instinct, are shy of human beings, yet so unchanged is this place from its ancient state of nature, altered to human purpose only by the presence of the cabin and the bridge, that one or another of these animals or birds is almost always visible from the cabin porch, sometimes a number of them at once. It is naive and sentimental for a man to think he can live as one with the creatures of river, wood and thicket, but in this one place, almost, he can. At the moment, I am irritated only by the beavers.

I am in this place now. I have been watching a pair of barn swallows. Every few daylight minutes for a week, they have been feeding their chirping young in their mud nest on a porch beam, and today I watched the chicks leave the nest one by one, clumsily trying to learn to swoop and dart in the air like swallows. It is getting late in the year for them. They have to find their wings quickly because they have a long trip south ahead of them, all the way to Mexico.

The sun will be going down soon, and the big brown trout will soon be swimming out from beneath the logjam on the river to sip their supper. A male pheasant in full plumage just strutted past the window without his harem. A white-tailed doe and her two fawns have been passing every evening, and I expect them presently.

I hear an owl hooting from the top of a not-yet-fallen, beaver-girdled cottonwood. A coyote is moaning somewhere in the dry hills that look down on this small, green, river bottom Eden. The moon is rising.

I love this place. When I am here, I think I would be happy never to leave it. Every trip has to end.